4th edition

geog.2

teacher's handbook

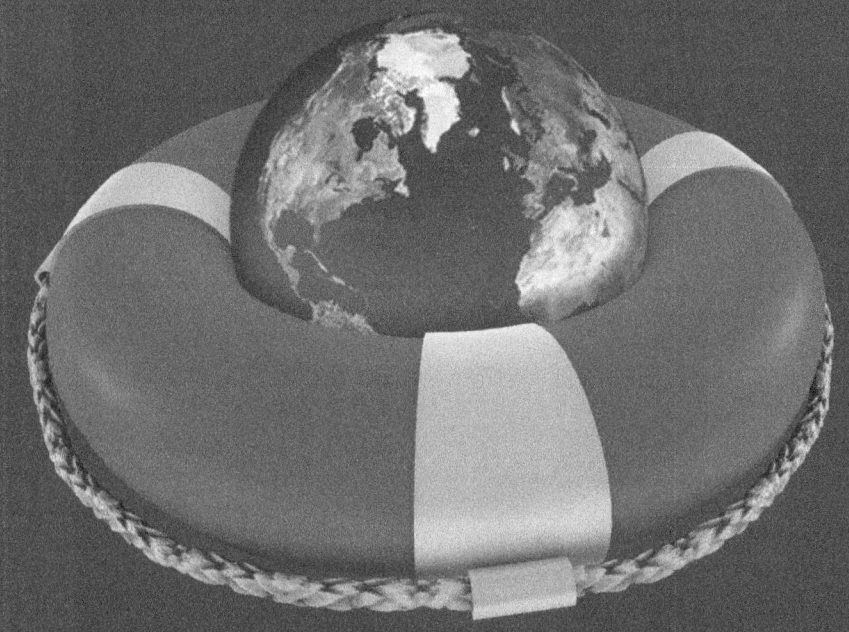

◆ starters ◆ plenaries ◆ objectives and outcomes
◆ answers ◆ further suggestions for class and homework

‹gillian burrell›

OXFORD
UNIVERSITY PRESS

Great Clarendon Street, Oxford OX2 6DP

Oxford University Press is a department of the University of Oxford.
It furthers the University's objective of excellence in research,
scholarship, and education by publishing worldwide.

Oxford is a registered trade mark of Oxford University Press
in the UK and in certain other countries

Author: Gillian Burrell

First published 2001

Second Edition 2005

Third Edition 2008

Fourth Edition 2015

British Library Cataloguing in Publication Data

Data available

ISBN: 978-0-19-839309-2

10 9 8 7 6 5 4 3 2 1

Printed in Great Britain by Ashford Print and Publishing Services, Gosport

Paper used in the production of this book is a natural, recyclable product made
from wood grown in sustainable forests. The manufacturing process conforms
to the environmental regulations of the country of origin.

Acknowledgements

The publisher would like to thank the following for permission to use
photographs and other copyright material:

Cover image by: Getty (globe); Shutterstock (lemon)

The publisher and author would like to thank the following for their
excellent contributions:

Andy Crawley, Catherine Hurst

Links to third party websites are provided by Oxford in good faith and for
information only. Oxford disclaims any responsibility for the materials
contained in any third party website referenced in this work.

Every effort has been made to contact copyright holders of material
reproduced in this book. Any omissions will be rectified in subsequent
printings if notice is given to the publisher.

Contents

About this course

geog.2 is the first book of *geog.123* – the complete geography course for KS3. The course covers the KS3 Programme of Study, and provides excellent support for assessment.

The course components

The course consists of:

For students

– three students' books – also available as *Kerboodle* online books

– three workbooks

For teachers

– three handbooks

– three *Kerboodles* of online lessons, resources, and assessment, including *Kerboodle* online students' books for teacher access

Find out more about the course components by looking at these panels.

The students' books

- Three books for the course
- Chapters divided into two-page units
- Chapter openers give the big picture – the big ideas behind the chapter – and the goals for the chapter
- Aims of unit given in student-friendly language at the start of each unit
- 'Your turn' questions at the end of each unit

The workbooks

- One for each students' book
- Support for each unit in the students' book
- Fill-in activities
- Ideal for homework and independent study

For more information, see page 17.

The teacher's handbooks

- One for each students' book
- Chapter overviews
- Help at a glance for each unit
- Ideas for starters and plenaries for each unit
- Outcomes for each unit
- Answers for 'Your turn' questions
- Further suggestions for class and homework
- Glossary

geog.123 provides a wide range of materials. The students' books are the core of the course. They combine a rigorous approach to content with a uniquely engaging style.

You can decide how to use the wealth of support materials, but notes in the teacher's handbooks will point you towards appropriate material in the workbooks and *Kerboodle Lessons, Resources, & Assessment*. The result is a truly comprehensive and flexible geography course – which we hope you will enjoy using.

You can access *geog.123* online. There are two purchasable options:

- *Kerboodle Lessons, Resources, & Assessment* (which includes teacher access to the *Kerboodle Book*, an online version of the students' book)
- student access to the *Kerboodle* Book

You can choose to use one or the other, or both – you decide what you and your students need.

Kerboodle Lessons, Resources, & Assessment

- A package to support each students' book
- Lesson presentations and supporting Lesson plans for each unit
- Interactive activities, and animations and video clips
- Editable and photocopiable differentiated Foundation and Extension worksheets for each unit, with answers provided
- Teacher access to the *Kerboodle Book* – the online version of the students' book – for front-of-class use
- Comprehensive support for assessment:
  - interactive auto-marked End-of-lesson assessments, with feedback – one for each unit
  - Extended assessment tasks, with mark schemes – one for each chapter
  - Exam-style questions, with mark schemes – one for each chapter
  - interactive auto-marked Self-assessment forms – one for each chapter
  - markbook and reporting functions
- Many resources are editable
- Upload and create your own content

For more information, see pages 12-16.

Kerboodle Book

- An online version of each of the students' books
- Includes a range of tools that allow students to annotate their book
- Can be accessed on a range of devices with internet connectivity, including iPads and other tablets – so students can have access anywhere, any time

For more information, see page 13.

Using this book

This book aims to save you time and effort! It offers full support for *geog.2* students' book, and will help you prepare detailed course and lesson plans.

What it provides

For each chapter of the students' book, this book provides:

1   a chapter overview

2   help at a glance for each unit, including answers for 'Your turn'

3   further suggestions for class and homework.

It also has a glossary at the back, covering the geographical terms the students will meet.

Please turn to the contents list on page 3 now, to see how this book is structured.
Then find out more about the three main components, below.

1   The chapter overview

This is your introduction to the corresponding students' chapter. Look at its sections.

Shows how the students' chapter relates to the KS3 Programme of Study.

Sets out the objectives and outcomes for the chapter, and the corresponding unit numbers.

Sets out the key ideas within, and behind, the students' chapter. The students' version of this is given in their chapter opening unit.

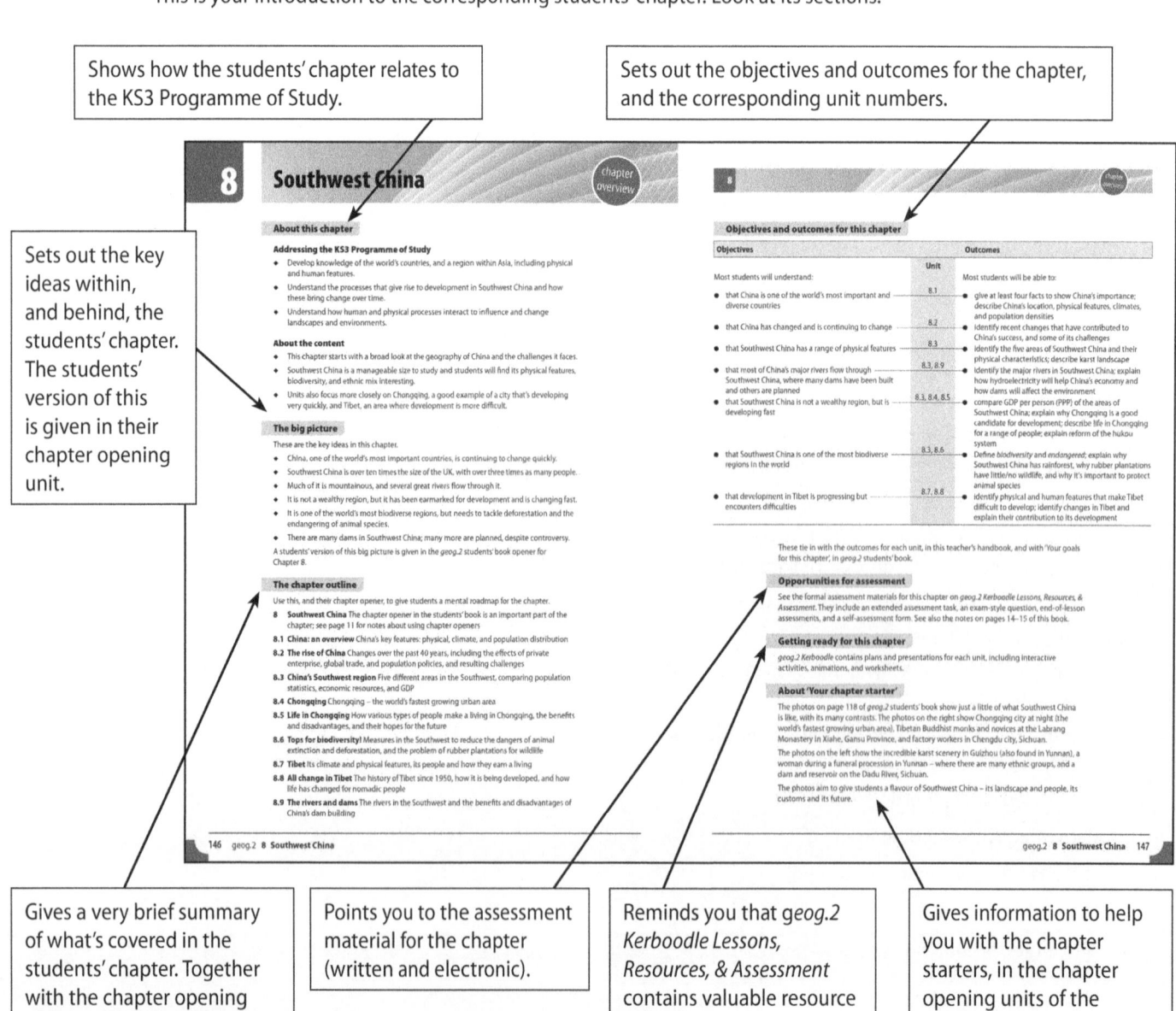

Gives a very brief summary of what's covered in the students' chapter. Together with the chapter opening unit in the students' book, it will help you give students a roadmap for the chapter.

Points you to the assessment material for the chapter (written and electronic).

Reminds you that *geog.2 Kerboodle Lessons, Resources, & Assessment* contains valuable resource material.

Gives information to help you with the chapter starters, in the chapter opening units of the students' book.

2 Help at a glance for each unit

These pages give comprehensive help for each unit of *geog.2* students' book.

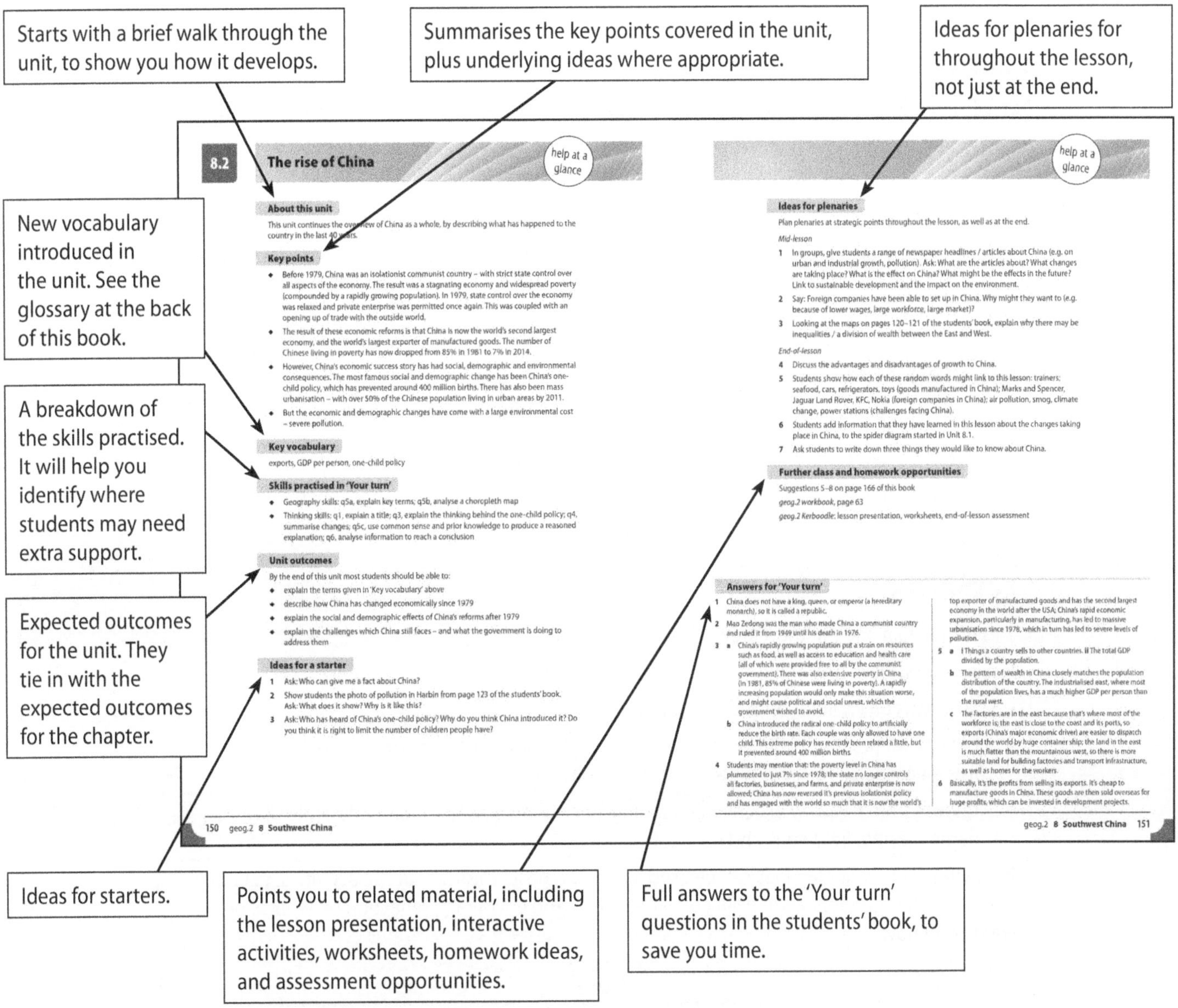

> Starts with a brief walk through the unit, to show you how it develops.

> Summarises the key points covered in the unit, plus underlying ideas where appropriate.

> Ideas for plenaries for throughout the lesson, not just at the end.

> New vocabulary introduced in the unit. See the glossary at the back of this book.

> A breakdown of the skills practised. It will help you identify where students may need extra support.

> Expected outcomes for the unit. They tie in with the expected outcomes for the chapter.

> Ideas for starters.

> Points you to related material, including the lesson presentation, interactive activities, worksheets, homework ideas, and assessment opportunities.

> Full answers to the 'Your turn' questions in the students' book, to save you time.

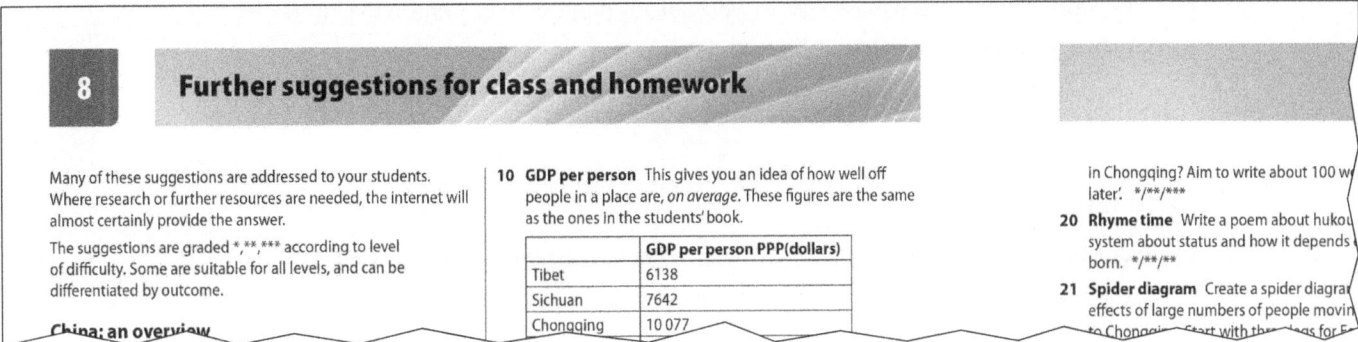

8.2 The rise of China *help at a glance*

About this unit
This unit continues the overview of China as a whole, by describing what has happened to the country in the last 40 years.

Key points
- Before 1979, China was an isolationist communist country – with strict state control over all aspects of the economy. The result was a stagnating economy and widespread poverty (compounded by a rapidly growing population). In 1979, state control over the economy was relaxed and private enterprise was permitted once again. This was coupled with an opening up of trade with the outside world.
- The result of these economic reforms is that China is now the world's second largest economy, and the world's largest exporter of manufactured goods. The number of Chinese living in poverty has now dropped from 85% in 1981 to 7% in 2014.
- However, China's economic success story has had social, demographic and environmental consequences. The most famous social and demographic change has been China's one-child policy, which has prevented around 400 million births. There has also been mass urbanisation – with over 50% of the Chinese population living in urban areas by 2011.
- But the economic and demographic changes have come with a large environmental cost – severe pollution.

Key vocabulary
exports, GDP per person, one-child policy

Skills practised in 'Your turn'
- Geography skills: q5a, explain key terms; q5b, analyse a choropleth map
- Thinking skills: q1, explain a title; q3, explain the thinking behind the one-child policy; q4, summarise changes; q5c, use common sense and prior knowledge to produce a reasoned explanation; q6, analyse information to reach a conclusion

Unit outcomes
By the end of this unit most students should be able to:
- explain the terms given in 'Key vocabulary' above
- describe how China has changed economically since 1979
- explain the social and demographic effects of China's reforms after 1979
- explain the challenges which China still faces – and what the government is doing to address them

Ideas for a starter
1 Ask: Who can give me a fact about China?
2 Show students the photo of pollution in Harbin from page 123 of the students' book. Ask: What does it show? Why is it like this?
3 Ask: Who has heard of China's one-child policy? Why do you think China introduced it? Do you think it is right to limit the number of children people have?

Ideas for plenaries
Plan plenaries at strategic points throughout the lesson, as well as at the end.

Mid-lesson
1 In groups, give students a range of newspaper headlines / articles about China (e.g. on urban and industrial growth, pollution). Ask: What are the articles about? What changes are taking place? What is the effect on China? What might be the effects in the future? Link to sustainable development and the impact on the environment.
2 Say: Foreign companies have been able to set up in China. Why might they want to (e.g. because of lower wages, large workforce, large market)?
3 Looking at the maps on pages 120–121 of the students' book, explain why there may be inequalities / a division of wealth between the East and West.

End-of-lesson
4 Discuss the advantages and disadvantages of growth to China.
5 Students show how each of these random words might link to this lesson: trainers; seafood, cars, refrigerators, toys (goods manufactured in China); Marks and Spencer, Jaguar Land Rover, KFC, Nokia (foreign companies in China); air pollution, smog, climate change, power stations (challenges facing China).
6 Students add information that they have learned in this lesson about the changes taking place in China, to the spider diagram started in Unit 8.1.
7 Ask students to write down three things they would like to know about China.

Further class and homework opportunities
Suggestions 5–8 on page 166 of this book.
geog.2 workbook, page 63
geog.2 Kerboodle: lesson presentation, worksheets, end-of-lesson assessment

Answers for 'Your turn'
1 China does not have a king, queen, or emperor (a hereditary monarch), so it is called a republic.
2 Mao Zedong was the man who made China a communist country and ruled it from 1949 until his death in 1976.
3 a China's rapidly growing population put a strain on resources such as food, as well as access to education and health care (all of which were provided free to all by the communist government). There was also extensive poverty in China (in 1981, 85% of Chinese were living in poverty). A rapidly increasing population would only make this situation worse, and might cause political and social unrest, which the government wished to avoid.
   b China introduced the radical one-child policy to artificially reduce the birth rate. Each couple was only allowed to have one child. This extreme policy has recently been relaxed a little, but it prevented around 400 million births.
4 Students may mention that: the poverty level in China has plummeted to just 7% since 1978; the state no longer controls all factories, businesses and farms, and private enterprise is now allowed; China has now reversed it's previous isolationist policy and has engaged with the world so much that it is now the world's

top exporter of manufactured goods and has the second largest economy in the world after the USA; China's rapid economic expansion, particularly in manufacturing, has led to massive urbanisation since 1979, which in turn has led to severe levels of pollution.
5 a i The total GDP divided by the population.
   b The pattern of wealth in China closely matches the population distribution of the country. The industrialised east, where most of the population lives, has a much higher GDP per person than the rural west.
   c The factories are in the east because that's where most of the workforce is; the east is close to the coast and its ports, so exports (China's major economic driver) are easier to dispatch around the world by huge container ship; the land in the east is much flatter than the mountainous west, so there is more suitable land for building factories and transport infrastructure, as well as homes for the workers.
6 Basically, it's the profits from selling its exports. It's cheap to manufacture goods in China. These goods are then sold overseas for huge profits, which can be invested in development projects.

150 geog.2 8 Southwest China   geog.2 8 Southwest China 151

3 Further suggestions for class and homework

These pages give a wealth of further suggestions for class and homework.
They have been graded *, ** or *** according to level of difficulty.
Some are suitable for all levels, and differentiated by outcome.

8 Further suggestions for class and homework

Many of these suggestions are addressed to your students. Where research or further resources are needed, the internet will almost certainly provide the answer.

The suggestions are graded *,**,*** according to level of difficulty. Some are suitable for all levels, and can be differentiated by outcome.

China: an overview

10 **GDP per person** This gives you an idea of how well off people in a place are, *on average*. These figures are the same as the ones in the students' book.

	GDP per person PPP(dollars)
Tibet	6138
Sichuan	7642
Chongqing	10 077

in Chongqing? Aim to write about 100 w[...] later'. */**/***

20 **Rhyme time** Write a poem about hukou[...] system about status and how it depends [...] born. */**/**

21 **Spider diagram** Create a spider diagra[...] effects of large numbers of people movin[...] to Chongqing. Start with the ideas for [...]

Planning your lessons around *geog.2*

Planning for high-quality lessons

Well-planned and well-structured lessons are a key requirement, for delivering high-quality teaching and learning in any subject, at any level. The *geog.123* course aims to make it easy to plan, structure, and deliver, high-quality lessons for KS3 geography.

Structure of a typical lesson

You will already be familiar with guidelines on structuring lessons. This shows a typical lesson structure.

STARTER

Purpose: To capture students' attention and focus the class. Use it as the lesson hook, or to find out what students know already about a new topic, or for quick revision of earlier work.

INTRODUCTION

Purpose: To prepare students for the activities ahead.

- If this is a new topic, tell students the topic objectives. Write these on the board.
- If it's a continuation of a topic, you can refer back to an objective as appropriate.

ACTIVITIES

This is the main body of the lesson.

Purpose: To achieve one or more of the topic objectives.

- Emphasis on exploration and investigation.
- Provide for practice in different types of skill: geographical, literacy, numeracy, thinking, listening, speaking, team-working, and ICT skills.
- Choose from a variety of activities: reading, answering questions, enquiries, role play, game playing, fieldwork, and ICT.

Plenaries: note that plenaries can be used as staging posts throughout the activities, to gain feedback, check understanding, link to earlier work, and encourage reflection on what is being learnt, and how.

FINAL PLENARY

Purpose: To round off and review what has been done, and to assess what has been achieved against the topic objectives. This is where you help students to:

- check, and crystallise, their understanding
- generalise, for example from an individual case study
- set work in context, and make links to work already done, or to be done in the future
- reflect on how they have learned, as well as what
- check how well they have achieved the topic objectives (self-assessment).

HOMEWORK

Purpose: To confirm, give practice in, and extend, what has been learnt in the lesson.

- The homework can lead on from the final plenary, and be the basis for a starter for the next lesson.

Planning around *geog.2*

Now see how the components of *geog.2* provide material for each part of your lesson.

STARTERS

- The 'Help at a glance' pages in this book have ideas for lesson starters.
- See further notes about starters, and resources for them, in this book.

OBJECTIVES

- The opening lines of each unit in the students' book give the purpose of the unit, in student-friendly language. The goals for each chapter are given in its opening unit.
- See also the objectives and outcomes given in this book.

ACTIVITIES

Using the students' book

- The text in the students' book provides the core information students need. Some lends itself to reading aloud, but try 'quiet time' too.
- You can let students work through the text uninterrupted, or break it up with 'Your turn' questions. (These generally follow the order of the text.)
- The questions give practice in literacy, numeracy, thinking, and geography skills.
- Some are ideal as whole-class questions with verbal response. Others can be worked through by students working alone, in pairs, or in small groups. The final 'Your turn' questions are usually open questions that challenge students to show what they can do.
- For students who finish early, check out 'Further suggestions for class and homework' at the end of each chapter in this book. Or select a worksheet from the *Kerboodle Lessons, Resources, & Assessment*.

Using *Kerboodle Lessons, Resources, & Assessment*

- The *Kerboodle Lessons, Resources, & Assessment* gives you a ready-to-play lesson presentation (with teacher's notes) for each unit plus interactive activities, animations and video clips.
- The *Kerboodle* also offers differentiated Foundation and Extension worksheets and an End-of-lesson interactive assessment (with feedback) for each unit.
- Much of the material is suitable for whole-class teaching using an interactive whiteboard or projector, and offers scope for vibrant and effective lessons.

PLENARIES

- The 'Help at a glance' pages in this book give ideas for plenaries, for throughout the lesson as well as at the end.
- See further notes about plenaries, and resources for them, in this book.

HOMEWORK

- 'Further suggestions for class and homework' at the end of each chapter in this book offer lots of ideas.
- Select a worksheet from the *Kerboodle Lessons, Resources, & Assessment*.
- The workbook provides support for every unit in the students' book.
- Use the End-of-lesson interactive assessment for each unit on the *Kerboodle Lessons, Resources, & Assessment*.
- Use other assessment materials on the *Kerboodle Lessons, Resources, & Assessment* – the Extended assessment tasks and/or the Exam-style questions.

More about starters and plenaries

Planning your starters and plenaries

Effective starters and plenaries need to be planned for. With planning, you can ensure that they'll help you to meet your lesson objectives, and that you won't have to rely on sudden inspiration in the classroom. But even where they are planned, you may want and need to modify them as you go along, in response to your students.

Our suggestions for starters and plenaries

The kinds of activities you feel comfortable with, for starters and plenaries, will depend on your teaching style, and the individual class. So the suggestions for starters and plenaries in this book are just that: suggestions! You may want to use some as described, or adapt them. Or they may provide inspiration for new ideas of your own.

The starters

- Most of these are intended for use with the students' books closed, before students have looked at the new unit. But they lead seamlessly into the work in the students' book.

- In some cases you may want to combine two starters to give a more extended one.

- A number of starters require the use of an atlas, and can be an excellent way of giving your students atlas practice that's fun.

- Other starters require both physical and mental activity – for example creating a graffiti wall on the board. This is a good way to get everyone involved.

The plenaries

- There are suggestions for plenaries for throughout the lesson, not just at the end.

- They have been chosen for a variety of purposes: to encourage feedback; assess understanding; promote reflection; build bridges with material already covered (or still to be covered), with other subjects, and with the real world; help crystallise what has been learnt; and see whether it applies to other situations.

- Some of the plenaries are single questions. You will find that you can readily combine some to make more extended plenaries.

- Some need more preparation than others. You might not want to choose these for every class, but it's a good idea to ring the changes, and keep your students surprised.

- Together with 'Your turn', the 'Ideas for plenaries' section is a rich resource to help you deliver fresh, exciting, and effective lessons.

Resources for starters and plenaries

Images

Many of the starters, and some plenaries, require images – mostly photos. There's a wealth of useful resources on the *Kerboodle Lessons, Resources, & Assessment*. You could use some of these to design your own starters or plenaries.

The interactive activities and animations and video clips on the *Kerboodle Lessons, Resources, & Assessment* also make great starters and plenaries.

The internet, of course, is an excellent source for other geographical photos and images. Please check with the appropriate people in your school regarding copyright issues.

Building a resource library

Some resources, such as photos, can be used over and over. You may want to create your own resource library. Laminating printed photos, and other resources (such as True/False cards), will extend their lives and save you time and effort in the future.

Using the chapter openers in the students' book

The chapter openers in the students' book are in effect the starters for new topics – and you can return to them as an end-of-topic plenary.

Below is a typical chapter opener.

Large photo to hook your students' attention (we hope!). The opening photos usually relate to specific material within the chapter, and are referred back to, at different points.

Gives the big underlying ideas for the chapter. These provide the context for new learning. At the end of the chapter they can be reviewed, to help crystallise the learning.

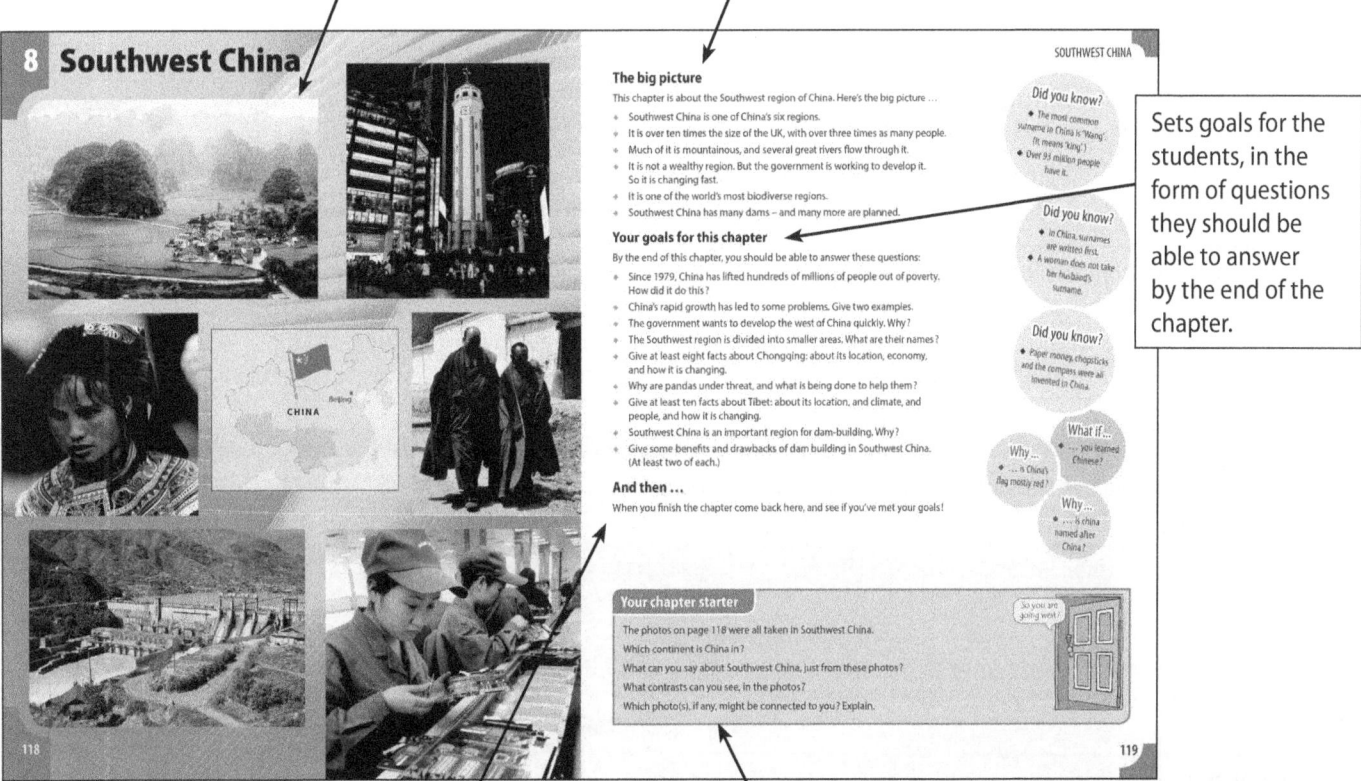

Sets goals for the students, in the form of questions they should be able to answer by the end of the chapter.

Invites students to revisit the goals at the end of the chapter. Note that the *Kerboodle Lessons, Resources, & Assessment* has an interactive students' Self-assessment form for each chapter, which refers to these goals.

Chapter starter questions, to get your students thinking. The 'Chapter overviews' in this book give information about the photos (where available), and some background for the starter questions.

Using the chapter openers

As you can see, the chapter openers can do quite a lot of useful work, so it's worth spending some time on them.

- 'The big picture' can be read aloud, and discussed.

- You can work through 'Your goals for this chapter' in advance, to find out what students know already. Most will probably be able to answer at least a couple of questions.

- Using the teacher-access *Kerboodle Book* in *Kerboodle Lessons, Resources, & Assessment*, you could display the chapter openers on the whiteboard.

- For some of the chapter starters (but not all) there are suggestions for related work, in the 'Further suggestions for class and homework' pages in this book.

- Then the next step is to give students a mental roadmap for the chapter, using the corresponding 'Chapter overviews' in this book.

About *geog.2 Kerboodle*

Kerboodle is an online resource. It offers two purchasable options:

- *Kerboodle Lessons, Resources, & Assessment* (which includes teacher access to the *Kerboodle Book*)
- student access to the *Kerboodle Book* – an online version of the students' book

You can choose to use one or the other or both – you decide what you and your students need. Each option is available as an annual licence for unlimited users.

Kerboodle Lessons, Resources, & Assessment

Lessons

There's a Lesson presentation for each unit in the students' book. There are resources attached to each presentation – including interactives, animations and videos, and worksheets. Each Lesson presentation is supported by a Lesson plan.

For each unit, the Lesson presentation provides engaging coverage of a particular learning objective – a key point or idea, or an important concept. It is provided to help you with part of the lesson – it is not intended to be the whole lesson.

You can add your own material to the Lesson presentations and the Lesson plans.

8.0 Southwest China

Help

What would you expect to find in China?

Front-of-class resources – interactives, animations and videos – are built into each presentation, helping you to create lively lessons.

LESSON   NOTES

OUP.com | Privacy Policy | Legal Notice | Cookie Policy | Support | Contact | Terms and Conditions

Tools   Digital Book   Back   1 of 3   Next

The Lesson plans are easily accessed from the Lesson presentations, and provide ideal support for NQTs and non-specialists.

The worksheets for each unit are attached to the presentation, so that they are easy to find and so that you can discuss them as a whole class.

Resources

Kerboodle includes a wealth of resources – you can use them as part of the Lesson presentations, or on their own as stand-alone resources to suit your particular needs.

*   Resources include items for front-of-class use, such as whole-class interactive activities and animations and videos.

*   Resources include differentiated worksheets that can be printed off and photocopied for use in class or homework – please see page 16 for more information and samples.

*   Teacher access to the *Kerboodle Book* is provided for front-of-class use. This allows you to focus your students' attention on particular maps, diagrams, or photos, or on particular pieces of text, during your lesson. You can use a range of tools as part of this, and you can save any annotations.

*   Upload your own resources – so that you can personalise your course.

Assessment

There's a comprehensive and flexible assessment package – please see pages 14-15 for details.

Kerboodle Book

The *Kerboodle Book* is an online version of the students' book.

Student access includes a range of tools that allow students to annotate their book.

Teacher access is included as part of the *Kerboodle Lessons, Resources, & Assessment* for front-of-class use.

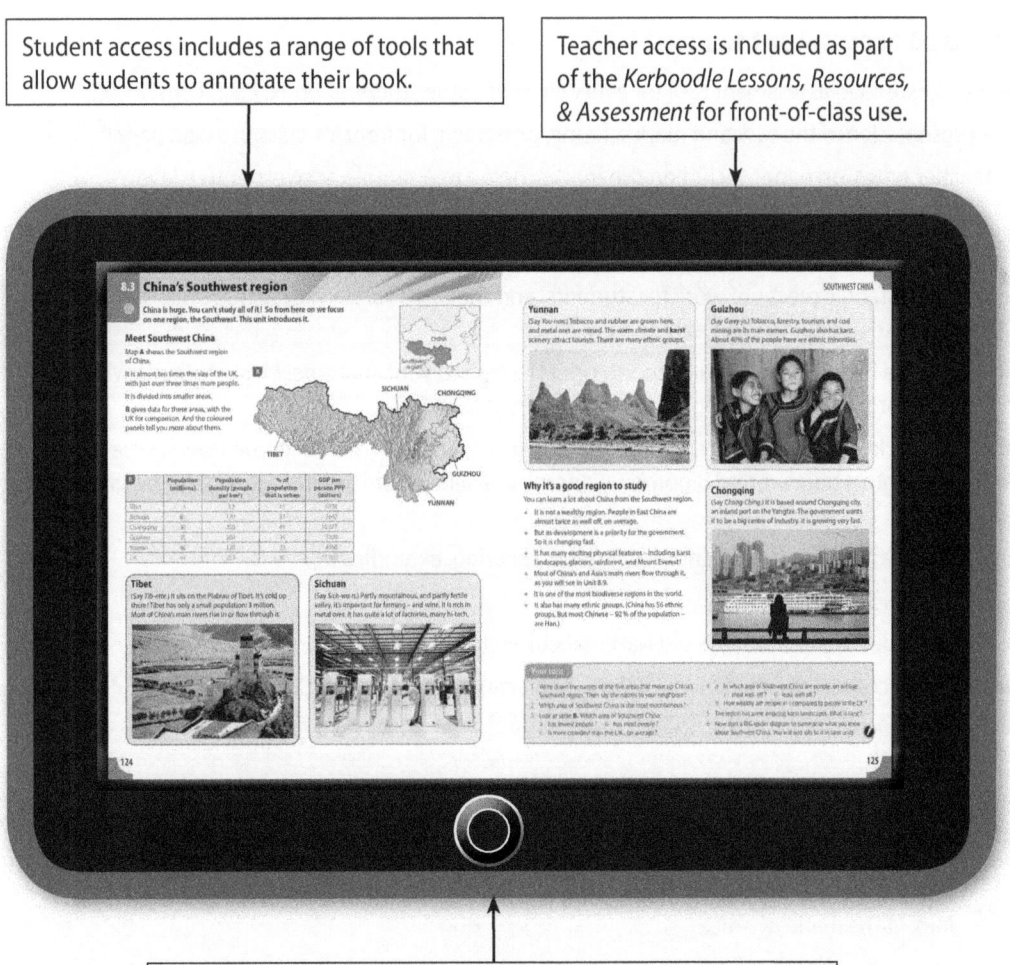

Can be accessed on a range of devices with internet connectivity, including iPads and other tablets – so students can have access anywhere, any time.

We hope the assessment package on *Kerboodle Lessons, Resources, & Assessment* will help you – whatever your approach to assessment, and however your school measures progress.

The comprehensive support for assessment includes:

- End-of-lesson assessments with feedback
- Extended assessment tasks with mark schemes
- Exam-style questions with mark schemes
- Self-assessment forms
- markbook and reporting functions

End-of-lesson assessments

There's an End-of-lesson assessment for each unit (double-page spread) in the students' book.

These are interactive, multi-question multi-screen formative assessments – students complete the questions on-screen, and receive feedback after each question. The questions focus on the content of the unit, and help test core knowledge.

Each assessment should take most students about thirty minutes to complete, and can be done either in class or for homework; they could be used promptly after the lesson, or some time later.

These assessments are auto-marked, with feedback, and the student outcome is given as a percentage and automatically entered into the markbook.

Extended assessment tasks

There's an Extended assessment task for every chapter in the students' book. Each consists of:

1 a presentation of the task and mark scheme, on-screen, for front-of-class use (see panel)

2 teacher notes, on paper, including the mark scheme and sample answers at two levels

3 student assessment material, on paper, including a student-friendly version of the mark scheme to help them achieve and progress

These are substantial pieces of work for students, and the tasks vary – they include decision-making exercises, enquiries, and extended writing.

You will need a lesson or part of a lesson to brief the task to your students. Most students will then need approximately two hours to complete the task.

The task is marked by you, using the mark scheme provided. Each mark scheme uses specially-written descriptors built around Bloom's Taxonomy and allows for student outcome to be given in terms of:

- a performance term (beginning/developing, securing, extending)
- a GCSE grade indicator
- or a level developed from the old National Curriculum Levels

You can easily convert the mark to a score so that it can be entered into the markbook.

The digital front-of-class presentations help you brief your students – you can:

- explain the task or question
- identify and explain the command language
- look at the mark scheme
- and view sample answers

– so that you can help students understand what's required, and how they can be successful.

Exam-style questions

These are KS3-appropriate. There's one Exam-style question per chapter. Each consists of:

1 a presentation of the question and mark scheme, on-screen, for front-of-class use (see panel)

2 teacher notes, on paper, including the mark scheme, guidance for adapting the question for lower and higher ability students, and sample answers at two levels

3 student question sheet(s), on paper

You will need part of a lesson to brief your students. Most students will then need approximately twenty minutes to write their answers.

The question is marked by you, using the mark scheme provided. Each mark scheme uses specially-written descriptors built around Bloom's Taxonomy – the mark scheme allows for student outcome to be given in terms of:

• a performance term (beginning/developing, securing, extending)

• a GCSE grade indicator

• or a level developed from the old National Curriculum Levels

You can easily convert the mark to a score so that it can be entered into the markbook.

Self-assessment forms

There's a Self-assessment form for every chapter in the students' book.

These are based on the 'Your goals for this chapter' on the chapter-opening spreads. They are completed on-screen, and should take about ten minutes. They are auto-marked, with the student response feeding automatically into the markbook.

The markbook

The markbook allows you to easily record and track progress.

For the End-of-lesson assessments and Self-assessment forms, student scores and responses are automatically recorded in the markbook. For the Extended assessment tasks and Exam-style questions, you can manually enter scores (the markbook records percentages only to allow quick comparison of performance) – guidance on how to do this is provided.

The markbook reporting functionality allows you to run reports on individual students, classes, and year groups across a single assessment or multiple assessments. You can also run diagnostic reports on the auto-marked assessments to see question-by-question performance across a group.

About the *geog.2* worksheets

geog.2 Kerboodle Lessons, Resources, & Assessment provides differentiated Foundation and Extension worksheets for each unit in the students' book. Answers are also provided.

Worksheets can be printed and photocopied – so they are ideal for cover lessons and homework.

The two worksheets for each unit are attached to the Lesson presentation – so you can see at a glance what's available to support that lesson. They can also be accessed as a separate *Resource* type.

Worksheets can be displayed on the whiteboard, allowing you to discuss questions with students.

8.4 Chongqing — foundation worksheet

Name _____ Class _____

1 Describe the location of Chongqing. Aim your work at a Year 2 student who does not know where China is.

2 Changes are taking place in Chongqing every day. Write a diary to show how the city changes in 24 hours. Try to include some information about how this might make residents feel.

3 If you were setting up a business in China, why might you want to locate it in Chongqing?

geog.2: 8 Southwest China

© Oxford University Press 2014 • This may be reproduced for class use solely within the purchaser's school or institution
Acknowledgements: http://www.oxfordsecondary.co.uk/acknowledgements

---

8.4 Chongqing — extension worksheet

Name _____ Class _____

1 Where is Chongqing? Write a detailed description, including reference to the continent, country and region Chongqing is in.

2 Be a town planner!

Deciding what to include in a new city can be very difficult. Make a list of **10 essential services** you think should be included in the city. When you are making your list, think about:

Young children   Teenagers   Parents   The elderly

1_____   2_____
3_____   4_____
5_____   6_____
7_____   8_____
9_____   10_____

3 Look at the list you made in Task 2. Put a number next to each idea so that you rank them in order of importance.

Now say why you've chosen your top three ideas.

4 Chongqing diary!

Changes are taking place in Chongqing every day. Write a diary over seven days to show how the city is changing day by day. Try to include some information about how this might make residents feel. Think about jobs, how the city looks and smells, pollution and community spirit.

geog.2: 8 Southwest China

© Oxford University Press 2014 • This may be reproduced for class use solely within the purchaser's school or institution
Acknowledgements: http://www.oxfordsecondary.co.uk/acknowledgements

---

The worksheets are provided as PDFs and as editable Word files – you can customise them to suit your students' needs.

In total, there are 134 worksheets – 67 Foundation worksheets, and 67 Extension worksheets.

Answers are provided as separate files.

About *geog.2 workbook*

The *geog.2 workbook* provides support for every unit (double-page spread) in the *geog.2* students' book.

The activities focus on core knowledge, locational knowledge, and skills. The workbook is ideal for homework.

A page of fill-in activities for every double-page spread in the students' book, to hand when you need it.

Perfect for homework and independent study, and great for cover lessons.

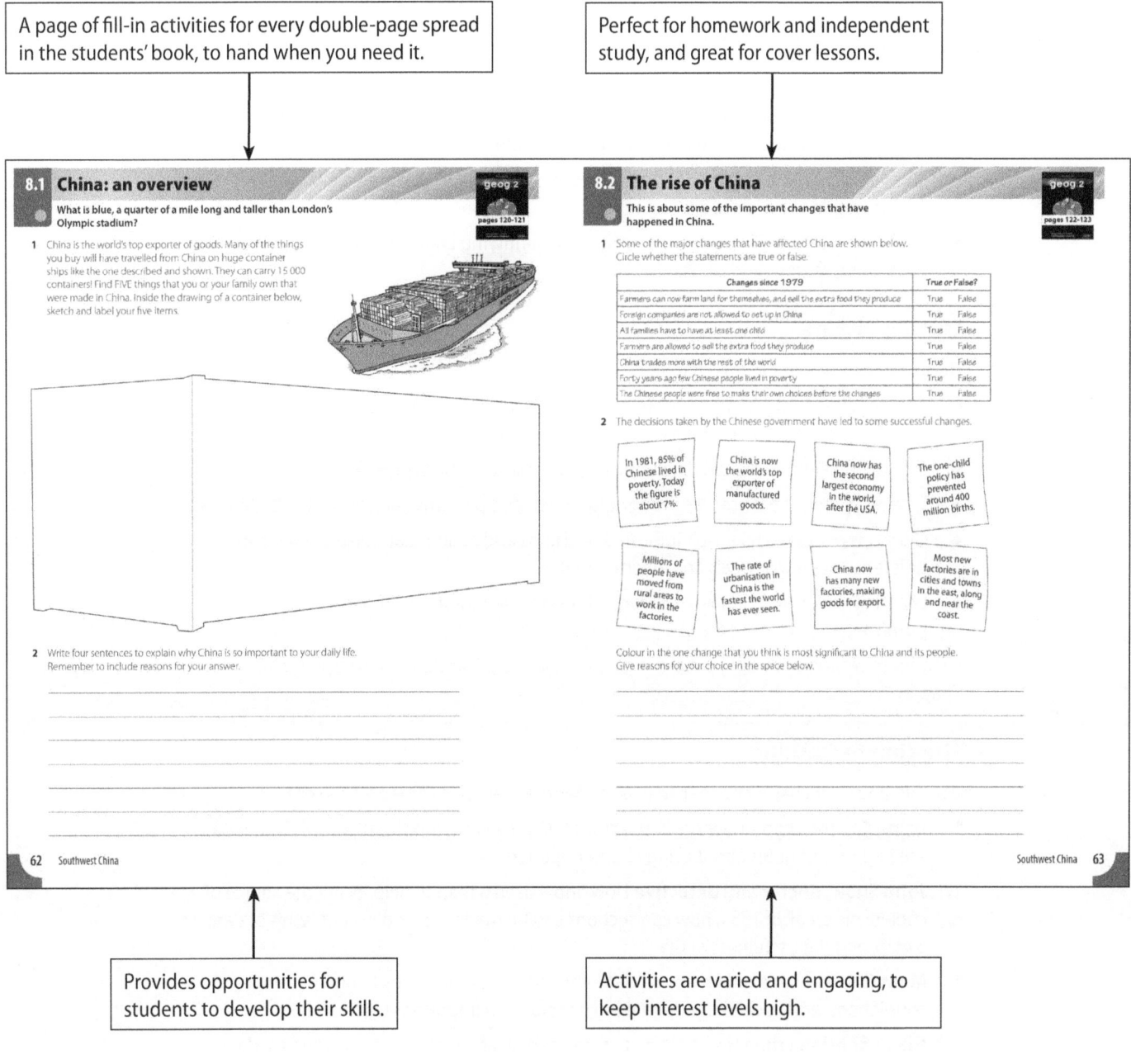

Provides opportunities for students to develop their skills.

Activities are varied and engaging, to keep interest levels high.

Using GIS

About this chapter

Addressing the KS3 Programme of Study
- ◆ Interpret maps, aerial photos, and GIS.
- ◆ Use GIS to view, analyse, and interpret places and data.

About the content
- ◆ This chapter starts by showing how John Snow identified the source of cholera by correlating two sets of data on a map, work that eventually led to the building of the London sewage system and improved public health.
- ◆ This very accessible beginning shows the basic principle of GIS and how its use can lead to very important decisions being taken.
- ◆ A range of uses for GIS is explored, including identifying crime hotspots and patterns, and suggesting reasons and decisions.

The big picture

These are the key ideas in this chapter.

- ◆ A geographical information system consists of a computer with GIS software and a map, and different layers of accurate data for the map area.
- ◆ GIS software allows related data to be displayed on a map very quickly.
- ◆ Different kinds of data can be brought together, and patterns and connections identified.
- ◆ GIS helps people to take well-informed decisions and action that make a significant difference to people's lives and environment.
- ◆ Learning about GIS is really important – for good geographers, as well as for many other purposes.

A students' version of this big picture is given in the *geog.2* students' book opener for Chapter 1.

The chapter outline

Use this, and their chapter opener, to give students a mental roadmap for the chapter.

1 **Using GIS** The chapter opener in the students' book is an important part of the chapter; see page 11 for notes about using chapter openers

1.1 **John Snow, doctor and detective** How Snow used a map to help locate the source of a cholera outbreak in 1854, how connections can be made across different types of data on a map, and the usefulness of GIS

1.2 **Meet GIS** Reading digital maps on different levels, how GIS helps to find patterns and correlations, and how it helps in making decisions on important topics

1.3 **GIS in fighting crime** How a map of crimes and an aerial photo can be used to identify patterns and crime hotspots, and to suggest reasons and solutions

1.4 **More about the data** How GIS depends on data, accurately presented in layers and in ways that facilitate making connections and decisions

1.5 **Other uses for GIS** Explores a range of uses for GIS and evaluates its usefulness

Objectives and outcomes for this chapter

Objectives		Outcomes
	Unit	
Most students will understand:		Most students will be able to:
● how different types of data can be shown on a map	1.1, 1.2	● identify the significance of text and different types of symbol on a map
● the meaning of *correlation*	1.1, 1.3	● define *correlation* and draw conclusions from correlating data on a map
● the basic principles of GIS	1.1, 1.2	● explain that GIS consists of a computer with GIS software, a map and accurate data about the map area
● what GIS can be used for and the importance of using it	1.1, 1.2, 1.3, 1.5	● name at least ten uses for GIS and explain why the outcomes might be important
● how to draw conclusions from studying data on a map and by comparing the map with an aerial photo	1.3	● identify the occurrence of different crimes, and suggest reasons and solutions, using data on a map and an aerial photo
● why data for GIS needs to be in layers and accurately positioned	1.4	● explain why different types of data need to be kept in separate layers; identify at least three methods of positioning data accurately on a map

These tie in with the outcomes for each unit, in this teacher's handbook, and with 'Your goals for this chapter', in *geog.2* students' book.

Opportunities for assessment

See the formal assessment materials for this chapter on *geog.2 Kerboodle Lessons, Resources, & Assessment*. They include an extended assessment task, an exam-style question, end-of-lesson assessments, and a self-assessment form. See also the notes on pages 14–15 of this book.

Getting ready for this chapter

geog.2 Kerboodle contains plans and presentations for each unit, including interactive activities, animations, and worksheets.

About 'Your chapter starter'

The man in the photo on page 4 of *geog.2* students' book, is in a traffic control and crime surveillance room, monitoring CCTV images. CCTV images are continuously monitored to manage traffic flows and congestion, and as part of crime reduction strategies - police are able to view incidents as they happen, and react quickly.

The image is an example of GIS in everyday use. If a crime is spotted on the screens being monitored, the maps can be used to pinpoint the location, and find the nearest police officers to deal with the crime as quickly as possible.

CCTV surveillance is common in many areas around the world. Whether we like it or not, we are all being watched.

About this unit

This unit explains how Doctor John Snow used a map to find the source of a cholera outbreak in London in 1854.

Key points

◆ In 1854, Doctor John Snow identified the source of a cholera outbreak in London by using a map to test a hypothesis – that cholera is transmitted by water, not air (as previously believed).

◆ Snow plotted two variables onto a street map of Soho: cholera deaths and the location of public water pumps (the only source of drinking water in that area). By doing this, he was able to spot a correlation between the two variables – and to identify that one particular water pump was the source of the infected water supply.

◆ The result of Snow's ground-breaking work was not only the shutting down of the infected water pump, but also the decision by the London authorities that a proper sewage system should be built right across the city. That original system is still in use today.

Key vocabulary

cesspool, cholera, correlation, sewage system, water pump

Skills practised in 'Your turn'

◆ Geography skills: q3, q5, map interpretation; q4, define a key term

◆ Thinking skills: q1, use common sense and general knowledge to construct a reasoned explanation; q2, use common sense and textual analysis to reach a conclusion; q6, q7, reach a reasoned conclusion

Unit outcomes

By the end of this unit most students should be able to:

◆ explain the terms given in 'Key vocabulary' above

◆ explain how Doctor John Snow used a map to reach a conclusion

◆ explain, with the use of a simple sketch, how the cholera outbreak began

Ideas for a starter

1   Show students the photos of Doctor John Snow, cholera bacteria and the water pump. Ask: What is the connection between the photos? Who was Doctor John Snow? What is cholera? What causes it? What are the symptoms?

2   Show students a video on cholera (e.g. Horrible Histories) or Doctor John Snow and the cholera outbreak of 1854, to introduce the topic. Students to note three things that stand out for them.

3   Introduce Doctor John Snow and his work and explain that he created a map like the one on page 7 of the students' book. Explain how cholera is caught. What does the map show? On which streets did most deaths occur? Are there any patterns?

Ideas for plenaries

Plan plenaries at strategic points throughout the lesson, as well as at the end.

Mid-lesson

1   Following on from starter **3**: You are Doctor Snow and you are investigating the causes of cholera. Now that you have plotted all the information on the map, you need to work out what it is telling you. Why are there clusters? What do you notice about the pattern? Based on what you know about how cholera is caught, where do you think the infection is coming from?

2   Ask: How might the map have looked if the cholera had been caused by 'bad air'?

3   Ask: What did Doctor John Snow think was causing cholera? How did he use a map to provide evidence to support this?

End-of-lesson

4   Imagine: You are Doctor Snow. What advice will you give to the people and authorities in London to stop the spread of cholera?

5   In groups, discuss: Do you think that Doctor Snow's way of solving the problem was a good one? Follow on with 'Your turn' question 7.

6   Think: Give one target you need to set for the next lesson, two skills you have used in this lesson and three things you have learned in this lesson.

Further class and homework opportunities

Suggestions 1–7 on page 30 of this book

geog.2 workbook, page 5

geog.2 Kerboodle: lesson presentation, worksheets, end-of-lesson assessment

Answers for 'Your turn'

1   There have been no cases of cholera in the UK for over 100 years. Cholera is a bacterial infection that is caused by contact with contaminated water. Cholera is generally found in areas with poor sanitation and poor food and water hygiene. This is not the case in the UK.

2   There was no proper sewage system so houses did not have flush toilets. Waste fell into cesspools – smelly pits under the house. These were only emptied when they got full.

3   The words tell us the name of streets and also of large buildings such as the workhouse. The red bars represent the number of deaths due to cholera at specific places; the taller the bar, the more people that died. The blue circles show us where the public water pumps were located.

4   A relationship between two different things.

5   There are no red bars close by, which means there were no deaths near to it.

6   Without information about the water pumps, it would have been more difficult to work out the cause. The information about the number of deaths would have helped to show where the largest numbers of people were dying. It wouldn't have helped with identifying the cause and showing a relationship with the cause.

7   Examples include: People at risk of flooding (location of houses and areas that have flooded previously); road safety near schools (location of accidents and schools); crime prevention (map of area showing houses, businesses, schools, recreation areas, and types of crimes in an area); air pollution and health (occurrence of different types of disease such as asthma and levels of air pollution).

About this unit

This unit uses a practical example to explain what a GIS (Geographic Information System) is.

Key points

◆ A GIS (Geographic Information System) allows the user to quickly add specific data onto a base map, using a menu, in order to look for patterns and correlations and make decisions.

◆ Flood risk maps and associated early warning systems are just one example of a GIS system being used in practice. There are many other examples, such as mapping crime hotspots, or planning new transport infrastructure routes to minimise the disruption, expense and number of complaints from the public, e.g. the route of the controversial High Speed 2 (HS2) rail line from London to northern England through the Chilterns.

Key vocabulary

data, GIS (Geographic Information System), software

Skills practised in 'Your turn'

◆ Geography skills: q1, define a key term; q5, map interpretation

◆ Literacy skills: q6c, write an emergency warning message

◆ Thinking skills: q2, q3, q4, q6, explain; q7, compare methods to reach reasoned conclusions; q8, apply knowledge to a new scenario

Unit outcomes

By the end of this unit most students should be able to:

◆ explain the terms given in 'Key vocabulary' above

◆ explain how a GIS system works, with at least two examples

Ideas for a starter

1 Using photos / maps, briefly introduce the topic of flooding, e.g. What are the causes of flooding? What are the effects of flooding? Why do we need to be able to predict flooding? How can we use maps to give us clues about flooding?

2 Imagine: You are a flood officer working for the local council and you have been told by your boss that a flood is on its way. What information do you need to know? Who do you need to inform? What actions will you need to take?

3 Show students a satellite image of an area that is likely to flood (i.e. with a river) and tell them that they have been asked to look into flood defences for the area. Ask: What do you know about this image? What do you want to know about this image? What other information might you need to know about the image?

Ideas for plenaries

Plan plenaries at strategic points throughout the lesson, as well as at the end.

Mid-lesson

1 Ask pairs to discuss and complete the following definition: Geographical Information Systems are…. Students feedback definitions to the rest of the class to come up with an all-encompassing definition.

2 Do 'Your turn' question 6 as a plenary.

3 Do 'Your turn' question 7 as a plenary.

End-of-lesson

4 Do 'Your turn' question 8 as a plenary.

5 Scaffolded discussion: What are the advantages of using GIS to warn local people about flooding? Are there any limitations / things that it can't help with? How could it be improved?

6 In small groups, ask students: What else might GIS be useful for? Note down as many ideas as you can. Think about other topics you have studied in Geography and how GIS might be useful. Collate ideas with a group discussion.

7 Learning wall: Write on sticky notes one thing you have learned about GIS in this lesson and one question you have from what you have learned. Stick the notes to the learning wall. Whole-class discussion about the questions and points learned.

Further class and homework opportunities

Suggestions 8–13 on page 30 of this book

geog.2 workbook, page 6

geog.2 Kerboodle: lesson presentation, worksheets, end-of-lesson assessment

Answers for 'Your turn'

1 A computer programme.

2 a People who have registered to receive flood warnings.

 b They are not at risk of flooding.

3 a Only a Level 2 flood is expected, so the flood officer only needs to know the area that will be affected by a Level 2 flood.

 b The flood officer only needs to know the houses / businesses that will be affected today rather than all the registered houses in the area or those that may be affected tomorrow. Only the houses that will be affected today need to be evacuated / warned immediately.

4 a It would not show any information about the level of floods.

 b It would just show a map of the area with no data on it.

5 From the pattern of the roads (densely packed, semi-circular roads), the location of schools and green spaces, the fact that names of the areas have a residential feel, the pattern of red dots indicates lots of houses.

6 a Area map, level 3, at risk today.

 b The purple area showing likely flooding will be wider. There will be more red dots as a larger area will be flooded.

 c Messages should include information about the level of flood (Level 3), the time the flood is expected (8 pm), and what people should do.

7 Examples might include: it shows a correlation more quickly; it allows you to see detailed information about the data (e.g. contact details for the people who will be affected); it allows you to see quickly who will be affected by different levels of flood; it allows you to contact the affected people more quickly by sending them a message to alert them.

8 Menus should include: area map; deaths from cholera; water pumps; message.

GIS in fighting crime

help at a glance

About this unit

This unit explores the use of GIS in fighting crime.

Key points

◆ Another example of a GIS system is that used by the police to identify crime hotspots and target suitable resources to address them. Certain areas might encourage particular crimes, which in turn require varied police responses. For example:

   – A city centre area where many bars and clubs are located might experience lots of fights and anti-social behaviour on Friday and Saturday nights. Therefore, the local police might consider it appropriate to deploy mounted patrols on horses to help maintain order and intimidate troublemakers.

   – By contrast, a particular residential street identified, using the GIS system, as suffering a lot of house burglaries – and which backs onto playing fields or rough waste ground – might be considered more suitable for foot patrols.

Key vocabulary

crime hotspot, postcode

Skills practised in 'Your turn'

◆ Geography skills: q1–q8, analyse a GIS map and aerial photo; q2, q5, q6, use four-figure map references; q3a define a key term

◆ Thinking skills: q1–q3, explain and give reasoned suggestions; q4–q7, use map skills and common sense to identify and analyse crime hotspots, and suggest reasons for them; q8, consider the role of aerial photos as part of a crime GIS menu

Unit outcomes

By the end of this unit most students should be able to:

◆ explain the terms given in 'Key vocabulary' above

◆ describe how and why the police usually use both street maps and aerial photos as part of their GIS systems

Ideas for a starter

1 Based on the previous lesson, ask: Can you tell us what Geographic Information Systems are? What might be the advantages of GIS over paper-based maps?

2 Discuss: What is a crime? Can you define it? Can you think of some examples of crimes? Students create a spider diagram showing examples of crimes, adding numbers to rank each crime based on severity, with 1 being the most severe.

3 Show students a variety of images taken from urban and rural areas. They describe each picture and say how it makes them feel. Ask: Is there likely to be crime in this area? Why?

Ideas for plenaries

Plan plenaries at strategic points throughout the lesson, as well as at the end.

Mid-lesson

1   Using the information from the map on page 10 of the students' book, students plot the data on a graph. Ask: What type of graph would be the most suitable?

2   Using the map, aerial photo, and graph plotted in plenary **1**, in groups students describe the pattern of crime across the whole map using geographical terms. Ask: Which crimes are most common? Which are the least common? Use 'Your turn' question 7 to identify crime hotspots and their reasons.

End-of-lesson

3   Ask: Do you think that the map on page 10 of the students' book shows all the crimes in the area? Support discussion about why it might not (i.e. crimes might not be reported for a number of reasons).

4   Do 'Your turn' question 8 as a plenary activity.

Further class and homework opportunities

Suggestions 14–24 on pages 30–31 of this book

geog.2 workbook, page 7

geog.2 Kerboodle: lesson presentation, worksheets, end-of-lesson assessment

Answers for 'Your turn'

1   **a**   They tended to take place outside places of entertainment (e.g. pubs, clubs, wine bars, restaurants) and may be the result of people drinking too much alcohol.

  b   Suggestions might include: regular police patrols; bars / clubs could employ door men; raising alcohol prices; anti-alcohol campaign; limit the number of pubs and opening hours; not selling alcohol to people who have had too much to drink.

2   **a**   Mugging

  b   There are lots of bushes / trees along the path where the muggings have taken place. These provide cover so that people might not be able to see what is going on.

  c   Suggestions might include: cutting down trees; cutting back trees; increasing police patrols along the path; public awareness campaign encouraging people not to walk in secluded areas after dark, not use phones or other expensive gadgets in public. The order that students place them in will vary but they should be able to justify their order.

3   **a**   A group of letters and numbers that locate a small area of houses and help with sorting mail, e.g. OX2 6DP.

  b   So that if things are stolen and then recovered by the police, the police are able to locate the area they were stolen from.

  c   The main crimes on that road were household burglary and repeat household burglary.

4   The houses on the right of Dante Avenue back onto the park and the footpath runs behind them. This makes it easier for burglars to get into and out of the houses without being seen. The houses on the left of Dante Avenue back onto other houses so it is more difficult to get into gardens without being seen.

5   **a**   1037. This is where an open air car park is located, so there are usually plenty of cars there, cars might be parked there for long periods of time, and owners might have left attractive items on display in their cars.

  b   1339. This is an area of fairly dense trees next to the railway. It is probably quite deserted so people can dump rubbish there without being seen.

6   These squares contain buildings (schools and shopping centre) that are likely to have large areas of wall, which are an ideal space for graffiti, and large groups are likely to hang out there and may vandalise things / graffiti walls if they are bored.

7   There are a couple of crime hotspots on the map:

  ◆   1137. This is the main shopping centre so there are a large number of businesses / shops in the area. There are also probably a lot of concrete walls and other areas that are ideal for graffiti.

  ◆   1438. This is where the schools are. There are car parks (i.e. lots of cars that could be broken into) and plenty of buildings (where windows could be broken by footballs, for example, and walls could be graffitied).

8   **a**   It is an exact match for the map and should score 10.

  b   If crime information was shown on the photo, it would be difficult to see it clearly.

  c   The photo helps the police to work out what the causes of crime might be. For example, in 1436 the map shows that there are a high number of muggings and the photo shows that the path is well covered with trees. The police need to know both the patterns and causes of crime so that they can work out ways of tackling or preventing the crime.

More about the data

help at a glance

About this unit

This unit provides more information about GIS and data.

Key points

- GIS depends on data. The system's purpose is to display different data on a base map, so that patterns and correlations can be identified – and actions planned in response.

- The data in GIS is organised in layers – each one with a particular theme, such as the cholera deaths in Unit 1.1. The number of layers can vary, depending on the complexity of analysis required (sometimes all layers will be turned on in the GIS menu, and sometimes only two or three).

- Each piece of data must appear at the right place on the base map, i.e. the correct latitude and longitude. Without this accuracy, any conclusions about correlations would be flawed.

Key vocabulary

correlation, data, GPS (global positioning system), latitude and longitude, layers, patterns, postcode

Skills practised in 'Your turn'

- Geography skills: q1, define a key term

- Thinking skills: q2, q3a, q4a, give a reasoned explanation; q4b, apply information to reach a conclusion; use common sense and prior knowledge to reach a reasoned conclusion

Unit outcomes

By the end of this unit most students should be able to:

- explain the terms given in 'Key vocabulary' above

- explain the importance of data in GIS

- explain why data in GIS is organised in layers, and how the layers work

- explain the importance of accurate geographical coordinates for each piece of data

Ideas for a starter

1   Ask for a volunteer to remind the class what GIS is and what they know about it.

2   Explain that GIS data is in layers with each layer containing specific information. Ask students to look back to Unit 1.2 about flood warning. What information was needed to warn people about the flood? Explain that these are the layers. What information was needed by Doctor Snow in Unit 1.1?

3   Recap lines of latitude and longitude: What is the question? Give students the answer and ask them to give you the question:

Answer	Question
They are imaginary lines found on maps that give an exact location.	What are lines of latitude and longitude?
They run from east to west and tell you how far north and south you are.	What are lines of latitude?
The equator	What is an example of a line of latitude?
They run from north to south and tell you how far east or west you are.	What are lines of longitude?
The Greenwich Meridian	What is an example of a line of longitude?

Ideas for plenaries

Plan plenaries at strategic points throughout the lesson, as well as at the end.

Mid-lesson

1   Ask students to identify and explain the differences between GIS maps and paper-based maps. Why are GIS maps so great? Are there any occasions when it might be better to use paper-based maps?

2   Do 'Your turn' questions 4 and 5 as a plenary.

3   Give students some other examples of how GIS could be used: e.g. where to locate an out-of-town shopping centre; where to locate a new wind farm / solar panel farm; measuring coastal erosion over time. What information would you need for your investigation? What layers would you need on your GIS map?

End-of-lesson

4   Ask: What does GPS stand for? What information does it give us? Why is it important in GIS?

5   Ask: What did you enjoy about today's lesson? What didn't you enjoy about today's lesson? What challenged your thinking the most?

Further class and homework opportunities

Suggestions 25–34 on page 31 of this book

geog.2 workbook, page 8

geog.2 Kerboodle: lesson presentation, worksheets, end-of-lesson assessment

Answers for 'Your turn'

1   Information about people or things that is collected for a particular purpose (e.g. names, addresses, age, number of schools in an area).

2   You might want to turn one of the layers off and, if they are in the same layer, you can't do this. You might want to look at each of the sets of data against other data to find other patterns / relationships.

3   a   GPS can give us an exact position of a person or object.

   b   A coordinate which tells us latitude and longitude

4   a   Students might hang out in and around fast food places after school. This means that there might be a higher number of students near to fast food places and this could increase the risk of an accident.

   b   Answers will vary depending on the location of students' area / school.

5   All this information would make a paper map hard to read and confusing. It would be harder to pick out relationships between different sets of data. You wouldn't be able to select certain layers of data if you wanted to look at specific relationships (e.g. you might just want to look at the number of pedestrians hit by cars in the last ten years and not those hit by bikes). If you wanted to add more data to a printed map, you would have to print a new version and it might become even harder to read.

Other uses for GIS

help at a glance

About this unit

This unit provides some additional examples of GIS.

Key points

◆ There are already hundreds of different uses for GIS – the only restriction is the human imagination.

◆ As technology continues to develop, the number of different uses for GIS is likely to increase substantially (unless a better system is developed!).

Key vocabulary

satellite image, sat nav, Google Earth

Skills practised in 'Your turn'

◆ Thinking skills: q1, reach conclusions and support them with evidence; q2, reach reasoned conclusions; q3a, make a reasoned selection; q3b, consider personal circumstances

Unit outcomes

By the end of this unit most students should be able to:

◆ explain the terms given in 'Key vocabulary' above

◆ describe at least two other examples of the use of GIS

Ideas for a starter

1 Say: We have seen how GIS is useful for flood wardens and the police. Think of some other examples where GIS might be really important (e.g. other emergency services, town planning, conservation).

2 With books closed and using the different examples of uses of GIS on pages 14–15 (and other examples), give students a description from which they have to guess who / what you are. Ask: Do you know what the connection is between the different things that have been described?

3 With books closed, show students pictures of a delivery driver, a ship's captain, a fire or ambulance crew and a professional football player. Ask: Which of these people would not use GIS in their job?

Ideas for plenaries

Plan plenaries at strategic points throughout the lesson, as well as at the end.

Mid-lesson

1   Do 'Your turn' questions 2 and 3 as a plenary.

2   Ask: What if we hadn't learned about GIS?

End-of-lesson

3   Ask: Who can talk for one minute on GIS without pausing, repetition or making a mistake? If scaffolding is needed, include some key terms on the board: compare / connection; data; software; computer; map; police; crime; layers; latitude; longitude; GPS.

4   Ask: What three things do you know now that you didn't know at the start of your work on GIS? What three things would you like to find out more about?

Further class and homework opportunities

Suggestions 35–41 on page 31 of this book

geog.2 workbook, page 9

geog.2 Kerboodle: lesson presentation, worksheets, end-of-lesson assessment

Answers for 'Your turn'

1   **a** and **b**

	Doing jobs more efficiently	**Making good decisions**
Parcel delivery	Helps to plot the most efficient and the quickest route.	Plots the best route so you don't end up going back on yourself.
Sending an ambulance	It allows the operator to locate the address instantly (rather than looking it up on a map) and see the nearest ambulance to save time.	Getting the nearest ambulance could save lives.
Windfarm / Saving chimps	Layering of the different data sets makes it easier to find a suitable site (otherwise you would have to look up a number of other maps and refer from one to another to make a decision), which would take longer.	Locates the wind farm in the best possible place to generate the maximum amount of energy but with the least impact. Locates the precise area that the chimps live in so it can be protected without moving the chimps.
Sat nav	It can choose the fastest route so you will get there more quickly. There is less risk of getting lost so making the journey quicker.	It allows you to choose the best route (e.g. fastest, shortest or avoiding tolls). It can detect a traffic jam so you can take an alternative route.

2   If access to the internet, a computer or other device goes down or a battery runs out, then digital information is lost. This may be crucial whether trying to save lives or to deliver parcels. In that case paper maps are a useful back up.

Digital maps often give a snapshot of a small area but don't show the big picture. You might want to look at a wider area when looking at different factors in choosing to site a wind farm, for example. When driving with sat nav, you may feel you have to follow the instructions because you can only see the immediate area around the route. With a map, you can decide where you want to go; for example, you might want to stop at a point of interest not far from your route.

3   **a**   Choices will vary.

   b   Students should consider what they might want to do in the future (e.g. jobs), their health (e.g. in older age), and the future of the environment / planet, and how GIS might help.

Many of these suggestions are addressed to your students. Where research or further resources are needed, the internet will almost certainly provide the answer.

The suggestions are graded *,**,*** according to level of difficulty. Some are suitable for all levels, and can be differentiated by outcome.

John Snow, doctor and detective

1 **Cholera** What is it? How do you get it? What are the symptoms? If you get it will you die? Find out! */**

2 **Convincing the council** Doctor John Snow convinced the council that the water from the Broad Street pump was the source of the cholera outbreak. Write a letter from the doctor to the council explaining this, and to ask that the pump should no longer be used. */**/***

3 **Panic!** When the cholera outbreak happened in 1854 people were terrified. Many closed up their homes and fled. Imagine you were alive at that time. Write a diary entry for the first few days in September 1854 as the cholera outbreak grows. */**/***

4 **Cholera twenty first century** Where have there been cholera outbreaks since 2005? Search online for 'cholera outbreaks' and colour in the countries which have had outbreaks on a world map. Describe the pattern of the outbreaks. Have there been any in the UK? **/***

5 **Write a commentary** Find a video about the cholera outbreak of 1854 in London and Doctor John Snow's involvement. Watch it once. Then turn the sound off and watch it again. Now write your own commentary for the video. **/***

6 **Maps are key!** Doctor John Snow could not have carried out his work on the cholera outbreak without a map. Create your own map – this time a concept map – to show why Doctor Snow needed a map. **/***

7 **Storyboard or strip cartoon** Write a storyboard or draw a strip cartoon to show how the cholera outbreak happened, how Doctor John Snow found the source of the outbreak, and how it was stopped. Use one frame for each event. */**

Meet GIS

8 **What is GIS?** Write a paragraph to explain what GIS is. You must include these words: data, GIS software, map, computer. Take a class vote to decide on the best explanation. */**

9 **GIS has …** one part, three parts, five parts? How many parts does it have? List them and say why each one is important. */**

10 **Flood warning!** You are the flood warden. You have used GIS to work out which addresses are at risk of flooding today. Write your message to the people at risk. Tell them the level of the flood, what time it is expected and what they should do. Hurry up, there's no time to lose! */**

11 **5 Ws** Look at the map on page 9 of the students' book. Come up with three really good W questions about the map (Who? Where? What? When? Why?) Share your questions in a small group and see who can answer them. */**/***

12 **Uses for GIS** There are many uses of GIS. Work in a small group and bounce ideas around. How many uses can you come up with? Make a spider diagram of your ideas. **/***

13 **Summary** Summarise what you learned in today's lesson in 50 words. Now 20 words, now 5. **/***

GIS in fighting crime

14 **Information is key!** Think of three different pieces of information about crime that the police might need to know in order to be able to fight it (things like – where it happened, and so on). Then look at the map on page 10 of the students' book. What does it show? How could it help the police to tackle crime? */**

15 **Which is more useful?** Compare the map and aerial photo of the same area on pages 10 and 11 of the students' book. Which is better at telling you what the area is like? Which one might be more helpful to the police when they are looking at crime? Why? Explain how the map and aerial photo are useful when used together. **/***

16 **Crime information** Who else needs information about crime? It's not just the police. People like the government, insurance companies and house buyers all want information about crime, but why? What information do they need? How would they find it useful? How might the map on page 10 of the students' book help them? **/***

17 **Crime in the local area** The local crime prevention officer has asked your class to write a report on crime in the local area. Using what you have learned in this lesson, work in groups and list the types of crime in the area, make a statement about the levels of crime (identify crime hotspots) based on information from the map and aerial photo. Recommend three ways of reducing crime in the area. Where do you suggest the police focus their patrols? Gather together the ideas from the different groups and discuss them. **/***

18 **How would you feel?** Imagine your house has been burgled (or perhaps it really has been). Some of your best things were taken. Write to a friend saying when it happened, what was taken, and how you felt about it. */**

19 **Mapping local crime** Walk around your local area, recording graffiti and vandalism on a map (use coloured dots and a key). Then search the local newspaper or internet for other crimes committed in the area over the last month, and mark these in too. Identify any crime hotspots, and suggest reasons. */**/***

20 **Using GIS to map crime** If you completed the previous activity, here's another. How could you use GIS to record the crimes you identified? How would it help you to identify crime hotspots? How could it help the police? What else would it be useful for? **/***

21 How safe does it seem? The class take digital photos of the local area, and arrange them in order from 'safe' to 'less safe'. The photos should concentrate on the built environment, not on people. Finally, write a list of characteristics that make a place feel unsafe. */**

22 Up your street Search online to find out how your area or neighbourhood compares with the national average in terms of crime. Search using terms such as 'up my street' or 'neighbourhood statistics up my street'. Is this what you expected? Make a short presentation to the class. ***

23 Crime prevention report Following on from the previous activity - you are the local councillor for your area. Using what you have learned about crime in your local area, write a report called *Crime in the local community, and how it might be prevented,* for the council. Your report must be formal and should include facts and figures. ***

24 How serious? Choose two crime reports from a newspaper, one for a serious crime, the other for an apparently less serious crime. Neither too gory! One could be about a financial crime, for example.

Ask two students to read the reports to the class. Then ask students to rate each crime on a scale of 1-10, where 10 is *extremely serious*. Record the scores on a tally chart on the board, and let students work out the average score for each. Discuss why people have different views about what is a serious crime. **/***

More about the data

25 What's the connection ... between a globe with lines of latitude and longitude marked on it, a postcode, a mobile phone and a GPS unit? Work it out, and then explain how they are useful to geographers. **/***

26 What is... a coordinate? Latitude and longitude? A postcode? GPS? Why are they useful (in connection with GIS)? **

27 GPS What does it stand for? What is it? Have you ever used GPS? What about in the car? Have you ever used a map app on a mobile (they use GPS)? Explain how map apps use GPS. ***

28 Which is better? When would it be better to use a paper map rather than a GIS map? Work in a small group. How many ideas can you come up with? Record your ideas as a spider diagram. Compare your ideas with the rest of the class. */**

29 Data What data would you need for the following?
 – Deciding where to build a windfarm
 – Deciding the order to deliver parcels for a delivery company
 – Deciding where to build a secondary school
 – Controlling traffic flows
 – Deciding the location of a new shopping centre **/***

30 Recall Work in a small group. Give out sticky notes. Write down a different thing on each sticky note to do with what you have learned about GIS and data in this lesson. Post your notes on a large sheet of a paper. */**

31 True/False Work in pairs. Make up five statements, each based on what you have learned in this lesson – some true, some false. Swap your statements with your partner. Where they have written false statements, correct them. **

32 Summary Summarise what you learned in today's lesson in 50 words. Now 20 words, now 5. **/***

33 How many things... can you remember about using GIS? No peeking in your book! Write down four things, you can remember. Now another three, then two more. And one final one – you can do it! **

34 What is the question? Make up five questions and answers about data and GIS for your partner. But here's the trick – you give your partner the answers. They have to work out what the question was! **

Other uses for GIS

35 How many uses? How many uses of GIS can you think of? Work with a partner and create a spider diagram of as many examples of GIS as possible. */**/***

36 True or false? Which of these statements are true, and which ones are false? For the ones which are false, write out a correct version.
 – GIS stands for Global Information System.
 – A GIS system has three parts to it – a computer, GIS software and a map.
 – GIS maps are made up of layers of data.
 – GPS stands for Global Positioning System.
 – GPS is used for finding locations in space. **

37 Odd one out Create sets of uses of GIS (say three uses in each set), but one is an odd-one out which doesn't use GIS. Give the sets to your partner and ask them to find the odd-one-out. Tricky! ***

38 Time's up! Work in pairs. You have to write for 30 seconds about GIS without stopping. When 30 seconds is up your partner takes over. And 30 seconds later you take over again, and so on. How long can you keep going for without stopping or repeating yourselves? **/***

39 Banned! Choose one use of GIS. It could be from pages 14-15 of the students' book, or another suitable example. Describe how GIS is used for that job or function. Sounds easy? Here's the catch! You can't use any of these words in your description: GIS, data, layers, software, map, computer. How easy it is now? When you have finished, swap your description with a partner. Can they work out the use of GIS you have described? **/***

40 GIS presentation Work in pairs and create a presentation about GIS suitable for the year below you. You need to explain:
 – what GIS is
 – what data you need and how it is organised
 – examples of what GIS is used for. **/***

41 GIS crossword Make up a crossword on GIS. Then you and your neighbour can swap and solve each other's. **

2 Population

About this chapter

Addressing the KS3 Programme of Study

◆ Develop knowledge of globally significant places, including Ethiopia and China, defining their population characteristics.

◆ Understand how population change interacts to influence and change environments, climate, and the weather, and how human activity relies on effective functioning of natural systems.

◆ Interpret a range of sources of geographical information, including maps and graphs.

About the content

◆ This chapter starts by giving an overview of population growth through history, including the basic principles of how population grows.

◆ It examines global population distribution and various reasons for global differences.

◆ It looks at the impact of population growth on resources, other species, and the environment, and offers predictions for the future.

The big picture

These are the key ideas in this chapter.

◆ The global population has been growing at an exponential rate for the last 250 years or so.

◆ Globally, the birth rate is higher than the death rate.

◆ Population is distributed in different densities around the world, largely dependent on natural factors such as climate.

◆ Population grows at different rates in different countries – *falling* in some – depending on birth rates, life expectancy, and migration.

◆ Our rising population has an impact on Earth's resources, on other species, and on the environment.

◆ Global population is predicted to rise until about 2050, but then start to fall.

A students' version of this big picture is given in the *geog.2* students' book opener for Chapter 2.

The chapter outline

Use this, and their chapter opener, to give students a mental roadmap for the chapter.

2 Population The chapter opener in the students' book is an important part of the chapter; see page 11 for notes about using chapter openers

2.1 Our numbers are growing fast How the world's population has grown, some reasons why, and speculation about the future

2.2 So where is everyone? Where population is distributed around the world and the influence of climate on population

2.3 The population of the UK How and why the UK population has changed over the centuries, explaining average life expectancy for men and women

2.4 Population around the world Population growth and life expectancy around the world, and why population is growing fastest in some of the poorest countries

2.5 Our impact on our planet How population growth impacts on Earth's resources and on other living things

2.6 What does the future hold? Different predictions for global population in 2050, including why it might fall, and trends, comparing Germany and Ethopia

Objectives and outcomes for this chapter

Objectives	Unit	Outcomes
Most students will understand:		Most students will be able to:
• how populations increase generally, and how and why global population has changed through history	2.1	• describe how and why global population has changed through history, with reference to a graph
• what *population density* and *life expectancy* mean	2.2, 2.3	• define *population density*, *life expectancy*, and other related key terms
• how and why global population density is uneven	2.2	• identify different population densities on a world map; compare population density with climate for various global locations; describe the impact of climate on population density
• how and why the UK population has changed through history	2.3	• identify at least six causes of population change in the UK, with reference to graphs
• how and why population growth is different around the world	2.4	• identify on a map where population is rising and falling; explain the impacts on population growth of women's education, government policy, and life expectancy
• how much we depend on Earth's resources	2.5	• identify at least two of Earth's resources and explain why we depend on them
• the impacts of population growth on the planet	2.5	• give examples of how population growth impacts on resources, other species and the environment, explaining why
• how global population might change in the future, and why	2.6	• evaluate different future trends in population growth
• the problems population change might bring in the future	2.6	• identify at least one problem resulting from population change in each of Germany and Ethiopia

These tie in with the outcomes for each unit, in this teacher's handbook, and with 'Your goals for this chapter', in *geog.2* students' book.

Opportunities for assessment

See the formal assessment materials for this chapter on *geog.2 Kerboodle Lessons, Resources, & Assessment*. They include an extended assessment task, an exam-style question, end-of-lesson assessments, and a self-assessment form. See also the notes on pages 14–15 of this book.

Getting ready for this chapter

geog.2 Kerboodle contains plans and presentations for each unit, including interactive activities, animations, and worksheets.

About 'Your chapter starter'

The world's population is growing rapidly. The newborn baby on page 16 of *geog.2* students' book, is one of around 360 000 babies born every single day around the world. How long this baby will live will depend on where she was born. Life expectancy varies dramatically, from 89 years in Monaco, to 49 in Chad. Average life expectancy in the UK is 80 years.

The number of babies she will have (known as the fertility rate) will also vary, depending on where she was born. The fertility rate is highest in Niger, at an average of 6.9 babies per woman, and lowest in Singapore, at less than one baby per woman (0.8). In the UK the figure is 1.9.

About this unit

This unit introduces students to the concept of global population increase and some of the main reasons for it.

Key points

◆ As long as the number of births is greater than the number of deaths, a population will increase. Natural increase = birth rate − death rate. (The birth / death rate is the number of live births / deaths per thousand people in a year.)

◆ Population increases exponentially (2, 4, 8, 16, etc.) rather than arithmetically (1, 2, 3, 4, etc.), which is how food supply increases. Thus, according to Malthus, the population size will eventually outstrip the available food supply. This will lead either to a correction in the population size (e.g. famine and death), or to new developments in food production to increase the food supply. This is one argument put forward for developing GM foods.

◆ For most of human history the population remained relatively low, but it began to increase dramatically as the Industrial Revolution, with its increased labour demands, took hold. Methods of food production also improved, e.g. selective breeding and more mechanisation to increase productivity. Thus, in little over 200 years, the population has increased from 1 billion in 1804 to over 7 billion today – and it's still increasing.

Key vocabulary

Industrial Revolution, population

Skills practised in 'Your turn'

◆ Geography skills: q6a, describe a key term; q7, analyse data

◆ Numeracy skills: q7, analyse a graph

◆ Literacy skills: q8, write a reasoned conclusion (a paragraph)

◆ Thinking skills: q3b, q4, q5, q6b, q8, apply common sense and prior knowledge

Unit outcomes

By the end of this unit most students should be able to:

◆ explain the terms given in 'Key vocabulary' above

◆ explain that population rises when there are more births than deaths

◆ describe the shape of the world population graph and say roughly what the present world population is

◆ give reasons for the population increase and why it might slow down

Ideas for a starter

1 With books closed, ask: About how many people do you think are on Earth right now? How fast is the world's population growing? Use an online world population clock to show students the number of births, deaths, and population growth so far today, and for this year. Note the number of births, and size of the world's population.

2 Draw a village and a flow chart on the board, as started below. Explain: Nobody moves into or out of this village. Ask students to help you fill the missing numbers in the boxes, and make up missing arrow labels. Ask: What happens to the population when more people are born than die? What happens to it when more die than are born?

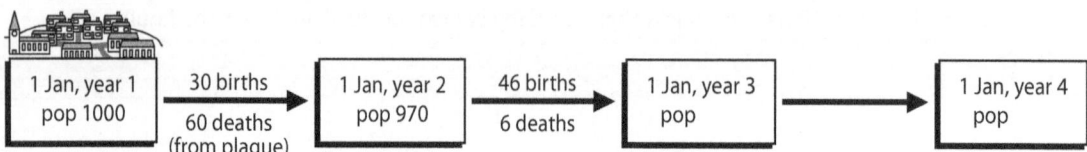

| 1 Jan, year 1 pop 1000 | 30 births / 60 deaths (from plague) | 1 Jan, year 2 pop 970 | 46 births / 6 deaths | 1 Jan, year 3 pop | | 1 Jan, year 4 pop |

Ideas for plenaries

Plan plenaries at strategic points throughout the lesson, as well as at the end.

Mid-lesson

1   Using the graph of world population on page 19 of the students' book, ask:
    - Why do the year numbers start at 10 000 and go down to 1 and then rise again?
    - What do BC and AD stand for?
    - How many years ago was 1000 BC?
    - In 1000 BC the population was 50 million – less than the UK's population today (64 million). What would it have been like with so few humans in such a big world?

2   Discuss the shape of the graph on page 19 of the students' book. Around when did the world population really start to take off? Why do you think that was?

End-of-lesson

3   Go back to the world population clock you used in starter **1**. Using the number of births, and size of the world's population you noted, students work out: a) how many people have been born during the lesson time b) the approximate world population at the end of the lesson.

4   Ask students to suggest, in pairs or small groups, the two key ideas in today's lesson.

Further class and homework opportunities

Suggestions 1–9 on page 46 of this book

geog.2 workbook, page 11

geog.2 Kerboodle: lesson presentation, worksheets, end-of-lesson assessment

Answers for 'Your turn'

1   The human population grows each year because there are more births than deaths.

2   **a**   It shows the increase in the world's population over time from 10 000 BC (Before Christ) to the present day. The *x* axis shows the year and the *y* axis shows the population in billions.

    b   The line rises very slowly at first – it is nearly flat – but starts to climb steeply around 1800 AD. (It's shaped a bit like the letter J.)

3   **a**   Hunter gatherers live by hunting animals and gathering wild fruit and seeds.

    b   Only a small number of plants were suitable for people to eat and plants were seasonal so food wasn't easy to come by. Hunter gatherers had to move around over a large area to get enough food. They were threatened by predators (e.g. tigers) or poisonous animals, such as snakes.

4   Farming meant that people were able to grow food and rear animals. This meant that people had more food and were able to live longer. Children had a better chance of survival. It also allowed settlements to grow, fed by the farms. The growth of settlements brought more people together so the birth rate began to rise.

5   Bronze was an excellent material for making tools and weapons as it was harder and stronger than the stone, wood and bone tools that had been in use. Bronze tools allowed people to clear large areas of land for farming and settlements and provided tools for farming. This enabled them to grow more food and live longer. Settlements brought more people together so the birth rate began to rise. Axes also allowed them to chop timber for constructing buildings and shelters, which protected them from danger.

6   **a**   The period from 1760 to 1840 when many new machines were invented and many factories were built.

    b   The new factories brought huge numbers of workers into towns. So the population of the towns exploded, which meant the birth rate also exploded as couples met and settled down together. The wealth brought by the Industrial Revolution helped to improve services, helped more children to survive and helped people to live longer.

7   **a**   1804

    b   It reached 2 billion in 1927, so it took 123 years to go from 1 billion to 2 billion.

    c   It was 3 billion in 1959 and 6 billion in 1999, so it took 40 years to go from 3 billion to 6 billion.

8   **a**   Students' answers should suggest that the world's population cannot continue growing at the same rate. Reasons would include the following problems that are exacerbated by a growing population: environmental problems, such as deforestation / loss of ecosystems, desertification, increasing levels of CO_2 emissions, global warming and pollution; pressure on resources (such as a lack of fresh water and food); consumption of resources faster than they are being replaced / over-consumption (fossil fuels); starvation, malnutrition and increased risk of disease.

    b   Answers could include: government policy (e.g. China's one child policy); education on family planning and birth control; spread of disease / epidemics / pandemics in less-developed countries due to overcrowding, poor sanitation, malnutrition and poor healthcare; famine / starvation / malnutrition due to poor diets, desertification, etc.

So where is everyone?

About this unit

This unit examines global population distribution and some reasons for it.

Key points

◆ Humans are distributed very unevenly across the planet – some areas are uninhabited, or very sparsely populated, and other areas are very densely populated.

◆ One reason for this uneven population distribution is the physical conditions of a location, e.g. the population is lower in mountainous and desert areas but higher near coasts and rivers (where there is flat land for agriculture, easier trade and transport routes and a reliable water supply).

◆ Another – related – reason is the climatic conditions in a given area, e.g. deserts are very hot (or cold) and dry, and the polar regions are extremely cold with low precipitation, which makes agriculture impossible.

Key vocabulary

population distribution, population density, densely populated, sparsely populated

Skills practised in 'Your turn'

◆ Geography skills: q1, explain key terms; q2–q5, analyse and interpret maps

◆ Thinking skills: q4, q5, apply information and prior knowledge to reach and explain conclusions

Unit outcomes

By the end of this unit most students should be able to:

◆ explain the terms given in 'Key vocabulary' above

◆ describe and analyse information provided on choropleth maps and reach reasoned conclusions based upon it

Ideas for a starter

1   Ask students to think back to last year. Who can remember what our ancestors had to think about in choosing where to settle? Do you think humans everywhere thought like that?

2   Ask students to move around the room, and stand in a spot where they feel comfortable. Say they are showing population distribution. Which parts of the room are densely populated? Which are sparsely populated? Why did you choose that spot? Perhaps because it's near a door (access), or window / radiator (climate / fuel), or a cupboard (resources), or friends (safety / security). Might people settle in different parts of the world for similar reasons? On the board, build up a list of factors that influenced where people settled.

3   Display photos of different types of environments from around the world (e.g. snowy mountains, coast, desert, green pasture land). Ask students to look at each one, make notes and describe each photo. Ask: Do you think a lot of people live there? Why / Why not? Would you want to live there? Discuss responses and try to draw out the different factors that might affect population distribution (e.g. physical, social and economic).

Ideas for plenaries

Plan plenaries at strategic points throughout the lesson, as well as at the end.

Mid-lesson

1   Look at the map on page 20 of the students' book. Ask: What is it about? Then do 'Your turn' question 2 as a plenary. Ask students to describe where most people tend to live and why.

2   Show a cartogram for world population (for example from the Worldmapper website). Ask: In what way is this map different from other maps? How does it work? Explain that a cartogram is a map where the sizes of places show data such as population, or wealth, not their actual land area. Which countries and continents are largest on the cartogram?

End-of-lesson

3   Display a photo showing refugees fleeing a war / famine. Ask: What is the picture showing? Try to elicit why they are refugees. How might war / famine affect population distribution?

4   Ask students to work in small groups to decide on three key points that they have learned about the world's population and its distribution.

Further class and homework opportunities

Suggestions 10–14 on page 46 of this book

geog.2 workbook, page 12

geog.2 Kerboodle: lesson presentation, worksheets, end-of-lesson assessment

Answers for 'Your turn'

1   a   Lots of people live there; it's crowded.

    b   Not many people live there; it's fairly empty.

    c   How people are spread or distributed around the country.

    d   The number of people per square kilometre.

2   Asia and Europe

3   a   Expect examples from among: India, Bangladesh, Japan, South Korea, Taiwan, UK, Germany, Netherlands, Belgium.

        (Note that population density varies greatly among these: about three times greater for Bangladesh than for India, for example. Note too that although China is densely populated in parts, it has a much lower population density overall than the UK – about 140 people per sq km compared with about 250 in the UK.)

    b   Expect examples from among: Greenland, Canada, Australia, Libya, Mongolia, Botswana, Namibia, Western Sahara, Mauritania.

4   a   Hot (close to the tropics) and very dry – no reliable rain.

    b   No, too dry; crops need water.

    c   Very low; people tend to settle where it's easy to find water and grow food. And it's a bit too hot at P for people too!

5

Place	Country	Climate	Population density	Reasons
P	Algeria	Hot; very dry (no rainfall in Sahara desert)	Very low	Too dry to grow crops; too hot for people to live; need water for settlements
Q	Canada	Very cold (on the Arctic Circle); fairly dry	Very low	Too cold for growing crops; climate difficult to live in
R	China	Mountain (colder as height increases)	Very low	Farming and access difficult in mountainous terrain
S	Russia	Cool, very cold in winter (inland, near the Arctic Circle); rain all year	Very low	Climate not good for farming; winter cold makes living conditions difficult
T	Brazil	Hot tropical rain all year	Very low	Thick rainforest so access difficult; deforestation reduces soil fertility

The population of the UK

About this unit

This unit focuses on the UK's population and how / why it has changed over time.

Key points

◆ The population graph for the UK mirrors the population graph for the world as a whole in terms of shape – with a steep increase from the Industrial Revolution to the present day.

◆ As well as natural increase (birth rate – death rate), the UK's population has been greatly affected by both immigration and emigration, particularly from the second half of the twentieth century onwards. Currently immigration into the UK far outstrips emigration, with the result that net migration to the UK in 2013–14 was about 243 000. The UK's population in mid-2014 stood at around 64 million.

◆ Another reason for the increase in the UK's population is increasing life expectancy. Women tend to live longer than men, on average, but life expectancy in the UK for both genders has increased steadily over the last century. In 2014, average life expectancy in the UK had reached 78.3 years for men and 82.7 years for women.

Key vocabulary

estimate, census, emigration, immigration, life expectancy

Skills practised in 'Your turn'

◆ Geography skills: q1, compare graphs / data; q4, define a key term

◆ Numeracy skills: q2, q3a, q5a, analyse graph data to reach conclusions

◆ Thinking skills: q3b, q5b, q6, apply common sense and prior knowledge to support reasoned conclusions

Unit outcomes

By the end of this unit most students should be able to:

◆ explain the terms given in 'Key vocabulary' above

◆ describe the population graph for the UK over the last 2000 years

◆ explain the impact of immigration / emigration and increasing life expectancy on the UK's population, particularly from the twentieth century onwards

Ideas for a starter

1   The following words are all terms that have been used so far. Ask students to unscramble them and work out what they are (solutions in brackets). Students to define each term.

   – optiolapnu (population)   – niotbirtsidu (distribution)

   – ydsneel (densely)   – rsthbi (births)

   – tadehs (deaths)   – psaylres (sparsely)

   – dynties (density)

2   Ask: What is a census? Do you know how often one is carried out? What kind of information about the population is collected? Who needs this information?

3   Use census information to find out the size of the population in your town before World War I. Ask: What was the population in your town after the war? How many people died during the war? What is the size of the population now?

4   Using atlases, students find a relief map of the UK and pick out areas where they think people are least likely to have settled. They outline these areas on blank maps of the UK and label and annotate them with their reasons. They compare their maps with a population distribution map of the UK to see how good their predictions were.

Ideas for plenaries

Plan plenaries at strategic points throughout the lesson, as well as at the end.

Mid-lesson

1 Using graph A on page 22 of the students' book, ask: Around when did the UK population start to increase rapidly? Why? Why did the population continue to grow? Elicit reasons such as improvements in farming (more food was produced); better nutrition, so people lived longer; plagues eliminated, with the help of vaccinations; rising standards of living (improved sanitation).

2 Life expectancy has increased over the years in the UK. Ask: What does this mean for the UK? Students to relate their own experiences with grandparents'. Discuss the implications (e.g. costs in terms of health and pensions, and benefits).

End-of-lesson

3 Give students the answers and ask them to work out the question.

Question	Answer
What does *population distribution* mean?	How the people in a country are spread around
What is population density?	The average number of people living in a place, per sq km
What is natural increase?	An increase in population where there are more births than deaths in a year (birth rate – death rate)
What is emigration?	When a person leaves a country to live elsewhere
What is the average number of years a new baby can expect to live for?	Life expectancy
What is it called when a person arrives in a country to live?	Immigration

4 Ask: How does the information collected in the census help the government? Think about the future as well as the present.

5 Ask students (in pairs) to suggest two key ideas in today's lesson and to write down one interesting question about the UK's population that has not been covered.

Further class and homework opportunities

Suggestions 15–16 on page 47 of this book

geog.2 workbook, page 13

geog.2 Kerboodle: lesson presentation, worksheets, end-of-lesson assessment

Answers for 'Your turn'

1 The population of the UK and Earth's population started to increase at about the same time. In both cases the population has grown rapidly since about 1760.

2 a The Black Death

   b World War I

3 a The UK's population increased rapidly.

   b An increase in wages would have given people more food and better diets. This would have helped them live longer and healthier lives.

4 The average number of years that a person can expect to live for.

5 a It increased by about 30 years.

   b Suggested answers may include: improved diet, improved health (e.g. vaccinations), improved hygiene.

6 a Smoking would increase the risk of contracting diseases, such as cancer, which can cause death and reduce life expectancy.

   b Heatwaves and extremes of temperature can cause heat-related deaths, particularly in elderly people who are more likely to suffer from illness due to heat. People with heart disease and lung disease are more likely to die in a heatwave. Severe heatwaves are likely to reduce life expectancy.

   c The development of new drugs would mean that we are able to treat cancer so people will live longer.

   d If everyone was well paid it would improve the quality of life and people would have money to pay for better food and the best medical treatment that they can afford.

7 Students' responses will vary.

About this unit

This unit examines population growth around the world and life expectancy.

Key points

◆ Overall, Earth's human population is growing at about 1.2% (about 80 million people) a year.

◆ However, population growth rates vary greatly between countries – with some even experiencing falling populations, e.g. Japan (with a population growth rate of –0.13%). Japan has a negative natural increase – with a very low birth rate of 8.07 births per thousand and a higher death rate (due to its large elderly population) of 9.38 deaths per thousand. Japan also has very minimal immigration to offset the negative natural increase.

◆ Japan is a rich, developed country. By contrast, poorer, less-developed countries tend to have much higher population growth rates. The highest of these are almost exclusively in Africa. For example, Uganda has a population growth rate of 3.24%. This is due to an extremely high birth rate of 44.17 births per thousand, compared to a death rate of 10.97. This has led to a high natural increase, which is only partially offset by a small negative net migration of –0.76 migrants per 1000 population.

◆ There also tends to be a correlation between population growth rate and life expectancy – with both indicators related to a country's wealth and level of development. Richer, more-developed countries, like Japan, have a higher life expectancy (85 years) and lower population growth. Poorer, less-developed countries, like Uganda, have a lower life expectancy (54 years) and higher population growth.

Key vocabulary

one-child policy

Skills practised in 'Your turn'

◆ Geography skills: q1, q5, q6, analyse map data

◆ Thinking skills: q2–q4, apply common sense and prior knowledge to produce reasoned explanations

Unit outcomes

By the end of this unit most students should be able to:

◆ explain the term given in 'Key vocabulary' above

◆ explain the correlations between population growth / life expectancy and a country's wealth / level of development

Ideas for a starter

1 Ask: What causes population to change?

2 Show students a picture of an advertisement / poster for China's one-child policy (i.e. one where the message is clear). Ask: What is the picture showing? Which country is it for? Have you heard about China's one-child policy? What do you know about it?

3 Explain China's one-child policy. Show a video about it and explain the effects that it has had.

Ideas for plenaries

Plan plenaries at strategic points throughout the lesson, as well as at the end.

Mid-lesson

1   Ask students to complete this table using the information learned in the lesson:

	Less developed country	More developed country
Population features (e.g. life expectancy / population growth)		
Examples of countries		

2   Ask: What will the world's population be like in 50 years' time? Why? Think about how it has grown in the past.

3   Ask: What are the advantages and disadvantages of China's one-child policy? Imagine you are an only child living in China. What are the advantages of being an only child? What are the disadvantages?

End-of-lesson

4   Write headings on the board: *Death rate rises; Death rate falls; Birth rate rises; Birth rate falls; No effect on birth rate or death rate.* Give students a list of statements to put under the correct heading, e.g.

–   War breaks out / A deadly disease epidemic spreads / Famine

–   Good healthcare available / Good lifestyle choices

–   Education on birth control / Methods of family planning provided / People get married later

–   No access to birth control methods / No family planning information

5   Ask: What new facts have you learned today? Has anything from today's lesson surprised you? Is there any fact or statistic that has stuck in your head?

Further class and homework opportunities

Suggestions 17–21 on page 47 of this book

geog.2 workbook, page 14

geog.2 Kerboodle: lesson presentation, worksheets, end-of-lesson assessment

Answers for 'Your turn'

1   a   Any three from: Mali, Niger, Chad, South Sudan, Eritrea, Oman, Tanzania, Zambia, Zimbabwe, Angola.

    b   Any three from: Spain, Portugal, Ukraine, Romania, Bulgaria, Latvia, Lithuania, Hungary, Greece, Croatia, Japan, Greenland.

2   Education means that women have more knowledge about family planning (i.e. education in the use of contraceptives and spacing out children), which helps to slow birth rates. Good education in the longer term means that women tend to marry later, have better jobs and have fewer children.

3   Fifty years ago, China's population was growing at about 2.4%. By allowing couples to have only one child, China reduced the country's birth rate and slowed the population growth rate.

4   More developed countries have access to more food, clean drinking water and health care, such as drugs and vaccinations against disease. People are better educated and able to make healthy lifestyle choices, e.g. about diet and exercise.

5   a   Africa

    b   Students may give a number of answers including: Mali, Niger, Nigeria, Democratic Republic of Congo, Angola, Zambia, Zimbabwe, Mozambique.

    c   Students may give a number of answers including: United States of America, Canada, Mexico, Chile, Argentina, Australia, United Kingdom, Germany, France, Italy, Japan, South Korea.

6   Answers could include: Mali, Niger, Chad, Angola, Zambia, Zimbabwe.

About this unit

This unit considers the impact of human population growth on the planet as a whole.

Key points

◆ The rapidly growing human population is putting a huge strain on resources, such as food, land, water, and different types of fuel and mineral reserves.

◆ Increasingly, disputes between countries are predicted to be focused on control of resources, rather than political power – whether it's oil, fertile agricultural land, or even water. For example, nine countries share the River Nile. An increasing level of dam building in countries upstream, particularly Ethiopia, is decreasing the water flow in countries downstream, particularly Egypt. The Egyptian economy is heavily dependent on water from the Nile, and the Egyptian government has been in dispute with Ethiopia about its dam-building programme.

◆ As well as affecting other people, human actions are also reducing the world's biodiversity – with habitats destroyed to provide land for food, settlements and mineral exploitation. Humans are also creating mountains of waste; causing air, ground and water pollution; and even causing global climate change.

◆ The solution? We must try to live more sustainably and think more about the planet's future.

Key vocabulary

acid rain, global warming, resources, sustainable

Skills practised in 'Your turn'

◆ Geography skills: q1a, define a key term

◆ Literacy skills: q1b, create spider diagrams; q3, create an imaginary conversation to make a point

◆ Thinking skills: q1b, q2, evaluate and explain the role and importance of different resources; q4, predict possible future problems; q5, evaluate a possible solution with reasoned arguments

Unit outcomes

By the end of this unit most students should be able to:

◆ explain the terms given in 'Key vocabulary' above

◆ explain the impact of humans on the world's resources

◆ discuss possible solutions

Ideas for a starter

1 Quick revision: About how many humans are there on Earth? About how many more will there be by the end of this lesson? How many more by this time tomorrow? By this time next week? (Calculators?).

2 Ask: What kinds of things will we need more of as the population rises? In pairs or small groups, students unscramble the following words:

– tarwe (water)　　　　　　　　　– laco (coal)

– cycletireit (electricity)　　　　　– lio (oil)

– porcs dofo (food crops)　　　　– sultana rag (natural gas)

Prompt students to think of other things and create a spider diagram. Could all these needs cause any problems?

Ideas for plenaries

Plan plenaries at strategic points throughout the lesson, as well as at the end.

Mid-lesson

1   Fill in the gaps: Provide some statements with gaps for students to fill in, e.g.
    –   When people have more money, they tend to produce _____ (more) waste.
    –   People in developed countries tend to have a _____ (larger) carbon footprint.
    –   Population growth rate is usually _____ (lower) in more-developed countries.
    –   Burning _____ (fuels) is helping to bring on _____ (global warming).

2   Ask students to write down three ways in which governments can help to reduce the amount of resources we use. Share ideas.

End-of-lesson

3   Scaffolded discussion: If women had only one child, what would happen to the population? Do you think governments should try to stop people having lots of children? Do you know anywhere this is happening? (China's one-child policy.)

4   Give students two minutes to work with a partner and write down three things that they have learned from this lesson and one interesting question that we have not covered today. (This could produce a good enquiry question for the class to follow through.)

Further class and homework opportunities

Suggestions 22–29 on page 47 of this book

geog.2 workbook, page 15

geog.2 Kerboodle: lesson presentation, worksheets, end-of-lesson assessment

Answers for 'Your turn'

1   a   Things we need to live or use to earn a living, e.g. food and fuel.
    b   The table on the right shows possible answers.

2   a   Of those resources, water and soil are the essentials for life: we can't live without water and food, and food needs soil. Wood also needs soil (and we can use wood for shelter and fuel). Oil and metals add greatly to our lives, but we could survive without them.

    b   We could run out of oil and metal ores. Earth contains a finite amount of these. At some point we may have extracted all we can access. But we won't run out of wood, water, and soil (although there may be shortages in places). We can grow more trees for wood. Water is continually recycled in the water cycle. Soil is continually forming, through the weathering of rock.

3   The pandas might see humans as their worst enemy, who'll kill them off in the end, by driving them from their territory. The baby panda might not find a partner when it grows up, so the species will decline.

4   a   Increased competition for food, water, fuel, housing; crowded conditions; strain on services (power, transport, education, health services, etc.); more waste (rubbish, sewage) to deal with; more pollutants; competition for resources could lead to wars.

    b   Habitats destroyed as humans spread, taking over more land for homes, faming, mining, transport, etc. Species will disappear. Intensive farming of some animals may be needed, which

Resource	I depend on it for …
Water	drinking, washing myself and other things, cooking, watering crops (indirectly)
Soil	food crops; crops that animals eat (indirectly); fibre crops for clothing (cotton, linen); trees
Wood	furniture, building materials, fuel
Metal ores	steel (from iron ore) used in cars, trains, buses, bridges, buildings, tins, washing machines, fridges etc; aluminium used for planes and drinks cans; aluminium and copper used in wires and cables; coins
Oil	fuel for transport; fuel burned in power stations and central heating systems; chemicals to make plastics, shampoo etc

often means poor conditions for them. Overfishing leading to breakdown of food chains and fish stocks in the oceans. Poisoning of wildlife by pollutants and pesticides needed for intensive farming.

5   Encourage students to discuss the pros and cons. Ask: Overall, how would people feel if this became the policy? You could point out that China has had a one-child policy since 1979, and parents who had more than one child faced fines and other penalties. Note that the one child policy is now being relaxed.

What does the future hold?

About this unit

This unit takes a look at what the future may hold for the human population by about 2050.

Key points

◆ It is always difficult to predict the future, so different scenarios have been put forward to forecast how the global population will change over the next 50 years or so. The most popular scenario is that the rate of population growth will slow down from its current level – and that eventually the population will begin to decrease.

◆ Possible reasons for this (apart from the ideas of Malthus, discussed in Unit 2.1) are that with increasing wealth, education and gender equality in the workplace, couples will wait longer to start a family – and will deliberately choose to have a smaller family. This is already happening in more-developed countries (where some, such as Germany and Japan, already have negative population growth rates), and it is predicted to extend to many less-developed countries as they develop further.

◆ As well as a falling birth rate – apart from in the poorest countries (particularly in Africa) – it is predicted that life expectancy across the world will rise, which will lead to an ageing population (already being experienced in countries such as Germany and Japan).

Key vocabulary

ageing population, working age population, young population

Skills practised in 'Your turn'

◆ Literacy skills: q1, q2, write a reasoned explanation

◆ Thinking skills: q1, reach a reasoned decision; q2b, q3, make reasoned predictions

Unit outcomes

By the end of this unit most students should be able to:

◆ explain the terms given in 'Key vocabulary' above

◆ explain two possible scenarios about global population growth

◆ explain some reasons for the most likely scenario

◆ describe likely population trends that different countries will face

Ideas for a starter

1 Give students figures for the size of the world's population for the last 50 years and get them to plot it as a line graph. Ask them to predict what the world's population will be for the next 50 years. Get them to compare their graph with the one on page 28 of the students' book.

2 Using the graph on page 28, ask: What was the population when you were born? One hundred years ago, the world's population was 4 billion – true or false? When was the world's population half of what it is now? If the world's population carries on growing at the same rate, it will be about 9.5 billion in 2040 – true or false? Everyone agrees how the world's population will grow in the future – true or false?

3 Display pictures of places where some retired people choose to live, including older people enjoying them (e.g. British seaside resort, Southern Spain, Florida). Ask: What do the pictures show? Why do elderly people live here? Would you like to live there when you are older?

4 Ask: Why do you think that governments might need to know about population change in the future?

Ideas for plenaries

Plan plenaries at strategic points throughout the lesson, as well as at the end.

Mid-lesson

1   Give students population structure graphs for two or more other countries – one with an ageing population (e.g. Japan) and one with a young population (e.g. India). Ask them to locate the countries on a map. Students should answer the following questions and annotate their graphs with labels. How many people are aged 0–14 for each country? Which country has the highest birth rate? How can you tell? Which country has the highest life expectancy? How can you tell? Which country will have the most elderly people to support?

2   Ask: What do you think is likely to happen to the world's population over the next 50 years? Why? Ask students to write a short summary.

End-of-lesson

3   Look back at the pictures from starter **3** and ask the questions again. Ask students to think of two benefits of an ageing population and two disadvantages.

4   In groups, ask students to think of four questions on what they have learned about predicting population growth, to ask another group.

Further class and homework opportunities

Suggestions 30–31 on page 47 of this book

geog.2 workbook, page 16

geog.2 Kerboodle: lesson presentation, worksheets, end-of-lesson assessment

Answers for 'Your turn'

1   Answers will vary. Most students might choose line 2, because they think Earth won't be able to support ever-increasing populations. In reality there are advantages and disadvantages to both lines:

   a   Line 1: Negative effects: increasing demand for / use of resources (e.g. food, energy, clean water), land cleared for housing and roads, overcrowding, more waste, increased pollution, global warming, species dying out. Positive effects: more effective use of resources will be needed to share them, many minds leading to advances in technology and medicine, economic benefits of more people (e.g. more taxes).

   b   Line 2: Negative effects: ageing population, so there are more elderly people who need to be supported by those who work and pay taxes, people have to work longer as there is less money to pay pensions, more money is spent on healthcare as we are living longer. Positive effects: less pressure on resources.

2   a   Ethiopia has the larger population. Germany's population has decreased by about 0.2% a year and Ethiopia's has continued to rise at about 3%.

   b   Germany: There will be an ageing population that will need to be supported by the working population. There won't be enough people to fill the jobs in the future as the birth rate is low. Ethiopia: The birth rate will still be high so young children

will need healthcare and education, which are expensive. When these children have their own children, the population will increase further. They may find it hard to get work when they are older as there are so many young people.

3   a   An asteroid of that size hitting Earth would have a huge amount of energy and hit Earth at great speed. It would be likely to wipe out life on the planet.

   b   A deadly disease could spread all over the world and kill a large number of people. It would result in an increase in the death rate and population decrease. This would recover over time.

   c   A third world war might cause a short-term increase in the death rate and a population decrease. After a war, there might be a baby boom and an increase in the birth rate and population growth.

   d   Mothers might consider having children (or more children) as they would benefit financially and the population size would increase.

   e   Sea levels are likely to rise which means there is more chance of flooding and loss of life as about a quarter of the worlds' population lives in the coastal zone. The population size would decrease.

Many of these suggestions are addressed to your students. Where research or further resources are needed, the internet will almost certainly provide the answer.

The suggestions are graded *,**,*** according to level of difficulty. Some are suitable for all levels, and can be differentiated by outcome.

Our numbers are growing fast

1   **How many people?** How do we know how many people there are in each country? How do we count them? Why do we need to know how many people there are? Can we really be sure of the *exact* number of people in each country, or the whole world? **/***

2   **Your great-great-great-grandchildren** Suppose you have two children, and they each have two children, and their children each have two children and so on. How many great-great-great grandchildren will you have? Around what year will those children be alive? (you could allow 30 years between generations.) Now what if two billion other people did the same as you? *

3   **A letter to your great-great-great grandchildren** Write a letter to your great-great-great grandchildren. It could be about anything you want. For example, you could ask questions about their lives, and tell them a bit about yours. *

4   **Natural increase** The table below shows the birth rates and death rates for different countries.

	Birth rate (per 1000 people)	Death rate (per 1000 people)	Natural increase
Angola	45	14	
Austria	9	9	
Cambodia	26	6	
China	12	7	
Ecuador	21	5	
Germany	8	11	
Mali	47	13	
Mexico	19	5	
Pakistan	26	7	
UK	13	9	

Source : The World Bank 2012

Work out the natural increase (birth rate – death rate) and fill in the last column of the table. **/***

5   **True or false?** Using the information and figures for natural increase that you worked out in the previous activity, state whether these statements are true or false. If they are false, then correct them.
   –   Austria has the lowest birth rate.
   –   Angola has the highest death rate.
   –   Angola has the largest natural increase.
   –   Germany's population is increasing.
   –   Cambodia has a higher natural increase than Ecuador. **/***

6   **How large?** Assume that the world's population carries on growing at the same rate as the line on the graph on page 19 of *geog.2* students' book. How big will the world's population be when you are 20, 40, 60 years old? **/***

7   **You as an ancestor** One day you could be an ancestor to millions of people. Explain why. Does it make you feel responsible? Should you look after the planet for them? *

8   **Falling population** Could it happen? Could the world's population fall? What might cause that? Write an article for a radio programme, or a blog, which tells what might happen when, and if, the world's population starts to fall. */**

9   **Our common ancestors** In 2004 a mathematician published a paper in *Nature* magazine proposing the theory that everyone alive today shares one common ancestor who lived about 3000 years ago. (He had worked this out by computer modelling.)

   Imagine you are that common ancestor. Write a letter to the human race today. For example you could point out things you think it is doing well, and things it is getting all wrong. **

So where is everyone?

10   **Spider diagrams** Create two spider diagrams. Write *Sparsely populated* in the middle of one, and *Densely populated* in the middle of the other. Think of as many factors as you can to add to your spider diagrams. */**/***

11   **How big?** Here's a list of the world's continents (excluding Antarctica): Asia, Africa, Europe, North America, South America, Oceania.

   Here are the populations of the continents (in millions, for 2013) – but they're in a different order to the continents listed above: 386, 739, 4140, 36, 995, 529. Your job is to match them up.

   And finally, why was Antarctica not included? **/***

12   **Taboo** Ask students to play taboo in small groups. One student should explain a key word to others in the group without using the banned (taboo) words.

Term	Taboo words			
Population density	People	Place	Number	Living
Population distribution	People	Located	Living	Country
Natural increase	Birth	Death	Rate	Rise

/*

13   **The top 20 countries** Find out the world's top 20 most populous countries by typing *top 20 countries population* into a search engine. Show the data as a bar graph. **

14   **Population check** Do drawings, or one big annotated drawing, to show you understand the difference between population, population distribution, and population density. **

The population of the UK

15 Natural increase Use the data in the table below to work out the natural increase (birth rate – death rate) in the population for England and Wales from 1995–2000.

Year	No. of births	No. of deaths	Natural increase
1995	648 138	569 683	
1996	649 485	560 135	
1997	643 095	555 281	
1998	635 901	555 015	
1999	621 872	556 118	
2000	604 441	535 664	

Source: ONS
/*

16 True or false? Using the figures for natural increase that you worked out in the previous activity, state whether these statements about the population of England and Wales are true or false. If they are false, then correct them.
– The number of deaths has increased over the period.
– The number of births has increased over the period.
– Generally, both the number of births and deaths have decreased over the period.
– Overall the population decreased between 1995 and 2000. **/***

Population around the world

17 Tweet! Write a tweet about China's one-child policy. You've only got 140 characters to explain what it is, why it was put in place, what impact it had. The best tweet will be the one that tells the most in the fewest characters! */**

18 Spider diagram Create two spider diagrams. One should show why life expectancy is lower in less-developed countries, and the other why it is higher for people in more developed countries. */**/***

19 Fewer? Think of a reason why it is better to have fewer children. Now think of another. How many reasons can you think of? How can governments control the number of children people have? Should they? */**/***

20 More? Think of a reason for having more children. Now think of some more reasons. Some countries have populations which are falling. Think of one way to encourage people to have more children. Now think of another. */**/***

21 Comparing population data Give students cards containing information about population growth in different countries. Use different coloured card for different countries. Data should include things like size of population, population growth rate, birth rate, death rate, life expectancy etc. In pairs or small groups, students compare the data and whoever has the highest value card wins. The student who wins needs to explain what the cards mean in terms of the development of the respective countries. **/***

Our impact on our planet

22 Poster Create a poster with a photo of huge numbers of people at the centre. Find as many examples of photos of different types of resources as you can and stick them around your central image. Add links to the photos to say what problems our increasing use of the resources might cause. */**/***

23 Defining resources Think of a definition of resources that a 10 year old would find easy to understand. Then think of a an interesting way to display or illustrate your definition. */**/***

24 Managing population Do we need to manage the number of people on our planet? Will our population growth cause problems? Have a small group discussion. **/***

25 Where does our waste go? Waste is an increasing problem, as the population grows. Students could work in groups and carry out an enquiry about where the waste that leaves their homes goes. ***

26 Reducing our impact Think of five ways you can reduce your personal impact on Earth. Then measure your own carbon footprint using an online carbon footprint calculator. First, make sure you know what a carbon footprint is. **/***

27 Plan an article You have been asked to write a magazine article on the effects of our growing population on the planet. Write a headline that will grab the reader's attention. Suggest an image that will create a big visual impact. Write down five points you want to make in your article. **/***

28 Is it all bad news? Create a spider diagram to summarise the effects of human population on Earth. Can you think of any positive impacts? */**/***

29 Those big questions Draw talking heads like the ones below on the board. The class discusses in groups, each group choosing one question, and gives feedback to the rest of the class. Do they reach the same conclusions? Are these conclusions about facts, or are they values? Would people everywhere agree with them? **

 'Whose planet is it, anyway?'

 'Who is responsible for the planet?'

What does the future hold?

30 Charity request You have been asked by a charity to create a short video about the effects of world population growth. Create a storyboard for your video giving background information about the level of growth (in the past, now and in the future) and explain the challenges and opportunities that it creates. It needs to be attention grabbing so that people will watch it. **/***

31 True or false? Write five statements about ageing populations, young populations and world population growth – some true, some false. Swap with a partner. Where statements are false, your partner should write out the correct version. **/***

3 Urbanisation

About this chapter

Addressing the KS3 Programme of Study

◆ Develop knowledge of globally significant places and how they provide a geographical context for understanding urbanisation and sustainable development.

◆ Understand, through exemplars in the UK, Africa, Asia, and the Middle East, the key processes in urbanisation and making sustainable environments.

◆ Understand how urbanisation influences and changes the environment.

About the content

◆ This chapter starts by looking at the Industrial Revolution, how it stimulated urbanisation, and how it affected cities like Manchester.

◆ The focus then moves beyond the UK to examine global patterns of urbanisation, and the benefits and disadvantages of living in urban areas, including in slums.

◆ Finally, it explores the concept of sustainability, through the example of Masdar City.

The big picture

These are the key ideas in this chapter.

◆ 300 years ago, only a small percentage of the world's population lived in urban areas.

◆ During the Industrial Revolution, people flocked into towns and cities to work in factories. This trend spread from the UK to other countries.

◆ Now 80% of us in the UK and 54% around the world live in urban areas.

◆ In many UK cities, population fell at the end of the 20th century, but is now rising again.

◆ The percentage of urban areas is lowest in Africa and Asia – but is growing quickly.

◆ There are disadvantages to urbanisation, and millions around the world live in slums.

◆ We are trying to make cities better, more sustainable places to live in.

A students' version of this big picture is given in the *geog.2* students' book opener for Chapter 3.

The chapter outline

Use this, and their chapter opener, to give students a mental roadmap for the chapter.

3 Urbanisation The chapter opener in the students' book is an important part of the chapter; see page 11 for notes about using chapter openers

3.1 How our towns and cities grew The process of urbanisation, the growth of towns and cities in the past, and populations in towns and cities today

3.2 Manchester's story – part 1 The urbanisation of Manchester from 1760, comparing the housing of mill workers and owners

3.3 Manchester's story – part 2 Reasons for the rise and fall of population in Manchester since 1801, pointing out similar trends across the UK

3.4 Urbanisation around the world Existing patterns of global urbanisation and the reasons for rising urbanisation in the future

3.5 Why do people move to urban areas? Push and pull factors, and why people around the world move to towns and cities

3.6 It's not all sunshine! Benefits and disadvantages of living in towns and cities, and how these places can become more sustainable

3.7 Life in the slums What it's like to live in a city slum and ways the problems of slums might be resolved

3.8 A city of the future? Masdar City – a purpose-built, research-driven sustainable city in UAE and what the planners set out to achieve

Objectives and outcomes for this chapter

Objectives	Unit	Outcomes
Most students will understand:		**Most students will be able to:**
the process of urbanisation	3.1	identify and explain the Industrial Revolution as the start of urbanisation
how and why a major UK city grew	3.2	identify factors that contributed to Manchester's success and urbanisation; describe the workers' housing
how populations have changed in UK cities over the last two centuries	3.3	describe how the population of Manchester has changed since 1801; explain why the population fell and then rose again in the last 90 years
what can be done to regenerate a modern city	3.3	give at least four examples of ways Manchester has stimulated regeneration; evaluate its success
how and why levels of urbanisation vary around the world	3.4	identify different levels of urbanisation around the world on a map; interpret changes in population from a bar chart; explain why urbanisation is important to governments
why people move to urban areas	3.5	define push factors and pull factors; identify at least three of each type of factor; rank push factors
why living in cities has disadvantages, as well as benefits	3.6	identify, rank, and evaluate three benefits and three disadvantages of living in a city
how we can make towns and cities more sustainable	3.6	define *sustainable*; identify at least five ways of making urban areas more sustainable
what it's like to live in a slum	3.7	identify the problems in slums; describe a dwelling in a slum; evaluate different ways to improve slums
the factors that might make a new city sustainable	3.8	rank aims for sustainability of a new city; identify reasons for sustainability measures; evaluate such measures for a UK context

These tie in with the outcomes for each unit, in this teacher's handbook, and with 'Your goals for this chapter', in *geog.2* students' book.

Opportunities for assessment

See the formal assessment materials for this chapter on *geog.2 Kerboodle Lessons, Resources, & Assessment*. They include an extended assessment task, an exam-style question, end-of-lesson assessments, and a self-assessment form. See also the notes on pages 14–15 of this book.

Getting ready for this chapter

geog.2 Kerboodle contains plans and presentations for each unit, including interactive activities, animations, and worksheets.

About 'Your chapter starter'

The photo on page 30 of *geog.2* students' book, shows an area of Tokyo, Japan, called Minato. Minato is densely populated, with 11 444 people per sq km (London has a population density of 5285 per sq km). Tokyo-Yokohama is also one of the world's largest megacities (those with over 10 million people) – its population is in excess of 37 million.

Tokyo has grown as a result of urbanisation – an increase in the percentage of people living in towns and cities. Urbanisation in the UK was driven by the Industrial Revolution, and Europe and the USA followed suit. From around 1950, as urbanisation slowed in Europe and the USA, it took off in Africa and Asia, including Japan.

How our towns and cities grew

About this unit

This unit introduces students to the development of settlements and the growth in urbanisation.

Key points

◆ The first hunter gatherers were nomadic, so they didn't develop any permanent settlements.

◆ However, with the development of farming about 12 000 years ago, small permanent settlements began to evolve. Some of these settlements started to grow in size, in order to provide markets and specialist ancillary services (such as carpenters and blacksmiths).

◆ With the advent of the Industrial Revolution in the UK in the late eighteenth century, new factories located in urban areas needed workers. In the countryside, increased mechanisation and changes to farming practices meant that many farm workers were no longer needed, so they began to move to the towns to find work in the new factories – leading to the process of urbanisation.

◆ Initially, this process of industrialisation and urbanisation spread from the UK across Europe and over to the USA. After the Second World War, other continents (especially Asia and Africa) began to experience increased urbanisation as their economies modernised and developed.

◆ Today, 54% of humans live in urban areas – by 2050 it's expected to be 70%. This figure will never reach 100%, because somebody needs to grow or raise the food we all eat!

Key vocabulary

industry, Industrial Revolution, market town, settlement, rural, urban, urbanisation

Skills practised in 'Your turn'

◆ Geography skills: q1, q2, q4, define key terms

◆ Literacy skills: q6, write a letter

◆ Thinking skills: q3, explain change; q5, use common sense and prior knowledge to reach a reasoned conclusion

Unit outcomes

By the end of this unit most students should be able to:

◆ explain the terms given in 'Key vocabulary' above

◆ explain the process by which settlements developed and evolved

◆ explain the link between industrialisation and urbanisation

Ideas for a starter

1 Show students a picture of a rural area, a town, and a city. Ask them to describe the pictures. What are the differences between them? See if they can come up with a definition for each one. Where would they want to live and why? Why do people live in big cities?

2 Show students pictures of rural areas in the UK. Ask: Why did parts of the UK change from this… to this?. Show them pictures of urban areas.

3 Ask: What was the Industrial Revolution? How did it affect the UK's population growth? How do you think it affected towns and cities?

Ideas for plenaries

Plan plenaries at strategic points throughout the lesson, as well as at the end.

Mid-lesson

1 What is the question? Give students answers and ask them to work out the question relating to the growth of towns and cities:

Answer	Question
Wild sheep	Which animals were the first to be domesticated?
Growing crops and rearing animals meant people could settle in one place.	How did farming help with the start of settlements?
A town where farmers and other trades would swap or sell the produce they didn't need or goods they had made.	What is a market town?
Machines were invented and factories sprang up. The factories needed workers so they poured in from rural areas.	Why did the Industrial Revolution cause the growth of towns and cities?
New crops, machinery, and methods of farming meant that fewer people were needed to produce more food.	What other reason caused people to move to towns and cities?
Africa and Asia	Where are the fastest growing cities in the world today?
70% of people	How many people will live in urban areas by 2050?

2 Students could do 'Your turn' question 3 as a plenary.

End-of-lesson

3 Ask students to write down: three things that helped cause urbanisation, two facts about urbanisation today, and one fact about urbanisation in the future.

4 Ask: What is the most interesting thing you have learned today? What fact / statistic is the most relevant?

Further class and homework opportunities

Suggestions 1–5 on page 66 of this book

geog.2 workbook, page 18

geog.2 Kerboodle: lesson presentation, worksheets, end-of-lesson assessment

Answers for 'Your turn'

1 People who live by hunting animals and collecting fruit and seeds. Hunter gatherers were always on the move looking for food.

2 a A place where individual dwellings are clustered together so that people live in one place

   b A place in which a market is held. A town grew up around the market.

3 New crops and ways of farming, such as increased use of machinery, helped to make farming more efficient so fewer farm workers were needed. The workers moved to the growing urban areas to work in the new factories. Improvements in agriculture meant that more food could be produced to feed the growing population (e.g. the workers).

4 a A built-up area such as a large town or city.

   b An area that is mainly countryside but that may have small towns and villages.

   c An increase in the percentage of people living in urban areas due to people moving from rural areas.

5 No, we are unlikely to be 100% urban. Reasons might include: Initially people will move to urban areas for work, better health care, and education so the percentage of people living in urban areas will grow. Over time, urban areas become crowded and polluted and may suffer from crime and traffic congestion so people start to move out. Also, with more people working from home and better transport making it easier to commute, people are able to live outside of urban areas. Also, someone has to grow our food!

6 Answers will vary but should be based on the information on pages 32–33 of the students' book.

Manchester's story – part 1

help at a glance

About this unit

This unit (and the following one) uses the example of Manchester to examine the development of industrialisation and urbanisation in the UK.

Key points

◆ As a result of the Industrial Revolution, Manchester evolved from a medieval market town into a major industrial city. In particular, the city developed and mechanised its existing textiles tradition in order to exploit the cheap raw cotton being imported into Liverpool.

◆ Manchester's industrial expansion required a massive increase in the number of workers, who came from all over the UK and Ireland to work in the new factories and mills.

◆ However, these new workers needed somewhere to live, which led to the rise of unscrupulous landlords, who built large quantities of poor-quality housing – all crammed together with poor sanitation and no running water. This congested housing inevitably developed into disease-ravaged slums.

Key vocabulary

cotton mill, slums, speculators, tenements, terraces

Skills practised in 'Your turn'

◆ Geography skills: q1, describe a location; q4, define and explain key terms
◆ Literacy skills: q3, write a newspaper report
◆ Thinking skills: q2, select factors for success; q4, use common sense and informed speculation to reach probable conclusions; q5, analyse text to reach reasoned conclusions

Unit outcomes

By the end of this unit most students should be able to:

◆ explain the terms given in 'Key vocabulary' above
◆ explain the process by which Manchester developed from a small market town into a huge industrial city
◆ explain the downsides of this massive expansion for the workers in particular

Ideas for a starter

1 Where am I? Give students clues about present-day Manchester.
   - I am home to the world's oldest railway station.
   - The world's first computer was built at the university here.
   - I am approximately 199 miles north west of London and about 34 miles east of Liverpool.
   - I am home to the UK's third biggest airport and have a modern city tram service.
   - I am connected to Liverpool by the M62 motorway and a famous ship canal.
   - I have two Premier League football teams. One of them was formed in 1887 by railway workers and the other was formed in 1880 by a church.
   - I am home to the UK's second biggest shopping centre: the Trafford Centre.

2 Use 'Your turn' question 1 to help students locate Manchester.

3 Follow on with 'Your turn' question 2a to see if students can identify how Manchester's location contributed to its growth.

4 Watch a video clip on urbanisation – search BBC Bitesize for a suitable clip.

Ideas for plenaries

Plan plenaries at strategic points throughout the lesson, as well as at the end.

Mid-lesson

1 Following on from starter **2**, do 'Your turn' question 2 so students can build on their understanding of the reasons for Manchester's growth.

2 In pairs, one student describes a back-to-back house or tenement in one of the slums in Manchester whilst their partner tries to draw it from the description. If more scaffolding is needed, give students some key words to include in their descriptions: cramped, narrow streets, sewage, pollution, cellar, toilet. Discuss: Why were back-to-back houses and tenements built in this way?

3 Discuss: What were some of the health dangers of living in a back-to-back house / tenement in Manchester?

End-of-lesson

4 Write an attention-grabbing newspaper headline to accompany one of the pictures on page 35 of the students' book.

5 Imagine: You are 15 years old and have just moved from a rural area to Manchester to take a job in a mill. Write a brief diary entry for today about your new life. Remember to include what it is like and how you feel.

6 Ask: Has anything from today's lesson appalled you or made you feel angry? What challenged your thinking? Was there anything you struggled with?

Further class and homework opportunities

Suggestions 6–10 on page 66 of this book

geog.2 workbook, page 19

geog.2 Kerboodle: lesson presentation, worksheets, end-of-lesson assessment

Answers for 'Your turn'

1 Manchester is located inland in the north west of the UK, to the east of Liverpool. It is located on the Manchester Ship Canal, which provides a link to Liverpool and its sea port.

2 **a** It was connected to Liverpool by river, so cotton could be brought to Manchester by boat. Canals (such as the Manchester Ship Canal) were built to transport coal for fuel, which helped the growth of the factories / mills.

  b Manchester had a history of weaving so workers already had skills, making it an ideal place to set up cotton mills. Famine in Ireland meant that people came for work. New machines were invented for spinning cotton and weaving.

3 Answers will vary. Students should write a balanced report of the city.

4 **a** People who take a risk and spend money in the hope that they will make lots of profit.

  b So that they could fit as many people in and earn more rent. Bigger houses would have meant purchasing more land and more building materials, which would have cost more money for the same amount of rental income.

  c Slums are areas of very poor housing built in urban areas. They are often overcrowded with poor living conditions (e.g. poor quality housing, poor sanitation).

  d Because of the introduction of machinery in agriculture there were fewer jobs in rural areas. With the growth of factories and mills there were plenty of jobs in Manchester so people stayed because there was work.

5 **a** It took place because the growth of factories and industry required people to work in them. So people had to move to where the jobs were.

  b The factory owners, merchants, landlords, speculators, and bankers gained the most. They made the most profit they could by keeping spending (e.g. wages, building costs) as low as possible or landlords fitted as many people into a house as possible in order to get more rent. With the profits they were able to move out of the crowded cities to large and comfortable homes, and afford education for their children and better health care for their families. They were able to improve their standard of living.

  c Answers should consider both the disadvantages and benefits. Whilst workers lived in poor conditions and earned low wages, they did have jobs and income. In rural areas they may not have had a job or, in Ireland, where some workers came from, they may have suffered and died from famine.

Manchester's story – part 2

About this unit

This unit continues using the example of Manchester to examine the process of deindustrialisation, decline and regeneration, which the UK's industrial cities experienced from the middle of the twentieth century onwards.

Key points

◆ Manchester's population continued to rise rapidly from the Industrial Revolution until approximately 1931, when it began to decline. This decline continued for the remainder of the twentieth century.

◆ The decline of Britain's industrial cities was largely due to cheap foreign competition, which undercut British factories and led to their closure. The closure of these factories, and Britain's deindustrialisation, led to a spiral of decline in many cities, including Manchester:

  – No factories means no work, so many people were forced to leave the city to try to find work elsewhere.

  – The loss of these workers' wages had a serious effect on the local economy, which went into decline as shops, pubs, etc. began to close.

  – As despair and desperation mounted, so did crime levels.

  – Once a city gains a reputation as dangerous and crime-ridden, businesses become reluctant to move there, so the downward spiral continues.

◆ However, Manchester has managed to halt the spiral of decline, and – through planning and investment – has started to regenerate itself as a service-based city (in particular: sport, entertainment, media and IT).

Key vocabulary

decline, regeneration

Skills practised in 'Your turn'

◆ Geography skills: q2, q4, define key terms

◆ Literacy skills: q1, write a short description

◆ Thinking skills: q2b, q3, q4b, q5, explain; q6, present a reasoned argument

Unit outcomes

By the end of this unit most students should be able to:

◆ explain the terms given in 'Key vocabulary' above

◆ explain the process of Manchester's decline

◆ explain how Manchester is now regenerating itself

Ideas for a starter

1 Draw an outline map of Britain on the board. With all books closed, ask five or six students to mark in where they think Manchester is, in one colour, and their own place in another. Ask the class which dots they think are (nearest to) correct. Then check against the map in the back of the students' book.

2 Using atlases, give students five minutes to give five geographical facts about Manchester. (This may help with starter **3** below.)

3 Recap: Ask students to give two reasons why urbanisation took place in Manchester and three effects of urbanisation on Manchester.

Ideas for plenaries

Plan plenaries at strategic points throughout the lesson, as well as at the end.

Mid-lesson

1   Ask: Why did the population of Manchester decline? Write *push factors* on the board. Ask students to look up *push factor* in their glossary. What push factors caused people to move away from Manchester? Why?

2   Ask: Why is the population of Manchester rising again? Write *pull factors* on the board. Ask students to look up *pull factor* in their glossary. What pull factors might attract people to Manchester today? Do you think Manchester's population will continue to rise? Why?

End-of-lesson

3   Ask: What are the benefits of people moving back into the cities? What are the disadvantages? Support a scaffolded discussion and ask students what they think are the effects on the social mix, services, housing, etc. Students create a mind map / spider diagram from the discussion.

4   Students tell their neighbour the most important thing and three other interesting new things they learned today.

Further class and homework opportunities

Suggestions 11–14 on pages 66–67 of this book

geog.2 workbook, page 20

geog.2 Kerboodle: lesson presentation, worksheets, end-of-lesson assessment

Answers for 'Your turn'

1   The population increased steeply from around 70 000 to 750 000. Between 1931 and 2001 it fell by approximately 350 000 to around 400 000. Since 2001 it has grown again. In 2011 it was approximately 510 000.

2   **a**   To fall gradually into a poor state.

   b   Other countries were able to make the same things more cheaply and sell them for less. Manchester's factories couldn't compete so they were forced to shut down. People lost their jobs, factories became derelict, and the rate of crime increased. People moved elsewhere to find work.

3   Answers could include: Old industrial areas became run down and disused. There was high unemployment and low morale amongst people with no work. New businesses didn't want to locate in Manchester. Housing also became run down and canals were dirty and polluted. Many people left the city to find new jobs and so lots of skills were lost. Crime rates rose.

4   **a**   To restore an area that was in a poor state and bring it back to life.

   b   Examples include: Spectators and fans will come and spend money on match days (e.g. in bars, restaurants, and hotels). Tourists will come to do tours of the football grounds and visit museums related to football (e.g. Manchester United Museum, National Football Museum). Income from tourists can be used to regenerate urban areas. Jobs are created (e.g. building / improving facilities; running facilities and jobs in hotels, bars, and restaurants; hosting the event). Other sporting events, such as the Commonwealth Games held in Manchester in 2002, might be attracted to the area with the development of world-class facilities. The Commonwealth Games also led to the redevelopment of run-down areas (e.g. Eastlands) and attracted businesses to move to the area.

5   Answers will vary depending on students' choices. The benefits identified should be both social and economic (e.g. improved environments / morale and income from businesses, visitors, and tourists).

6   Yes, Manchester's population is growing. Reasons include: People are moving back to Manchester because modern housing has been built, it has lots of things to do (e.g. shopping, entertainment, music, culture, restaurants), and the environment has been improved. New businesses are locating to Manchester due to new industrial parks (e.g. Trafford Park) being built and improved transport links (e.g. the tram service and the UK's third biggest airport).

Urbanisation around the world

About this unit

This unit examines the different levels of urbanisation around the world.

Key points

◆ Overall, 54% of the global population currently lives in urban areas, but levels of urbanisation vary significantly around the world.

◆ The most urbanised continents are North and South America, and Australia. This is not because South America and Australia are covered in towns and cities, but because the harsh conditions in those places (e.g. the Amazon Rainforest, Andes Mountains and Atacama Desert in South America, and the extensive hot deserts in Australia) mean that most of the population is restricted to living in urban areas along coastlines or rivers. Even in the USA, a large proportion of the population lives near the east and west coasts, rather than in the prairies of the mid-west or deserts of the southwest.

◆ The least urbanised continents are Africa and Asia, but urbanisation in those two continents is rising quickly, e.g. Uganda currently has an urban population of 15.6%, but the rate of urbanisation there is 5.74% (in the UK it is 0.76%); in Laos, the urban population is 34.3% and the rate of urbanisation is 4.41%. Therefore, by 2050, the urbanisation map for these two continents will have altered considerably.

Key vocabulary

(No new vocabulary)

Skills practised in 'Your turn'

◆ Geography skills: q1, analyse a choropleth map

◆ Numeracy skills: q2, analyse a bar graph

◆ Literacy skills: q1d, write an informative sentence

◆ Thinking skills: q3, use common sense and prior knowledge to reach a reasoned conclusion

Unit outcomes

By the end of this unit most students should be able to:

◆ describe current patterns of urbanisation around the world

◆ explain that over half of the world's urban dwellers currently live in towns and cities with fewer than 500 000 residents

◆ explain how and why the global urbanisation map is likely to change by 2050

Ideas for a starter

1 Ask: Why do people want to live in cities? Students independently think of reasons and then discuss with a partner. Ask: Why did people move to Manchester?

2 Ask: Who can remember what percentage of the world's population lives in urban areas? What percentage of the world's population do you think will live in urban areas by 2050? Why do you think this?

3 Search for the 'BBC interactive map of urban growth' online. Use it to show how urban growth has changed. For each period of time, ask students questions relating to the changing data. What is the population of city X? Has it increased or decreased? What has happened to the percentage of population in city / rural areas? Which continents have seen the highest urban growth over time?

Ideas for plenaries

Plan plenaries at strategic points throughout the lesson, as well as at the end.

Mid-lesson

1 Split the class into four groups and give students blank outline maps of the world. Using the interactive map in starter **3**, ask one group to plot the top five largest cities in 1955, the second group should plot the next five largest cities in 1955. The remaining two groups should do the same for the top ten cities in 2015. The location on the map should include a label with the name of the city and the population. Compare the maps. Ask: What do you think will be the top ten cities in 2050? Why?

2 Ask: Why is the percentage of people living in urban areas in less developed countries increasing so rapidly? In pairs, students think of two reasons. Encourage them to think not only about migration but also the reasons for natural increase. They contribute their ideas to a whole-class discussion.

3 Ask: Will the percentage of population living in urban areas in the UK and other more developed countries increase in future? In pairs, students think of two reasons. They contribute their ideas to a whole-class discussion.

End-of-lesson

4 In small groups, students complete the following sentences to summarise the topic:

- In the 1950s most people lived in … Not many people lived in …
- Today …
- The main differences between 1950 and today are …
- This is because …
- By 2050, it is predicted that …

5 Ask: Is life in cities always great? Students contribute to a whole-class discussion on some of the benefits and disadvantages of living in cities.

6 Use 'Your turn' question 3 as a plenary discussion.

Further class and homework opportunities

Suggestions 15–19 on page 67 of this book

geog.2 workbook, page 21

geog.2 Kerboodle: lesson presentation, worksheets, end-of-lesson assessment

Answers for 'Your turn'

1 a Africa

b Brazil, Argentina, Chile, Venezuela

c i Ethiopia, Niger, Uganda, Malawi, Rwanda, Burundi, Nepal, Papua New Guinea, Sri Lanka

ii Answer is the same as for **c i**.

d In Russia 60–80% of the population live in urban areas and most cities have populations of between 1 and 5 million, except Moscow which has a population of between 5 and 10 million. All of Russia's cities are located in the west of the country.

2 a Approximately 7 billion

b Approximately 9.2 billion

c It has increased considerably from approximately 0.7 billion to nearly 4 billion.

d There will be fewer people. In 2010 there were approximately 3.4 billion people in rural areas. In 2050 this is likely to be 3 billion.

3 So that it can provide the necessary services, such as health care, schools, and public transport and deal with issues that face rural areas (e.g. unemployment).

Why do people move to urban areas?

About this unit

This unit uses case-study examples from different continents to explain the push and pull factors that bring people from rural to urban areas.

Key points

◆ The reasons why people move from rural to urban areas (or vice versa) can be divided into push and pull factors.

◆ Push factors reflect problems in rural areas, e.g. poverty, a lack of educational opportunities, a lack of reliable jobs, poor healthcare, or climatic factors such as regular flooding or forest fires.

◆ Pull factors reflect positive things / opportunities in urban areas, e.g. increased opportunities for work, education and entertainment, or a regular and higher wage that can provide economic security.

Key vocabulary

pull factors, push factors

Skills practised in 'Your turn'

◆ Geography skills: q1, define key terms

◆ Thinking skills: q2, identify push and pull factors in a text; q3, order factors; q4, use common sense and prior knowledge to identify push and pull factors from a different perspective

Unit outcomes

By the end of this unit most students should be able to:

◆ explain the terms given in 'Key vocabulary' above

◆ give – and explain – examples of different push and pull factors that draw people to urban areas

◆ give – and explain – examples of different push and pull factors that draw people away from urban areas

Ideas for a starter

1 Show students a photo of a big city (e.g. Shanghai, Mumbai, Mexico City), a person who might live there, and give them an appropriate name (e.g. Ling / Jas / Cezar) to set the scene. Imagine: You are thinking of moving to city x to find work. What questions would you want to ask Ling / Jas / Cezar about their city before deciding to move there?

2 Use a fictional character who lives in a rural area in a less developed country and who is trying to decide whether to move to a city. Give students (in small groups) cards containing background information about the character and statements outlining push and pull factors. Students sort them into reasons to move and reasons to stay in order of importance. They should make a decision within their group and explain it to the rest of the class.

3 Show students a video on rural–urban migration for a developing country. Students note three reasons why people want to move to a city. Explain push and pull factors. Ask: Can you think of any reasons that might stop people from leaving rural areas?

Ideas for plenaries

Plan plenaries at strategic points throughout the lesson, as well as at the end.

Mid-lesson

1 Give students cards and ask them to sort them into push factors or pull factors for moving from rural to urban areas:

Push factors	Pull factors
Little or no access to schools, clean water, and power	Belief that the quality of life is better
Droughts or supply of food is poor	More jobs
Traditional ways of life	Better housing and healthcare
Poverty	More schools
War	

2 Do 'Your turn' questions 2 and 3 as a plenary.

3 Using the information from pages 40–41 of the students' book, students create a spider diagram showing the push factors that might force people to move away from rural areas and the pull factors that might attract people to urban areas. Ask: Can you think of any others to add?

End-of-lesson

4 With students in small groups, ask: If lots of people moved from rural areas to cities, what challenges might this cause in the cities? What effects might this have on the rural areas? Each group shares their ideas with the whole class.

5 Following on from plenary **3**, students create a spider diagram showing the push factors that might force people to move away from cities and the pull factors that might attract people to rural areas.

Further class and homework opportunities

Suggestions 20–23 on page 67 of this book

geog.2 workbook, page 22

geog.2 Kerboodle: lesson presentation, worksheets, end-of-lesson assessment

Answers for 'Your turn'

1 a Push factors (e.g. unemployment) are the reasons that people leave a place.

b The reasons (e.g. employment opportunities) that attract people to a place.

2 a and b

Names	Push factors	Pull factors
Sylvie	Remoteness / lack of services / amenities Too quiet Boredom No career opportunities	Career opportunities Contacts for her work
Three friends	Lack of employment Lack of services / amenities	Employment Better wages Football More fun Education
Lan	Poverty Lack of services / amenities	Employment opportunities More wealth
Shimaz	Poverty Lack of freedom (i.e. she'd be married)	Employment opportunities More wealth Better services Freedom Financial independence / own money
Osakwe	Flooding Crop failure	Potential for a better life Education Family Potential for employment

3 Answers will vary. Poverty is an important push factor, as is lack of employment and lack of services / amenities.

4 a Pollution; traffic congestion; poor environmental quality; people no longer need to work in the city (i.e. retirement); declining industry / derelict inner city areas; poor quality housing.

b Cost of land may be cheaper so they may be able to afford larger houses; better quality of life (i.e. closer to the countryside and clean and quiet area); lower crime rates; good transport and communication with the city.

It's not all sunshine!

About this unit

This unit examines the benefits – and problems – of living in urban areas. It also investigates different ways of making urban life more sustainable.

Key points

◆ There are many benefits to living in urban areas, but there are also many disadvantages. These disadvantages may eventually become push factors that drive people back to rural areas.

◆ The benefits (pull factors) of living in urban areas include: a good variety of well-paid work; good educational opportunities; good healthcare; good transport links; a wide variety of entertainment and social possibilities.

◆ The disadvantages of living in urban areas include: higher levels of crime and pollution; social isolation, because people are so busy and caught up in their own lives; a much higher cost of living than in rural areas; bland concrete rather than green spaces; crowds and congestion.

◆ Many of the disadvantages listed above could be – at least partially – reversed by making urban areas more sustainable. Pollution and congestion could be reduced by cutting car use and encouraging people to use eco-friendly public transport. The creation of more green spaces, cycle paths and social options for young people could help to reduce street crime and make the urban living experience more enjoyable and less of a concrete jungle.

Key vocabulary

sustainable

Skills practised in 'Your turn'

◆ Geography skills: q4, define a key term

◆ Thinking skills: q1, consider and order benefits; q2, consider disadvantages and reach a conclusion; q3, empathy; q5, q6, consider possible arguments

Unit outcomes

By the end of this unit most students should be able to:

◆ explain the term given in 'Key vocabulary' above

◆ identify and explain possible benefits and disadvantages to living in urban areas

◆ explain a variety of options to make urban life more sustainable

Ideas for a starter

1 Imagine: You are a young woman living in a rural area in Sichuan in south east China. Your family relies on rice farming for income. Over the last few years the price of rice has fallen and your family is struggling. Your brother has written to tell you there are good work opportunities in the factory where he works in Shanghai. He has sent you some pictures of the city. (Give students some pictures showing a prosperous city and wealth.) In pairs, students think of three reasons why they might want to move to Shanghai.

2 Odd one out: Show students a series of pictures of the advantages of living in urban areas (e.g. good shops, a hospital, a tram / bus, a cinema). Mix in a couple of pictures showing some of the disadvantages (e.g. pollution, traffic congestion, crowds, graffiti). Ask students which are the odd ones out (i.e. the disadvantages) and why.

Ideas for plenaries

Plan plenaries at strategic points throughout the lesson, as well as at the end.

Mid-lesson

1 Do 'Your turn' questions 1 and 2 as a plenary.

2 For any aspect of sustainable development (energy-efficient homes, cutting car use, going greener, providing more for young people to do), students create a poster outlining ways in which they can make towns and cities more sustainable, and the benefits.

End-of-lesson

3 Following on from starter **1**, imagine: You decide to move to the city but find that it isn't so great. Your cousin back home is also thinking of moving there. Using the information on page 42 of the students' book, write a text message of 140 characters to explain some of the things about living in the city that are not so good.

4 Students create a spider diagram / mind map to show the effect that people have on towns and cities. For each one, they try to think of some ways to reduce the effect that people have and to make urban life more sustainable.

5 Ask students to think of five things they do that are sustainable and five things that aren't. They discuss these with a partner. Ask: What can you do to change the things that aren't sustainable?

Further class and homework opportunities

Suggestions 24–26 on page 67 of this book

geog.2 workbook, page 23

geog.2 Kerboodle: lesson presentation, worksheets, end-of-lesson assessment

Answers for 'Your turn'

1 **a** and **b** Answers will vary, but students might consider benefits relating to employment, education, health services and transport to be the most important, but benefits relating to entertainment may be the most appealing. For each of their chosen benefits, they explain why it would be strong enough to pull them into / keep them in a city. For example, well-paid jobs mean you have a better income and can enjoy other benefits of urban areas (e.g. shopping and going out).

2 **a** and **b** Answers will vary but they might consider pollution, crime, noise, and competition for housing / jobs to be important factors. For each of the disadvantages they have chosen students should explain why it would stop them living in the city. For example, pollution may affect their health (e.g. asthma).

3 **a** and **b** Generally, the factors that older people might consider to be important are likely to be different to those of younger people. The three push factors that an older retired person is more likely to choose are: crime; many people feel isolated / people don't know their next-door neighbours; more expensive than living in rural areas.

4 Something that can be carried on into the future (e.g. use of a natural resource) without negative effects on the environment, the economy, or people's quality of life.

5 There are a number of ways that green roofs can make a city more sustainable:

◆ Drainage: They absorb water (so that it doesn't just run off concrete / tiles, etc.) and help to prevent flooding.

◆ Plants absorb carbon dioxide, which is a greenhouse gas, and other harmful gases too (e.g. nitrous oxide).

◆ They can provide a habitat for animals, such as nesting birds, and plants.

◆ Dry soil provides insulation and can reduce energy costs.

◆ A green roof provides green space, which is more pleasing to look at than a traditional roof.

6 Answers will vary depending on the place in which students live. Specific suggestions might be based on the ways listed on page 43 of the students' book.

About this unit

This unit concentrates on slum life in developing countries and what can be done about it.

Key points

♦ About 860 million people (one-third of the urban population in developing countries) live in slums. With the rate of urbanisation in Africa and Asia now so high, this figure is likely to grow significantly by 2050, when about 70% of humans are expected to live in urban areas (a rise from 54% today). Much of that increase will be in Africa and Asia – and many of those people will end up in slums, as a result of poverty.

♦ As an example, according to census figures, the slum population of India more than doubled between 1981 (27.9 million) and 2001 (61.8 million), despite strong economic growth in the country as a whole. India's financial capital, Mumbai, has an estimated 6.5 million slum dwellers (55% of the city's population). To provide some contrast, the entire population of London in the 2011 census was 8.17 million. India's urban population in 2011 was 31.3%, and its rate of urbanisation is 2.47%, so India's slum population is likely to increase significantly.

♦ The example of India shows how difficult it is to address the slum problem, when so many extra people (usually poor) are arriving in developing cities every day.

Key vocabulary

self-help, shanty town, slum

Skills practised in 'Your turn'

♦ Geography skills: q1, q5, define key terms; q4, create an explanatory labelled diagram

♦ Thinking skills: q2, q6, consider problems and possible solutions; q3, analyse and compare photos

Unit outcomes

By the end of this unit most students should be able to:

♦ explain the terms given in 'Key vocabulary' above

♦ explain what conditions are like in a modern, developing-world slum

♦ explain how the authorities are tackling the problem in different countries / cities

Ideas for a starter

1 Display a series of pictures of Rio showing sites that tourists might see (Copocabana beach, Sugarloaf Mountain, etc) and one that they might not (the favellas). Ask: Where am I? Which picture is the odd one out? Why?

2 Using photos of slums in developing countries lead a discussion on what students see. What types of houses are there? Where do people get their water from? How do they shop? Explain what a slum is. Ask: What do you think and feel about these places? Vote: Would you want to live here?

3 With students' eyes closed, read the description of Osakwe's life in Lagos at the bottom of page 44 of the students' book. Ask them to describe the images that this conjures up.

Ideas for plenaries

Plan plenaries at strategic points throughout the lesson, as well as at the end.

Mid-lesson

1 Show students an aerial photo of a shanty town. Ask them to describe its location, its size, shape, and any features such as rivers. Now show them a recent Google Earth image of the same shanty town. Ask: What shape is it? Has it grown? How has it grown? Are there any other changes that have taken place? Does it look more permanent? Have the homes been improved? Is there any evidence of services having been installed?

2 Discuss: How is life in a shanty town different from your life?

End-of-lesson

3 Ask: Are all slums places with unhappiness and little hope? Have you heard of the film *Slumdog Millionaire*? Do you know what it's about? Explain the basic plot of the film and that the people making the film found real positives in Dharavi, the slum in which it was filmed. Find and show video clips of life in Dharavi to support this. Have a discussion on both the benefits and disadvantages of living in slums.

4 Ask: What skills have you developed?

5 Ask: What was the most surprising thing you learned today? What really challenged your thinking?

Further class and homework opportunities

Suggestions 27–29 on page 67 of this book

geog.2 workbook, page 24

geog.2 Kerboodle: lesson presentation, worksheets, end-of-lesson assessment

Answers for 'Your turn'

1 An overcrowded area of poor housing found within an urban area.

2 a Overcrowding; no basic sanitation in the shack; have to share a nearby latrine. Rubbish is everywhere, (causes unpleasant smells) attracts flies and dogs, and could cause disease. No schools.

b If Osakwe could find more work he would be able to find them a place of their own. If the rubbish could be removed, it would prevent his children from getting ill.

3 a Similarities include: lots of houses crammed into an area; pollution; people living in a few rooms; no running water and shared toilets; rubbish thrown everywhere; no electricity (i.e. no evidence of power lines in the pictures).

b Differences include: houses are more temporary in the pictures on pages 44–45 of the students' book. In Manchester, factories and industry were next to the housing, there are few or no factories in the pictures on pages 44–45. Shops are less formal in the pictures (e.g. the hair salon) compared to Manchester. In Lagos there is stagnant water outside the shacks, and no roads in evidence.

4 Suggested labels:

a Roof / side of the building – corrugated tin / metal; upstairs: scrap wood / timber; stairs / balcony: scrap timber/bamboo; downstairs; mud walls / concrete.

b Not very big. The average size of a shack is about 3.5 by 3.5 metres.

c Space for sleeping on the floor, mattresses (and maybe beds), an area for sitting with a small table, a small area for cooking.

d Bathroom; toilet; electrical goods (e.g. TV, washing machine); heating; lights; formal furniture (e.g. dining table).

5 a A shanty town is a poor area where houses are just shacks.

b Favela is the name for a slum in a South American city.

6 Students' choices will vary. Some of the improvements include:

C Improvements: People have access to reliable services, such as water, electricity, and sewage, and a cleaner environment.

D Improvements: People can stay in their houses and don't have to move. Homes are improved by providing access to basic services and so day-to-day life is improved. People are given training to learn the skills to improve their homes.

E Improvements: People can stay in their houses and not have to move. They can stay near to people they know but the cable car allows them to get to the city for jobs and schools.

A city of the future?

About this unit

This unit introduces the example of a custom-made sustainable city in Abu Dhabi as a possible vision of the future.

Key points

◆ Masdar City, in the UAE, is a brand-new city that has been designed to be as sustainable as possible. It is at the forefront of research into urban sustainability.

◆ Although it is located in the Arabian Desert, and therefore has conditions that differ from those of many other cities, a great number of Masdar City's sustainability aims are still applicable elsewhere, e.g. reducing the use of fossil fuels, minimising waste and traffic congestion, and allowing for a high population density.

◆ Many of the solutions adopted at Masdar City are also applicable elsewhere (but maybe not the wholesale use of desalination plants!). The extensive use of solar panels, and the installation of sensors for taps and light switches, could be used universally. Equally, the development of green, open public spaces and street layouts that help to regulate temperature and airflow could be adopted in new urban developments elsewhere, in order to improve the pleasure of the urban experience.

Key vocabulary

desalinating, solar power, recycling, renewable resource

Skills practised in 'Your turn'

◆ Geography skills: q1, provide location information; q4, define key terms

◆ Thinking skills: q2, evaluate and order aims with reasons; q3, suggest reasons; q5, q6, evaluate ideas and make selections with reasons; q7, decide

Unit outcomes

By the end of this unit most students should be able to:

◆ explain the terms given in 'Key vocabulary' above

◆ describe the main features of Masdar City

◆ evaluate the features and make reasoned selections and comments

Ideas for a starter

1 Show students pictures relating to a sustainable city using solar power (e.g. the Sun, a solar panel, a city (Masdar City). Ask: What do the pictures show? What is the link? Give them the clue: energy.

2 Recap: What challenges do cities face? Create a spider diagram showing the challenges that cities face. Students consider the following headings: Energy, Transport, Waste, etc.

3 Do 'Your turn' question 1 as a starter.

4 Show a video or section of a video on Masdar City (e.g. from YouTube). Ask students to note down three ways in which Masdar City is sustainable. Take feedback.

Ideas for plenaries

Plan plenaries at strategic points throughout the lesson, as well as at the end.

Mid-lesson

1   Revisit the spider diagram created in starter **2**. For each challenge, students think of solutions and where possible relate them to the example of Masdar City. They can also add additional challenges faced by Masdar by virtue of its location and note the solutions that have been implemented.

2   Ask: What is the perfect sustainable city for the future? In small groups, students design their ideal sustainable city, using sketches, pictures, etc. What features did they include? Students present their designs to the rest of the class and share best ideas.

3   Imagine: You work for a company that creates promotional videos. The UAE government has asked your company to create a video about Masdar City. It will be used to the sell the benefits of Masdar as a sustainable city to the rest of the world. Design and present a storyboard for the video.

4   Ask: What might be the effects of building a city in a desert? Scaffold discussion to draw out some of the possible advantages and disadvantages.

End-of-lesson

5   Do 'Your turn' questions 6 and 7 as a plenary.

6   Students speak for a minute without pausing, going off topic, or giving incorrect information on the topic: How can cities be made sustainable?. Their explanation should include the following key words: energy-efficient, waste, pollution, transport, green roofs, quality of life, Masdar City.

Further class and homework opportunities

Suggestions 30–32 on page 67 of this book

geog.2 workbook, page 25

geog.2 Kerboodle: lesson presentation, worksheets, end-of-lesson assessment

Answers for 'Your turn'

1   Abu Dhabi City is the capital city of the United Arab Emirates (UAE). Its address is: Abu Dhabi City, United Arab Emirates, Arabian Peninsula, Asia.

2   **a and b** Masdar City's main aim is to be a sustainable city (with a low carbon footprint) powered by renewable energy. Therefore the aims relating to reducing the use of fossil fuels and creation of greenhouse gases (e.g. say no to fossil fuels, car-free streets, minimising waste) would be the most important. Reducing the use of fossil fuels will have the biggest impact in reducing emissions and the creation of greenhouse gases.

3   **a** To minimise wastage of resources (i.e. taps being left running / dripping taps / lights being left on unnecessarily) and to ensure that only the amount of water / electricity actually needed is used.

   b To reduce the amount of emissions (e.g. carbon dioxide, which is a greenhouse gas that contributes to global warming). This meets its aim of saying no to fossil fuels.

4   Solar power: Energy that is generated from sunlight (via photovoltaic (PV) cells). Renewable resource: A resource, such as solar energy or wood, that can be replaced naturally over time. Desalination: The process of removing salt from seawater to turn it into drinking water.

5   **a** In the UK we can copy ideas relating to the reduction of fossil fuels, providing electric public transport, making it easier to walk between places, and minimising waste.

   b Ideas around keeping cool, as the climate is not as hot as in the UAE.

   c Relying on solar power for electricity would be difficult in the UK as we would only generate enough solar power at certain times of the year. What about winter? The process of desalination also needs sunlight.

6 and 7 Answers will vary.

Many of these suggestions are addressed to your students. Where research or further resources are needed, the internet will almost certainly provide the answer.

The suggestions are graded *,**,*** according to level of difficulty. Some are suitable for all levels, and can be differentiated by outcome.

How our towns and cities grew

1 **How did it happen?** How did the change from hunting and gathering, to farming, mark the beginning of settlements? Write a text to explain it. */**

2 **Crossword** Make up a crossword with clues about some of the key words in this unit. Here's a clue to get you started: A period between 1760 and 1840 when machines were invented, factories were built and population grew. Answer - Industrial Revolution. Now, write clues for these – hunter gatherers, urban, cities, town, rural, urbanisation. */**

3 **Order, order** Put this sequence of events about the growth of towns and cities into the correct order.
   – Machines are invented in the Industrial Revolution.
   – People move from rural areas to the cities to find jobs.
   – Market towns grow up.
   – Factories spring up.
   – Better farm machinery produces more food.
   – New forms of transport develop.
   – People grow crops and rear animals, so begin to cluster together in one place.
   – Farm workers lose their jobs.
   – People start trading produce or goods they don't need. **/***

4 **Rural or urban?** What is the difference between rural and urban areas? Choose one term and draw a mind map of all the things you can think of related to that term. Which do you live in? If you live in an urban area would you prefer somewhere more rural? Or vice versa? Why? **

5 **Presentation time** Where is your nearest big town or city? How did the Industrial Revolution affect its growth? Find out, and prepare a presentation to show your class. ***

Manchester's story – part 1

6 **Life in the eighteenth and nineteenth centuries** Look at the images of Manchester (in 1857, and terraced housing) on pages 34 and 35 of the students' book. Work in pairs and describe the scenes. What do the pictures show? Who would have lived and worked there? Would you have wanted to live there? Why? What was life in Manchester like back then? */**

7 **Imagine …** You are one of the children working in the mill in the photo on page 35 of the students' book. It is the nineteenth century. Tell the person taking the photo what you are doing, how long you work and why you are not at school. Tell them what your home life is like and what your hopes are for the future. **

8 **Industrial Revolution – advantages and disadvantages** The Industrial Revolution had many effects. What advantages and disadvantages did it have on: employment, economic development, population growth, health? List them. **/***

9 **Industrial Revolution – advantages and disadvantages** A more scaffolded version of the previous activity. The Industrial Revolution had many effects on employment, economic developement, population growth and health. Sort these advantages and disadvantages into the correct category: plenty of work in factories; only factory owners grew wealthy; pollution; couples met in cities and had children; disease spread easily because of overcrowding; only the wealthy benefitted from improved health services; children had to work in mills; people who lost farming jobs found work; working conditions were poor; industry grew; the economy grew; no running water/shared toilets; health services improved, people lived longer; more wealth was created; overcrowded living conditions.**/***

10 **Manchester 1857** The painting on page 34 of the students' book shows Manchester in 1857. Write a newspaper article to describe how Manchester grew from a large town of 17 000 people in 1760, to a city of over 300 000 dominated by industry. Write your article in the style of newspapers of the time (do some research to find out what they were like, and what the language was like then). */**/***

Manchester's story – part 2

11 **Redevelopment** Give students photos of areas of Manchester which have been redeveloped. Ask them to describe how the city has changed, and why it has changed. */**/***

12 **True or false?** Look at the graph of Manchester's changing population on page 36 of the students' book. Decide if these statements are true or false. If they are false give the correct version.
   – Manchester's population peaked in 1931.
   – Manchester's population is now larger than ever.
   – From 1931-71 Manchester's population fell by about 200 000.
   – Manchester's population is continuing to fall.
   Now write another two statements (true ones!) about Manchester's population based on the graph. */**

13 **Push or pull?** Give students cards with the following push and pull factors on them. The push factors are those which contributed to Manchester's fall in population, the pull factors include those which have contributed to Manchester's recent rise in population. Ask students to sort the factors. Leave some cards blank for students to add some factors of their own.

Push: Other countries began to make things more cheaply; Factories shut down; People lost their jobs; Crime rates rose; High levels of pollution.

Pull: Old industrial areas cleared to make way for new businesses; Improved transport links (e.g the tram service); Run-down housing replaced with modern housing; New services and facilities (e.g. restaurants, bars, shops); Financial support from the government for businesses. */**/***

14 Manchester's story – summary Write a summary of the growth (and decline) of Manchester in 50 words. Now write it in 15 words. Can you do it in 10? **

Urbanisation around the world

15 The world's biggest cities are … Find out! Research the world's 10 biggest cities. Draw a bar graph to show how big they are. Locate them on a world map and then describe their distribution. **

16 2050 Following on from the previous activity, find out which will be the world's biggest cities in 2050. Draw another bar graph and locate them on a world map. Compare your graph and map with those in the previous activity. Describe any changes in terms of size, or location of the biggest cities. **

17 Good? What are the advantages of living in cities? Choose a more developed country and a less developed one. Work with a partner and do some research and find out some of the advantages of living in cities in your named countries. Produce an exuberant poster of all the good things about living in the cities. **

18 Or bad? What are the disadvantages of living in cities? Choose a more developed country and a less developed one. Work with a partner and do some research and find out some of the disadvantages of living in cities in your named countries. Produce a poster of all the bad things about living in the cities. Your poster should reflect the bad things. **

19 Wordsearch Create a wordsreach for your partner. Include the following words which are used in this unit: urbanisation, cities, Shanghai, Birmingham, London, rural, urban, Africa, Asia. *

Why do people move to urban areas?

20 Imagine You live in a rural area in the UK and want to move to your nearest city. What do you need to know before you move? What questions do you need to ask? Where will you find the information you need? Now, you've found the answers – do you still want to go? */**

21 Imagine You live in a city in the UK and want to move to the countryside. What do you need to know before you move? What questions do you need to ask? Where will you find the information you need? Now, you've found the answers – do you still want to go? */**

22 Interview Choose one person from page 40–41 of the students' book (not Osakwe). Work with a partner and write the questions and answers for an interview with them. Ask them why they moved to the city and what their life is like now. **/***

23 Odd-one-out Prepare sets of odd-one-out for your partner based on the push and pull factors that encourage people to leave rural areas and move to cities. How many sets can you come up with in five minutes? **

It's not all sunshine!

24 Define sustainable Who can come up with the best definition of the word 'sustainable' – without just copying the definition in the students' book? **/***

25 Making cities more sustainable Create a poster or a presentation on how cities can be made more sustainable. Use the ideas on page 43 of the students' book, and research some more ideas of your own. Explain what the different ideas are, how they make cities more sustainable and what benefits they bring. */**/***

26 Sustainable cities Find a video online about a sustainable city. You can choose from Copenhagen, Curitiba, Malmo or Vancouver. Note down at least four things which have been done to make the city sustainable. **/***

Life in the slums

27 Living in Kibera Look at the photo of Kibera on page 44 of the students' book. Use the five Ws to ask the people in the photo about their life. Think of at least one question about the way they live (social environment), one about their financial situation (economic question), and one about the area they live in (natural environment). **/***

28 Shanty town living Look on You Tube for a video of life in a shanty town (e.g in Rio de Janeiro, or in Nairobi). Watch the video and pick out two facts that strike you in some way. Why did you pick out those two facts? How did they make you feel? How would you feel if it was you living in the shanty town? */**/***

29 A day in the life of… Imagine you lived in the slum in photo B on page 44 of the students' book. Write a description of a day in your life (don't just copy Osakwe's description – it will be spotted!). Who do you live with? What is it like there? What do you see, hear, smell? What do you like about living there? What is bad about living there? Then read your day to a partner. */**/***

A city of the future?

30 Desalination How does it work? The water for Masdar City is obtained by desalinating sea water. Is it a sustainable way to produce fresh water for a city in a desert? **/***

31 Masdar City should never have been built What is wrong with building a brand new sustainable city? Some people think it would be better to make existing cities more sustainable, rather than build new ones. What do you think? Work in small groups and be prepared to put someone in the hot seat to take questions on the view that Masdar City should never have been built. ***

32 Field trip Plan a week-long field trip to Abu Dhabi to find out about Masdar City. How will you get there? Where will you stay? What do you want to find out? Tell us your plans. **

4 Coasts

About this chapter

Addressing the KS3 Programme of Study

◆ Understand, through the use of detailed place-based exemplars, the key processes relating to coastal landforms and human use of coastal areas.

◆ Interpret maps and diagrams.

◆ Interpret Ordnance Survey maps, including using grid references.

About the content

◆ The chapter starts by explaining how waves form and how they shape the coastline, introducing key terms and various landforms.

◆ It uses Newquay as an exemplar, through an OS map and photos, of human activity in coastal resorts.

◆ It looks at the causes and effects of the storm surge of winter 2013/14, and the specific case of Happisburgh, to introduce the sea defences that can be used and the factors involved in deciding which places to defend and which to allow the sea to destroy.

The big picture

These are the key ideas in this chapter.

◆ Our coastline is continually shaped and changed by physical and human processes.

◆ The waves shape and change the coast by eroding, transporting, and depositing material. The result is special coastal landforms.

◆ We humans also change the coast, through the way we use the land and sea.

◆ Places along the coast are at risk from flooding and erosion by the sea. With climate change, this will become a bigger problem.

◆ There are ways to protect places from the sea, but they cost a lot.

◆ In future, only parts of the coast will be protected. The sea will be allowed to destroy others.

A students' version of this big picture is given in the *geog.2* students' book opener for Chapter 4.

The chapter outline

Use this, and their chapter opener, to give students a mental roadmap for the chapter.

4 Coasts The chapter opener in the students' book is an important part of the chapter; see page 11 for notes about using chapter openers

4.1 Waves and tides What they are and what causes them

4.2 The waves at work How waves erode, transport, and deposit material

4.3 Landforms created by the waves The landforms you find along the coast, created by the waves – some through erosion, some through deposition

4.4 The coast and us The ways we use places along the coast and the sea

4.5 Your holiday in Newquay Brushing up on OS map skills, at this surfing resort

4.6 Under threat from the sea Reasons for the storm surge along the east coast in December 2013 and the areas easily eroded by the sea

4.7 How long can Happisburgh hang on? How and why the coast at Happisburgh (pronounced *Haisbro*) is being nibbled away by the sea

4.8 Protecting places from the sea Ways of protecting places from the sea and factors in deciding which places to protect

Objectives and outcomes for this chapter

Objectives	Unit	Outcomes
Most students will understand:		Most students will be able to:
• that our coastline is shaped by both physical and human processes	all	• give examples of physical and human processes that shape the coastline
• what causes waves and tides	4.1	• explain that waves are caused by the wind, and say how its strength, duration, and fetch affect them; explain that the tides are caused by the pull of the moon (and to a lesser extent, the Sun) on the sea
• how waves shape the coast	4.1, 4.2, 4.3	• describe the processes of erosion, transport, and deposition by the waves
• that the action of waves leads to characteristic coastal landforms	4.2, 4.3	• name, describe, and identify the coastal landforms covered in the chapter; explain how they are formed
• that we use the coast in different ways, some directly related to the sea	4.4, 4.5	• give at least six examples of ways we use the coast; and say what special functions a coastal town can have
• that erosion is causing serious problems along some parts of the coast	4.6, 4.7	• point out the main stretches of coast where erosion is a problem; describe the problems at Happisburgh
• that there are things we can do to protect the coast from erosion	4.7, 4.8	• give at least four ways to protect coastal places from erosion
• that the current strategy is to defend the coast in a sustainable way	4.8	• explain why the government does not want to protect all the places at risk of erosion; say what the current strategy is for defending the coast

These tie in with the outcomes for each unit, in this teacher's handbook, and with 'Your goals for this chapter', in *geog.2* students' book.

Opportunities for assessment

See the formal assessment materials for this chapter on *geog.2 Kerboodle Lessons, Resources, & Assessment*. They include an extended assessment task, an exam-style question, end-of-lesson assessments, and a self-assessment form. See also the notes on pages 14–15 of this book.

Getting ready for this chapter

geog.2 Kerboodle contains plans and presentations for each unit, including interactive activities, animations, and worksheets.

About 'Your chapter starter'

The coast is where the land meets the sea. Why does it look so different in different places? It's largely down to geology, and how hard or soft rocks are.

The Old Man of Stoer (photo **A** page 48 of *geog.2* students' book) is a stack made of sandstone, around 1.2 billion years old, and resistant to erosion. Morston Marshes (**B**) on the Norfolk coast, are located in an area where the rock is a mix of materials deposited by melting glaciers around 400 000 years ago, and easily eroded. Sennen Beach (**C**) nestles in a sandstone area surrounded by granite. Handfast Point and Old Harry (**D**) are formed from chalk (the remains of a band which stretched between Purbeck and the Isle of Wight).

Waves and tides

About this unit

This unit provides an introduction to waves and tides.

Key points

◆ Waves are caused by wind dragging on the surface of the water.

◆ The length of water the wind blows over is called the fetch. The stronger the wind, the longer it blows for, and the longer the fetch, the larger the waves will be.

◆ Waves break at the shore, giving turbulent water called swash. The water that rushes up the sand is called the uprush; it then rolls back into the sea as backwash.

◆ When the uprush is stronger than the backwash, material is added to the beach. If the backwash is stronger than the uprush, the beach is eroded.

◆ The moon and Sun exert a gravitational force on Earth, so they draw the seas upwards on the side facing them. At the same time, on the opposite side of Earth, the seas are pulled outwards by a centrifugal force. As a result, the water level falls everywhere else around Earth.

◆ These rises and falls in water level are called tides. There are high tides at any given place twice a day, and low tides in between.

◆ As the moon orbits Earth, and Earth orbits the Sun, the combined pull of the moon and Sun changes, so the heights of the tides change too.

Key vocabulary

backwash, fetch, high tide, low tide, prevailing wind, swash, tidal range, tides, uprush, wave, wind

Skills practised in 'Your turn'

◆ Geography skills: q2, analyse information on a diagram; q3a, q4, define key terms; q5–q7, analyse photos

◆ Literacy skills: q1, write explanatory sentences; q7, write a diary entry

◆ Thinking skills: q5–q6, use evidence to draw conclusions

Unit outcomes

By the end of this unit most students should be able to:

◆ explain the terms given in 'Key vocabulary' above

◆ explain that waves are caused by wind dragging on the water's surface

◆ explain that tides are caused by the pull of the moon and Sun on the sea

Ideas for a starter

1 Show images of different types of waves (small and large). Ask: Why are some waves larger than others?

2 Show video clips of waves breaking on the shore. Ask students to describe what happens as a wave reaches the coast. They should describe not only what they hear but also what they see.

3 Make waves by blowing on the surface of water in a shallow tray, with a straw.

Ideas for plenaries

Plan plenaries at strategic points throughout the lesson, as well as at the end.

Mid-lesson

1 Ask: How do we use waves and tides? Can waves do us harm?

2 Ask students to list three ways they think waves affect our world. Discuss answers as a whole class.

3 With books closed, get students to finish the following sentences: Waves are caused by … The fetch is … Low tide is when … High tide is when … Tidal range is caused by …

End-of-lesson

4 Countdown: On the whiteboard, list some anagrams / scrambled-up words, and clues relating to tides and waves. Give students 30 seconds (with their books closed) to unscramble them. Have an animation of a clock ticking on the whiteboard. Examples of anagrams might be:

◆ Uh spur: the water that rushes up the sand beach after a wave has broken.

◆ Cab hawks: the water that rolls back into the sea after a wave has broken.

◆ Tide owl: the lowest sea level during a day.

◆ Edit high: the highest sea level during a day.

◆ Delta grain: the drop in sea level from high to low tide.

◆ Inland view grip: the dominant wind direction in an area.

Further class and homework opportunities

Suggestions 1–5 on page 86 of this book

geog.2 workbook, page 27

geog.2 Kerboodle: lesson presentation, worksheets, end-of-lesson assessment

Answers for 'Your turn'

1 The stronger the wind speed, the more energy it will have and the larger the waves will be. The longer the wind blows, the more energy it will have, which will cause larger waves. If the wind has been blowing over a large distance (fetch), it will have more energy and result in bigger waves.

2 a B, because it is the strongest, with the longest fetch.

   b A, because it is light, like C, but has a shorter fetch.

3 a Prevailing wind: the wind that blows most often. South west wind: the wind that blows *from* the south west.

   b Winds from the south west have a long fetch, over the Atlantic Ocean. If they are strong too, this means there will be high waves along the south west tip of England.

   c Surfers like big waves. South west England and Wales can get big waves because of the long fetch of the prevailing south west wind. So they're good places for surfing schools.

4 a Swash is the water that rushes up the beach when a wave breaks.

   b Uprush is the water which rushes up the beach after the wave has broken.

   c Backwash is the water that runs down the beach.

5 a Uprush is stronger. There is a large beach. If the uprush has more energy than the backwash, material is carried onshore and left there, building up a beach.

   b Morston Marshes (photo **B**) looks as if it gets hardly any waves (look at all the low grassland).

6 a Tides are the rise and fall of the sea. As the moon travels around Earth, it attracts the sea and pulls the water upwards. (The Sun also attracts sea that's turned towards it but to a lesser extent, since the Sun is much further away.)

   b The mud / sand would be covered by water and the boats would be floating.

   c The water would be further up the sand, so there would be less beach to see.

   d The photo was taken at high tide. The sea reaches the cliffs and no beach or shore is visible.

7 Students should write a diary entry in response to this question.

The waves at work

About this unit

This unit explores how waves shape the coastline.

Key points

- ◆ Waves continually shape the coastline by eroding, transporting and depositing material. Weathering helps this process by making erosion easier.
- ◆ The waves erode rock by: hammering into the cracks at high pressure (hydraulic action); dissolving any soluble material (solution); and flinging pebbles and sand at it, which scrape it away (abrasion). They then knock rock fragments together, so that they get smoothed and worn away (attrition).
- ◆ The end products of erosion are pebbles (shingle), sand, and mud.
- ◆ The way waves roll in and out, and their direction, means that most eroded material is carried *parallel* to the shore. This is called longshore drift. (Some is carried out to sea.)
- ◆ Beaches form in sheltered areas where the waves deposit sand or shingle.
- ◆ Some resorts have groynes (barriers of wood or stone) down the beach, to stop sand being carried away by longshore drift.

Key vocabulary

erosion (erode), transport, deposition (deposit), weathered (weathering), hydraulic action, solution, abrasion, attrition, shingle, sand, longshore drift, groynes, prevailing wind

Skills practised in 'Your turn'

- ◆ Geography skills: q1–q2 name and describe key terms; q4, q5, analyse a photo and a diagram
- ◆ Thinking skills: q3, q6, use evidence to reach a conclusion

Unit outcomes

By the end of this unit most students should be able to:

- ◆ explain the terms given in 'Key vocabulary' above
- ◆ describe the processes of erosion, transport, and deposition by the waves
- ◆ say that weathering helps to make erosion easier

Ideas for a starter

1 Show a video of waves at work.

2 Show a picture of a house at the edge of a cliff. Ask: If you owned this house, would you be worried?

3 Show students an aerial photo of a beach with sand built up behind groynes. Ask: What does the photo show? How might this have happened?

4 Show beach trophies; shells, pebbles, old bits of net from fishing boats. Say: I found these on a beach. How did they end up there?

Ideas for plenaries

Plan plenaries at strategic points throughout the lesson, as well as at the end.

Mid-lesson

1 If you did not use starter **1**, show the video of the waves at work.

2 With books closed, give students cards of the main erosion processes and their definitions. In pairs or small groups, students match the process to the definition.

Process	Definition
Abrasion	Pebbles and boulders are pounded against a cliff face. Over time this wears away the rock.
Solution	Water dissolves soluble material from the rock.
Attrition	Rocks knock against each other and break into smaller pieces. The rock breaks down to become shingle and sand.
Hydraulic action	Water is trapped in cracks in the rock. This helps to break it up.

3 With books closed, students create a mental map on the whiteboard of processes that contribute to coastal erosion. They nominate others to explain each term.

4 Revisit the aerial photo of a beach (in starter **3**) with sand built up behind the groynes. Ask: Why is there sand one side but not on the other? What would happen if the groynes weren't there? Where would the sand go? Where do you think it would end up?

5 Do 'Your turn' question 6 as a plenary.

End-of-lesson

6 Referring back to starter **2**, ask: What will happen next? Why do you think this?

7 Ask students: Which is the odd one out in each of the following lists? Why?
   – hydraulic action, attrition, longshore drift, abrasion.
   – hydraulic action, solution, attrition, deposition.

8 Discuss: Is the sea making the British Isles smaller?

9 Give students two minutes, with a partner, to think of one interesting question about the waves at work that has not been covered today. (This could produce a good enquiry question for the class to follow up.)

Further class and homework opportunities

Suggestions 6–8 on page 86 of this book

geog.2 workbook, page 28

geog.2 Kerboodle: lesson presentation, worksheets, end-of-lesson assessment

Answers for 'Your turn'

1 They erode, transport, and deposit material.

2 Three from: hydraulic action, solution, abrasion, attrition.

3 **a** **Y**. It is smoother, because any projections on its surface have been worn away through knocking against other particles.
   b Attrition

4 **a** To stop the beach being eroded.
   b Yes; more sand has built up on one side of each groyne (the side facing the waves) than the other; this shows they are working.
   c From the south west towards the north east; the longshore drift flows past the groynes from that direction and some of the sand gets trapped.

5 **a** South east
   b A is not sheltered enough. The waves are eroding material.
   c B is sheltered so sand is deposited.
   d From the erosion of rocks; at least some would have come from the rocks at A.

6 No. There are different types of rocks; some are harder, and these erode more slowly than softer rocks. Also wave action around the coast varies, depending on the amount of exposure to, or shelter from, the winds, as well as other local conditions (e.g. tides, currents).

Landforms created by the waves

About this unit

This unit explains the various landforms that waves create along the coast, through eroding and depositing material.

Key points

- ◆ Erosion and deposition by waves result in different coastal landforms.
- ◆ Waves erode different types of rock at different rates. Hard rock erodes more slowly than adjacent soft rock. The result is headlands and adjoining bays.
- ◆ Waves carve notches in a cliff face. When these get deep enough, the overhanging cliff topples into the sea. So the cliff face recedes, leaving a wave-cut platform of rock.
- ◆ Waves can attack cracks in headlands, enlarging them into caves. In time these wear right through to form arches. Arches collapse, leaving pillars called stacks, which wear away to stumps.
- ◆ Sand carried by longshore drift may be deposited in bays, forming beaches. Or in the sea, where the coast changes direction sharply, forming spits.
- ◆ Silt and mud collect in the sheltered area behind a spit, forming a salt marsh.

Key vocabulary

headland, wave-cut notch, wave-cut platform, bay, cave, arch, stack, stump, beach, spit, salt marsh

Skills practised in 'Your turn'

- ◆ Geography skills: q1, identify processes that created different landforms; q2, q3, make annotated sketches of photos to aid explanations; q4, use an annotated sketch to make a prediction
- ◆ Thinking skills: q2, q3, explain; q2, q4, predict

Unit outcomes

By the end of this unit most students should be able to:

- ◆ explain the terms given in 'Key vocabulary' above
- ◆ identify, and sketch, the coastal landforms that have been covered in this unit
- ◆ explain how they are formed
- ◆ draw an annotated sketch of a coastal landform from a photo
- ◆ show, by means of a sketch, that they understand that different rock types erode at different rates

Ideas for a starter

1. Show photos or a video of different coastal landforms. Ask students to describe what they see. Why do you think we get all these different landforms?
2. Look at the photos on page 48 of the students' book. Ask: Why do you think they are all so different? Can you name any of these landforms?
3. Show students photos of the following features: cave, arch, stack, stump. Ask: How might they have been formed? Are they part of a sequence? Follow with starter **4**.
4. Show a before and after picture of the rock arch in Porthcothan Bay, Cornwall that was destroyed in the 2014 storms. Ask students to identify the differences between the before and after pictures, and explain what happened.

Ideas for plenaries

Plan plenaries at strategic points throughout the lesson, as well as at the end.

Mid-lesson

1   Ask students to write their own glossary for the terms and features learned today (headland, wave-cut platform, bay, arch, stack, cave, beach, spit, salt marsh).

2   Ask: What is the link between abrasion, solution, attrition and hydraulic action? Ask students to explain the differences between the four processes.

3   Using the photos on page 48 of the students' book, ask: Can you name the landforms in the photos? What will happen at **A**, eventually? Look at photo **D**. These chalk cliffs are retreating at a rate of about 60 cm a year. Why? What can you say about chalk and its resistance to erosion? How long will it take the cliffs to retreat 10 metres? (16.6 years).

End-of-lesson

4   What am I? Describe the features covered in the lesson (headland, wave-cut platform, bay, arch, stack, cave, beach, spit and salt marsh). Students have to guess what feature you are.

5   Give students the following lists of landforms caused by erosion and deposition. Ask them to find the odd ones out:

–   wave-cut platform, spit, arch, cave

–   spit, salt marsh, headland, beach

Further class and homework opportunities

Suggestions 9–15 on page 86 of this book

geog.2 workbook, page 29

geog.2 Kerboodle: lesson presentation, worksheets, end-of-lesson assessment

Answers for 'Your turn'

1

Landform	Created by ...	
	erosion	deposition
headland	✓	
wave-cut platform	✓	
bay	✓	
cave	✓	
arch	✓	
stack	✓	
beach		✓
spit		✓
salt marsh		✓

2   **a**   Students sketch and label the landforms in photo **A**. Note that the photo shows several wave-cut notches.

b   First the waves eroded a hollow in the rock of the headland. This deepened to form a cave. (In fact two caves may have formed opposite each other, because waves at a headland get bent around or refracted, attacking the headland from both sides.) Then the cave eroded right through, leaving an arch.

c   Students add a dotted line to their sketch to show where there was once another arch.

d   It will be completely eroded away.

3   **a**   Their final sketch should look like this but larger.

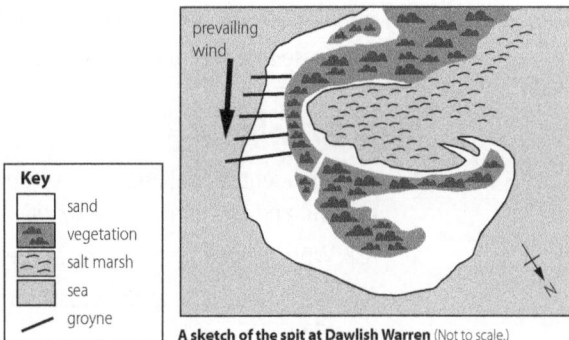

A sketch of the spit at Dawlish Warren (Not to scale.)

b   South west. The direction the spit grows *from* is the wave direction, which in turn tells you wind direction. Then use the N arrow.

4   Their sketch should look something like this. Students should add notes to explain what has happened.

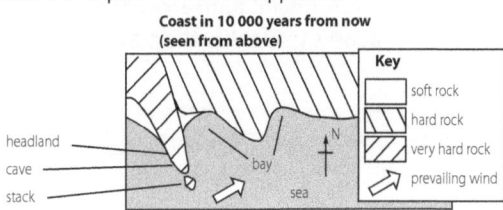

The coast and us

About this unit

This unit discusses the many different ways in which people use the coast.

Key points

◆ The sea shapes and changes the coast, and so do we – via the different ways in which we use it, e.g. for recreation (such as beach holidays, fishing, diving); as a source of valuable primary resources (fish / seafood, sand / gravel for building, and seawater to produce sea salt); or for trade or access through ports and ferry terminals.

◆ Coastal settlements are likely to have specific functions related to the sea, which bring related employment, e.g. fishing settlements provide employment for the fishermen, as well as the workers in the onshore fish-processing plants, the traders who sell the fish on to wholesalers and supermarkets, and the lorry drivers who transport the processed fish inland (as well as the local fishmongers and fish and chip shops in every coastal town).

Key vocabulary

ports, seaside resorts, primary sector, secondary sector, tertiary sector

Skills practised in 'Your turn'

◆ Geography skills: q2, q5, use photos to identify coastal uses and different sectors of the economy; q3, use a map to identify ports; q4, draw a sketch map from a mental map

◆ Literacy skills: q2, unscramble words

◆ Thinking skills: q1, q7, q8, q9, use common sense and prior knowledge to construct a reasoned explanation and argument; q3, q4, use general knowledge to name ports and seaside resorts; q5, classify coastal jobs by sector of the economy

Unit outcomes

By the end of this unit most students should be able to:

◆ explain the terms given in 'Key vocabulary' above

◆ give at least six examples of ways in which we use the coast

◆ say what special functions coastal settlements can have

◆ recognise that we humans shape and change the coast through how we use it

Ideas for a starter

1 Show students aerial photos of settlements located next to the sea (e.g. with a port or harbour and farming). Ask: Why was the settlement located here?

2 Ask: Who has been to the coast? Where? What did you do there?

3 Ask: What can we do at the coast? Students create a graffiti wall about how we use the coastline.

4 Give students different types of human activities that take place on the coast (e.g. snorkelling, sailing, surfing, birdwatching, sunbathing, boating, deep-sea diving, fishing) and ask them to act out the activity. Others have to guess what the activity is.

5 Where am I? Read out clues about seaside resorts (e.g. famous landmarks, facts about the place, information about the geographical location). Students use the information and atlases to identify the place.

Ideas for plenaries

Plan plenaries at strategic points throughout the lesson, as well as at the end.

Mid-lesson

1 Do 'Your turn' question 2 as a plenary. Ask: What does each photo show? What do they have in common? Then students complete the question working alone or in pairs.

2 Write the following headings on the board: *Tourism, Industry, Leisure, Energy, Other*. Ask students to think of as many examples of uses of coastlines for each heading as possible.

3 Ask: Do you think having a coast helps the UK's economy? How? Can you think of a way it might help it in the future (think energy)?

4 Write on the board: *The sea affects the coastline and so do humans*. Ask: In what ways does the sea affect the coastline? In what ways do humans affect the coastline? Which do you think affects it the most? Which can be controlled? Introduce the idea that there may be conflicts (looked at in more detail later in the chapter).

End-of-lesson

5 Ask students to think of a use of the coast for every letter of the alphabet. The first student gives a use starting with A, the second student gives a use starting with B, and so on.

6 Give students types of activities done on the coast and ask them to describe them without using the word itself. Others have to guess the activity that is being described. Types of activity could include: hotels, amusement arcades, port / harbour / docks, wave energy generation, industry, farming, rambling, bird watching.

7 Ask students to identify three uses of coastal areas, two possible problems with the use of coastal areas, and one question they may still have.

Further class and homework opportunities

Suggestions 16–17 on page 86 of this book

geog.2 workbook, page 30

geog.2 Kerboodle: lesson presentation, worksheets, end-of-lesson assessment

Answers for 'Your turn'

1 a Access to the sea for fishing, trade, travel by boat, water for washing; defence against enemies arriving by sea; milder winter climate due to the warming effect of the sea in winter; and along the coast you might find some flat land for farming. Some early settlers might have wanted a sea view, for enjoyment.

   b The reasons that still apply today, are underlined above. People are still employed in fishing, trade and travel by sea (in fishing fleets and at fishing ports, cargo ports and ferry terminals); and in defence and coastal protection (the navy, and coastguard service); and in farming along the coast. Many people retire to the coast specifically for the milder climate, and sea views.

2 **A** seaside resorts **B** fishing **C** ports **D** farming **E** industry **F** homes **G** defence **H** dredging

3 a Six out of the ten – London, Glasgow, Edinburgh (at Leith), Liverpool, Manchester (via a ship canal to the sea), and Bristol – had ports that helped them grow. But changes in shipping led to decline in several ports. The old ports in Glasgow and Manchester have closed.

   b Some other ports: Aberdeen, Cardiff, Dover, Felixstowe, Grimsby, Tees/Hartlepool, Hull, Milford Haven, Plymouth, Portsmouth, Southampton, Swansea, Tyneside.

4 a Students could name resorts they have visited, or use the map on page 139 of the students' book to suggest resorts.

   b Students can check their sketch map against the map on page 139.

5 a photos **B, D** and **H**

   b photo **E** (an oil refinery at Grangemouth in Scotland**)**

   c **A, C** and **G**; although **A** does not show anyone working, day trippers and people on holiday at the seaside rely on services.

6 Examples include: deep-sea fishing, beach guard, diving crew taking tourists diving, surfing instructor, lobster farmer, sailor in the navy or on a container ship or ferry, harbour master, oil rig worker, worker on sea dredger.

7 Because it is an island, Britain has had a long history of exploring, sea trading and naval warfare, eventually leading to the growth of the British Empire. It was able to import cheap raw materials from around the empire. When the Industrial Revolution got under way, Britain was able to export goods all over the world. Much later the discovery of oil and gas in the North Sea helped to boost its economy.

8 A coast makes travel abroad, and transporting goods more expensive; insularity – we may not bother to learn other languages; risk of coastal erosion and drowning of low lying coasts as sea levels rise.

9 Students' responses will vary.

About this unit

This unit employs an OS map as the basis for an introduction to Newquay – one of Cornwall's premier seaside resorts and the main home of UK surfing.

Key points

◆ An OS map can help the reader to identify coastal landforms.

◆ It can also inform the reader about transport routes and available facilities, such as camp sites, the tourist information office, and tourist attractions like National Trust properties and Newquay's aquarium.

Key vocabulary

(No new vocabulary)

Skills practised in 'Your turn'

◆ Geography skills: q1–q7, read an OS map, interpret OS map symbols, use grid references, use the map scale, match photos to an OS map; q6a, draw a sketch map of a route from the OS map

◆ Numeracy skills: q6b, a simple time calculation

◆ Literacy skills: q1, write explanatory sentences based on map and photographic data; q8, write a blog entry

◆ Thinking skills: q2, use prior knowledge to reach conclusions; q3, analyse a photo to reach a reasoned conclusion; q5, q6, plan a route and a schedule; q7, consider the possible benefits and problems of increasing the number of flights into Newquay, and whether this would be sustainable; q8, plan a blog, including illustrations

Unit outcomes

By the end of this unit most students should be able to:

◆ identify coastal landforms on an OS map

◆ compare a photo to an OS map to identify a place

◆ draw a sketch map of a route from an OS map

◆ recognise that you can tell a great deal about a place from an OS map

Ideas for a starter

1   Students ask questions to determine your location (Newquay) and you answer only yes or no. Alternatively, place clues and images relating to Newquay on the whiteboard with the question, Where am I? For example: photo of Newquay as a seaside resort; I face the North Atlantic; I am about 280 miles south west of London; map with Cornwall highlighted; picture of people surfing and Volkswagen camper vans; I am the surf capital of the UK.

2   Ask students to locate Newquay on a map of the UK. Ask them to give you five geographical facts about it.

3   Give students bingo cards with six to eight OS map symbols related to coasts on them. Display the symbols on the whiteboard and students cross them off their card. The first student to cross off all the symbols shouts 'Bingo'.

Ideas for plenaries

Plan plenaries at strategic points throughout the lesson, as well as at the end.

Mid-lesson

1 Ask students to write a story (or some statements) about a holiday in Newquay where some words are replaced by map symbols. Start with the following sentences. Give students a key depending on ability.

During the summer holidays we went to Newquay. We stayed at a [campsite symbol] near Trencreek. On the first morning we went to the [tourist information symbol] to get some information and directions.

End-of-lesson

2 Read some statements about features and symbols on the map. Students decide whether they are true or false, and, if false, give the correct answer:

- Fistral beach is the longest beach in Newquay. (False: Tregurrian or Watergate Beach is the longest.)
- Trevelgue Head is east of Towan Head.
- Towan Head is north east of Pentire Point East.
- You could pitch a tent at 792608. (False: This site is only for caravans.)
- You can visit animals at 820615.
- Horse Rock is 2 km from Zacry's Island. (False: It is approximately 0.5 km).

Further class and homework opportunities

Suggestions 18–25 on pages 86–87 of this book

geog.2 workbook, page 31

geog.2 Kerboodle: lesson presentation, worksheets, end-of-lesson assessment

Answers for 'Your turn'

1 Students should be able to say that it has cliffs, and looks rocky and irregular, with a number of headlands, many beaches, and several little islands. Some may note that it faces north west.

2 a Headland

b The waves eroded softer rock (or perhaps similar rock but with weaknesses in it) on either side, leaving the headland jutting out.

c Trevelgue Head; and also the places with Point in the name – Pentire Point East, Berryl's Point, Griffin's Point, Stern Point.

d The rock at a headland must be quite hard and resistant to erosion.

3 It may be a very big stack! It probably formed as a result of erosion forming a cave, then an arch and finally a stack.

4 Crantock, Fistral, Lusty Glaze, and, at the top right, part of Tregurrian or Watergate beach.

5 a There is plenty of choice. (Their choice will affect their answers for question **6**.)

b Things to do: swimming, surfing, walking, lolling on the beach, playing golf, climbing cliffs; visiting the aquarium, zoo leisure park or sports centre (represented by the blue figure in a circle). There's also eating out and shopping.

c 816617

d i Slightly more than half a kilometre (500 metres).

ii Southwest.

6 a The answer depends on their choice of campsite.

b The answer will depend on the distance from the campsite.

7 a 8665

b i More customers for the businesses in Newquay: hotels, B&Bs, restaurants, the zoo, aquarium etc – in other words, more money coming into the town. As a result, some facilities will improve and new services will start up. The place will become even livelier.

ii It could get overcrowded, which might make life worse for the residents. Aircraft noise could be a problem. More air traffic will bring an increase in road traffic in the area too – and both produce carbon dioxide, which is linked to global warming.

c i Students should give reasons.

ii Students should make up their own minds.

8 You could ask what differences there might be in writing a blog compared with writing a report for the head teacher, for example.

help at a glance

About this unit

This unit examines the storm surge that battered the UK's coastline in December 2013.

Key points

◆ A storm surge is a large surge of seawater that can overwhelm coastal defences and flood low-lying inland areas. It can also dramatically increase the rate of erosion on coasts consisting of mainly soft rock, such as those of Humberside and East Anglia.

◆ A storm surge is caused by a combination of low air pressure, high tides and strong winds – and, therefore, is more common in the winter months, when powerful storms can hit the UK.

◆ This is what happened in December 2013, when a storm surge battered much of the UK's east coast and caused flooding in several places, as well as some dramatic coastal erosion.

◆ The power of the storm surge was magnified as it headed down the North Sea coast, because the North Sea is quite shallow, and narrows as it approaches the English Channel, so the waves were funnelled and increased in size. As a result, the Thames Barrier had to be closed to protect London.

Key vocabulary

coastal erosion, low air pressure, storm surge, Thames Barrier

Skills practised in 'Your turn'

◆ Geography skills: q3a, define a key term; q3b, write an explanation based on a diagram

◆ Literacy skills: q2, write explanatory sentences; q5, write letters

◆ Thinking skills: q1, explain what causes big waves; q3b, apply knowledge to explain a physical result; q4, use common sense and prior knowledge to reach a reasoned conclusion

Unit outcomes

By the end of this unit most students should be able to:

◆ explain the terms given in 'Key vocabulary' above

◆ describe what happened to the UK's coastline, especially the east coast, in December 2013

◆ explain the reasons for the storm surge in December 2013

Ideas for a starter

1 Show photos of the floods and destruction caused by the storm surge in December 2013. Ask: What damage can you see? What might have caused it? Who is likely to have been affected? Explain it was caused by the storm surge. Can you name any of the parts of the UK that were affected?

2 Show students the BBC News video clip 'What creates a storm surge?' for an explanation of what caused the storm surge in December 2013.

3 Read an extract from a newspaper report about the storm surge and the effects on people (e.g. houses falling into the sea / homes being flooded). Ask: How did the article make you feel? Students share their thoughts. Alternatively, ask students to select a sentence that resonates with them.

Ideas for plenaries

Plan plenaries at strategic points throughout the lesson, as well as at the end.

Mid-lesson

1   Ask: What lessons can be learned from the storm surge of December 2013?

2   Ask: Is there anything that could have been done to save the house in Hemsby?

3   Ask: Why do people buy houses in areas that are under threat from the sea?

4   A similar storm surge happened in 1953 but the effects were far more devastating. Ask: Why do you think that the 2013 storm surge was less damaging?

End-of-lesson

5   Give students 30 seconds to complete the following sentence:

A storm surge is caused by .... .

Other students can put up their hands to challenge if there are any pauses, repetition, or incorrect information.

6   On the board, write the headings: *Cause, Effect*. Students suggest and add causes and effects of the storm surge under the headings.

7   Ask: Why is money spent protecting some areas under threat from the sea, but not others?

Further class and homework opportunities

Suggestions 26–28 on page 87 of this book

geog.2 workbook, page 32

geog.2 Kerboodle: lesson presentation, worksheets, end-of-lesson assessment

Answers for 'Your turn'

1   Strong winds created big waves.

2   **a**   The low pressure over the UK caused the air to rise. This draws the sea level up with it.

   b   At high tide the water level is at its highest.

3   **a**   A big surge of water is caused when there is low pressure, high tides, and strong winds at the same time.

   b   Parts of the east coast are composed of soft rock that was easily eroded in the storm surge. The North Sea gets narrower and shallower as you move south along the east coast. This caused the surge to grow. Point X on the map had the longest fetch, resulting in the largest waves. It is a low-lying flat area and, even though the sea defences have been improved, they were still unable to protect the coast in some places.

4   Protecting London is given high priority because if it flooded it would have both a national and international impact. London is the capital city of the UK and has a high population density. It is the home of central government and a popular tourist destination. It is also the largest centre of economic activity in the UK and a leading global financial centre, bringing billions of pounds into the economy each year. The London Underground is an important part of London's travel network and if it flooded, it would cause huge disruption.

5   **a**   Letters could mention the damage it has caused, what has been lost, the disruption caused and also the emotional effects that they feel.

   b   Responses will vary.

About this unit

This unit uses the example of Happisburgh on the Norfolk coast to explain the effects of coastal erosion – both the physical effects and their human consequences.

Key points

◆ Happisburgh is located on the north Norfolk coast, in an area that suffers from severe coastal erosion (particularly during winter storms). This has led the cliffs there to recede dramatically – and many homes to fall into the sea.

◆ The erosion is severe along this coast because the cliffs consist of sand above clay, which means that they are very soft; easily waterlogged and weakened by rain; and vulnerable to strong waves.

◆ Hard-engineering is not possible along this coast, because the population size and economic worth of the Happisburgh area does not justify the expense, so attempts have been made to slow the erosion down. However, those attempts have proved fruitless and Happisburgh will soon completely disappear into the sea.

Key vocabulary

groyne, revetment, rock armour

Skills practised in 'Your turn'

◆ Geography skills: q1, provide detailed location information; q3, analyse photographs; q4, compare photographs

◆ Numeracy skills: q5, calculate based on known data

◆ Literacy skills: q6, write a persuasive letter

◆ Thinking skills: q2, explain cause and effect; q4, reach conclusions based on evidence; q7, use common sense and prior knowledge to assess the human consequences of coastal erosion

Unit outcomes

By the end of this unit most students should be able to:

◆ explain the terms given in 'Key vocabulary' above

◆ explain why the coastal erosion at Happisburgh is so severe

◆ explain which types of coastal defences have been employed in Happisburgh to try to slow down the erosion – plus how they work and how effective they have been

◆ describe the human effects of coastal erosion

Ideas for a starter

1 Show students photo **A** on page 62 of the students' book. Ask: Why do people build homes in such a risky place?

2 You could ask 'Your turn' question 4a as a starter.

3 Show students a video clip of erosion at Happisburgh. Ask them to pick out two key facts that resonate with them. How would they feel if it was them living on Beach Road at the top of the cliffs? What defences have been used to protect the coast and how successful have they been?

Ideas for plenaries

Plan plenaries at strategic points throughout the lesson, as well as at the end.

Mid-lesson

1 Start a flow chart on the board, like this one. Ask students to suggest sentences for some of the boxes, using your starter words. They can add more boxes on both branches if they like. Encourage them to use as many correct terms as they can (e.g. hydraulic action). At the end, students complete / modify the flow chart on the board, with feedback from the class.

2 Put the following headings on the board: *Cause of erosion, Effect of erosion*. Ask students to think of examples of each for Happisburgh.

3 Ask students to work in pairs to create a table of the advantages and disadvantages of building coastal defences at Happisburgh. Then ask them to classify them as economic, social and environmental.

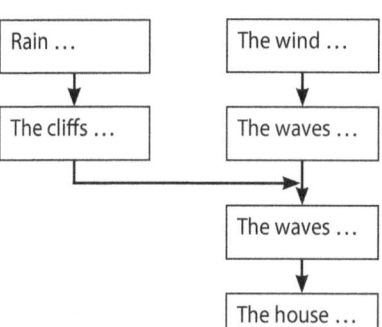
Why Bryony's house was at risk

End-of-lesson

4 Following on from plenary **3**, ask students to discuss the advantages and disadvantages of the defences against erosion at Happisburgh, role-playing a meeting between the residents, who want the defences repaired / replaced, and North Norfolk District Council, which has a managed retreat policy.

Further class and homework opportunities

Suggestions 29–31 on page 87 of this book

geog.2 workbook, page 33

geog.2 Kerboodle: lesson presentation, worksheets, end-of-lesson assessment

Answers for 'Your turn'

1 Students should be able to say that Happisburgh is located on the east coast of England, which meets the North Sea, on the bulge north of London (or below the Wash). They may also be able to say that is in North Norfolk, north east of Norwich.

2 a The cliffs are made of easily-eroded materials: sand and clay.

b Rain soaks into the soft cliffs and weakens them. The weaker they are, the more easily eroded they are.

c Strong north winds coming down the North Sea (a long fetch) will drive big waves against the soft cliffs, eroding them rapidly.

d Gale force winds created exceptionally large waves. The surge grew higher as it moved south, so Happisburgh got the full force of the waves. The soft cliffs could not stand up to the waves and collapsed.

3 a i Groynes; they prevent sand being carried away by longshore drift; the sand in turn helps protect the cliffs against erosion, since it absorbs some of the energy of the waves.

ii Revetments; they make the waves break early, reducing their energy, so the waves won't erode the cliffs so fast.

b Rock armour; again the waves batter against it and lose some of their energy.

4 a Students should have noticed that Beach Road has got shorter over the 16-year period and that several of its houses have disappeared. Bryony's house is right on the edge of the cliff by 2012 and the houses further inland have gone (been demolished). Further along the cliff a group of buildings that stood on the cliff edge have also gone and the caravan park is now much closer to the sea. By 2012 there was a much bigger bite out of the coastline in the foreground of the photo and some of the beach has disappeared altogether. The groynes have disappeared. The revetments appear to be in worse shape. The 2012 photo shows rock armour put down in an attempt to slow erosion.

b Expect students to conclude that the barriers have not been completely effective, because the coast has continued to be eroded, and more houses and more of Beach Road have fallen into the sea. However, without the barriers the impact might have been even worse.

5 2021

6 Reasons for wanting to move it might include: loss of land, property, and possessions (and possibly lives) to the sea. With less space for caravans to rent out and fewer caravans, the caravan park owner's income will be reduced. Removing the caravan park will clear the land at the top of the cliff and will help with the government's decision of managed retreat for this coastline. Tourism is important for Happisburgh's economy and if the caravan park is lost tourists won't have anywhere to stay and the local economy will suffer.

7 Cliff erosion will have social, economic, and environmental effects, such as: loss of beach for recreation; loss of property and reduction in value; loss of possessions; loss of agricultural land; loss of tourism; no compensation from insurance companies (as cliff retreat is not covered by policies) or from the government; threat to wildlife (e.g. loss of breeding grounds of rare birds that nest in the cliffs); increased risk of flooding; loss of community (e.g. leaving friends and family behind if they have to move).

About this unit

This unit examines and assesses different ways of protecting the coast and the problems that planners face when making their decisions.

Key points

◆ There are a number of different ways of protecting coastlines, ranging from recurved stone sea walls to wooden groynes. Some (like rock armour) are designed to soak up the waves' energy, thus reducing their ability to cause damage, whilst others (like revetments) are designed to keep the sea away from vulnerable cliffs. Both approaches have been used at Happisburgh but without success.

◆ Unfortunately, all coastal defences cost a great deal of money. Also, unless they are constantly maintained and strengthened (which those at Happisburgh have not been), they do not provide a long-term solution.

◆ In addition, the effects of climate change are predicted to raise sea levels and increase the severity of storms, both of which are likely to overwhelm the existing defences.

◆ Therefore, coastal planners have been forced to make hard decisions about which parts of the coastline are worth protecting – and how. Many stretches of the coast, like Happisburgh, are being abandoned to the sea.

Key vocabulary

artificial reef, beach nourishment, sea wall

Skills practised in 'Your turn'

◆ Literacy skills: q3, write reasoned replies to different opinions

◆ Thinking skills: q1, assess different forms of coastal defences; q2, use prior knowledge to produce a reasoned explanation; q4, produce a persuasive plan

Unit outcomes

By the end of this unit most students should be able to:

◆ explain the terms given in 'Key vocabulary' above

◆ consider the different options available to protect coasts

◆ explain the problems faced by planners when considering how to protect a coastline – and whether it's worth protecting at all

Ideas for a starter

1   Ask: Who can remind us about what's happening in Happisburgh? Do you think it's the only place in the UK where this is happening? Why do you think that?

2   Show a set of named images of coastal erosion around the UK. Ask students to describe what is happening. With the use of atlases, students locate the places on a map.

3   Show a set of images of named coastal defences around the UK. Ask students to describe them. Again, ask students to locate the places on a map.

4   Show students three photos: one with houses close to a cliff edge, one with a rocky coastline with scrubland / moorland, and one of a busy beach with lots of development behind the beach. For each photo, ask: What can you see in the photo? Does this area need to be protected? Why?

5   Ask: Is building sea defences a good idea? Take a vote. What will they protect? Who do you think pays for them?

Ideas for plenaries

Plan plenaries at strategic points throughout the lesson, as well as at the end.

Mid-lesson

1   Give students photos of different types of sea defence and ask them to match each one to the defences mentioned on page 64 of the students' book.

2   Imagine: You work for North Norfolk District Council and are responsible for coastal defences. You need to decide which types of defences are most appropriate for Happisburgh and why. You have received costs from the contractors who will be building the defences (see page 64 of the students' book). Which defences will you recommend?

3   Discuss: Global warming is likely to lead to higher sea levels and storms. Should we protect coastal settlements whatever the cost? If so, who should pay for the work?

End-of-lesson

4   With books closed, using a blockbuster-style grid, ask students questions about sea defences: e.g. What SW is curved in shape to reflect the waves away? What RA are boulders that soak up the waves' energy? What W is a revetment built out of? What BN is the process of adding more shingle to a beach?

5   Give students a grid like the one below. They should show their understanding of the words in the grid using a traffic light system: red is no understanding, orange is some understanding, green is full understanding.

	1	2	3	4	5	6
1	Sea wall	Storm surge	Swash	Conflict	Transport	Abrasion
2	Headland	Groynes	High tide	Backwash	Bay	Sand
3	Deposition	Longshore drift	Hydraulic action	Stack	Attrition	Stump
4	Low tide	Cave	Fetch	Artificial reef	Arch	Tidal range
5	Wave-cut platform	Erosion	Revetment	Salt marsh	Beach	Spit
6	Solution	Shingle	Happisburgh	Uprush	Beach nourishment	Rock armour

Further class and homework opportunities

Suggestions 32–40 on page 87 of this book

geog.2 workbook, page 34

geog.2 Kerboodle: lesson presentation, worksheets, end-of-lesson assessment

Answers for 'Your turn'

1   a   Sea walls

    b   Artificial reef

    c   Groynes, revetments and beach nourishment

    d   Beach nourishment

2   The cliffs at Happisburgh are made up of sands and clays. They are soft and crumble easily when rainwater soaks into them. A sea wall would not stop this happening.

3   Answers dependent on students' opinions.

4   Ideas might include: raffle it or auction it as a unique disappearing property; let it out as a holiday home with a difference; persuade the council to pay you compensation.

Many of these suggestions are addressed to your students. Where research or further resources are needed, the internet will almost certainly provide the answer.

The suggestions are graded *,**,*** according to level of difficulty. Some are suitable for all levels, and can be differentiated by outcome.

Waves and tides

1   **Ships a-sailing**   Collect images of historic British sailing ships, including warships, cargo ships, and ships used on explorations. Then move on to steam ships, then to modern vessels. You could include Royal navy ships, submarines, container ships and cruise liners. You could show them on a timeline along the classroom wall, with a short paragraph about each one. Pupils could work in groups for this, each group researching a period of history.   */**/***

2   **Sea fever**   Find John Masefield's poem *Sea Fever* and read it to the class. What does the last stanza mean?   **

3   **Cargoes**   The sea means trading. Find John Masefield's poem *Cargoes* and read it to the class.   **

4   **A stormy read**   There are many thrilling stories about storms at sea. Find a really exciting passage and read it to the class. Your English teacher may be able to suggest one?   **

5   **Oceans**   How many are there? And how can you tell where an ocean begins and ends? Shade in and label the oceans on an outline world map. Add interesting facts about each.   *

The waves at work

6   **What is weathering?**   Ask students to create a poster about weathering. (They may have met it in science by now.) Their poster should include: three labelled diagrams showing physical, chemical and biological weathering *or* three annotated photos of examples of different types of weathering; three paragraphs explaining each type of weathering; and an example of where each can be found around the school. They should include a paragraph which explains why weathering makes the work of waves (erosion) easier.   ***

7   **Longshore drift demo**   Students can demonstrate longshore drift using a small ball and themselves. They need to stand in two parallel rows facing each other. A throw from one row represents the uprush, and a throw from the other row the backwash.   *

8   **A poem about longshore drift?**   Ask a student to read *Beachcomber* by George Mackay Brown (find it on the internet). Ask students to illustrate it.   **

Landforms created by the waves

9   **Stump – the movie!**   Divide a sheet of A4 paper into 6 equal parts. In each part draw one stage in a sequence to show how a stump forms. Make your drawings the same size and put them in the same position, leaving space on the left to staple them. Cut up the sheet. Staple the drawings together (in the right order) slightly staggered, so that the bottom one sticks out furthest to the right. Flick them and watch the stump develop.   */**

10   **My life as a grain of sand**   You started life as a silica crystal embedded in rock in a cliff (sand is made of silica). What happened to you? Where are you now? Tell your story in any form you like – as prose, a poem, or a strip cartoon.   **

11   **Adopt a headland**   Choose a dramatic headland from a map of the British Isles. Research it and see if you can find out something about the geology of the area. Write a report with a map and photos.   ***

12   **Study a spit**   This is a variation on the previous activity. Choose one of Britain's spits, such as the Sandbanks spit in Poole Harbour, or Spurn Head. Find an aerial photo of it and draw a sketch. Draw a map to show its location. Is it used for anything? If so , describe it. And describe what the environment is like, and what there is to do there.   **

13   **Famous coastal landforms**   Collect images of famous British coastal landforms (for example Beachy Head). Stick them on cards and write a paragraph about each one. Then stick them around a map of the British Isles, with the locations of the landforms marked on it.   **

14   **Get sketching**   Laminate a set of colour photos of coastal landforms. Try for at least 10 or 12 different images. Give them out to pairs of students to identify and sketch. They should add a paragraph to say how the landforms were formed.   **

15   **Make a model**   How would you make a realistic model of the coast, showing different coastal landforms? Students could work in groups to design and create the best model.   */**/**

The coast and us

16   **Another poem**   Try *maggie and milly and molly and may* by E E Cummings. An internet search will find it.   **

17   **Coastal settlements around the British Isles**   Many coastal settlements have one main function, linked to the sea, for example cargo port, seaside resort. Students should each choose a coastal settlement (all different), anywhere in the British Isles. Encourage students to explore the whole coastline, and choose places they know nothing about. They should research their choices, e.g in terms of population, main function, what the place is like, and find at least one photo of it. They should write their information on cards, using their own words and include the photo. They then need to mark their settlements on a large blank wall map of the British Isles, and arrange the cards around it linked by thread or coloured string etc.   **

Your holiday in Newquay

18   **Seaside poem/rap**   Make up a poem or rap about why everyone loves being by the sea, or about a seaside holiday you had.   */**/***

19 Write a cinquain It's a poem with only five lines – but there's a snag. There are rules for what goes in each line, and how many syllables.
1st line: the thing that the poem is about (2 syllables)
2nd line: describes the thing (4 syllables)
3rd line: an action related to the thing (6 syllables)
4th line: a feeling related to the thing (8 syllables)
5th line: refers back to the thing (2 syllables)
For example:
The coast
Pale yellow sand
White waves break in blue sea
I feel so free and happy here
Seaside
Have a go! */**/***

20 A holiday brochure for Newquay Make a fold-out holiday leaflet to encourage people to visit Newquay. It should include a sketch map of the resort, a map of how to get there, photos and information about things to do. **

21 Or a holiday brochure for … Ask students to produce a brochure like the one in the previous activity, but for a different resort. Encourage students to choose different resorts around the British Isles. Their leaflets could be displayed on the wall around a map of the British Isles. **

22 Go surfing! Surfing is a popular activity. Use the internet to find out about surfing in the UK. Write an information sheet about it. Mention the equipment you need, plus any dangers you need to be aware of. Add a map of the British Isles showing where the best places to surf are. **

23 Go …! Like the previous activity, but choose another sport you'd prefer, that you can do at, or off the coast. It could be windsurfing, diving, coasteering or … ? **

24 Seaside safety The seaside can be dangerous. Strong currents can carry poor swimmers away. Design a poster for display at the seaside with advice about swimming safely. **

25 Make up your ideal British seaside resort Give it a name, say where it is on the coast, and draw a sketch map for it. Do drawings to show land use in it, and say a bit about different activities you can do there. *

Under threat from the sea

26 Imagine … You are out in a boat as the storm surge sweeps down the North Sea. What can you see and hear? How do you feel? Write down the main words you think of in the shape of a huge wave – a wordle. */**

27 1953 In 1953 a devastating storm surge hit England's east coast. What happened? Why was it so bad? How did it compare with the storm surge of December 2013? Find out! **/***

28 Falling into the sea Parts of England's east coast are easily eroded. Why? Prepare a presentation for a year 7 student about which parts of the coast are affected and why they are eroding so fast. **/***

How long can Happisburgh hang on?

29 If only it could talk… Imagine you are Bryony's house. It's a dark, stormy winter's evening – 5 December 2013. Write a monologue about your life, all the stresses and strains of living on Beach Road and what happened on 5 December. */**

30 Happisburgh field sketch Draw a field sketch based on the lower right photo on page 63 of *geog.2* students' book. Annotate your sketch to show how the coast is protected and how it has been eroded. */**/***

31 A TV report on Happisburgh Your TV company has sent you to Happisburgh to interview people living there. Prepare a storyboard and script for a 90-second TV news report. Say who you interviewed and what they said about how erosion affects them. Your storyboard should show the images you'll use for each section of audio. Can you shoot the video too? */**/**

Protecting places from the sea

32 Is beach nourishment a good idea? Find out more about beach nourishment, and where it's used in the UK. Do you think it's a good idea? Is it sustainable? Give your answer in an interesting form: for example as interviews with an engineer and an environmentalist, or an interview with the sea, or as a 'serious' strip cartoon. ***

33 No more defences It's the year 2050. Global warming has caused rising sea levels around the British Isles, and many more storms. Every year, more coastal defences are shattered. You are the minister in charge of the coast. You've decided there will be no more sea defences. So, what will you do about all the people living on eroding coastlines? Write an action plan. ***

34 Dredging from the sea Huge quantities of gravel are dredged from the sea bed. Some people think it may be contributing to erosion. Find out more and give your findings as a radio report or a 'serious' strip cartoon. ***

35 What about the Norfolk Broads? People say the sea must not be allowed to breach the Norfolk Broads. Find out what the Broads are, and why they are important. Then write a unit on them, based on the units in *geog.2* students' book. You can even add questions. **/***

36 Compensation? Should people who lost their homes through coastal erosion be given compensation? Hold a class debate. **/***

37 The sea has the final word Pretend you're the sea. Make up a monologue, a poem or a song, about humans and their efforts to keep you at bay. */**/**

38 Alphabet run Do an alphabet run from A-Z, with a word to do with coasts and the sea for each letter. *

39 Coasts crossword Make up a big crossword about all the terms you have met in this chapter. Then swop yours with your partner, and fill theirs in. **

40 Marine mind map Create a big colourful mind map about coasts and the waves and everything else you have covered in this chapter. Give it a nautical look! *

About this chapter

Addressing the KS3 Programme of Study
- Understand the key processes involved in weather and climate.
- Understand the key features of UK weather.
- Interpret local weather maps and global climate maps.
- Communicate geographical information using maps.

About the content
- This chapter starts by explaining what weather is, what causes it, and various key terms.
- It looks at the features of weather in the UK, using weather maps and symbols.
- The difference between weather and climate is established, and the factors influencing climate explored.
- The final unit looks at different climates around the world.

The big picture

These are the key ideas in this chapter.
- Weather is the state of the atmosphere around us at any given time. Its different components, such as temperature, can be measured.
- All weather is caused by one thing: the Sun heating Earth unevenly. Most weather occurs in the troposphere.
- The weather in the UK is changeable because different air masses move over us. They have different characteristics (warm or cold, damp or dry).
- Climate is the 'average' weather in a place. It is worked out by taking weather measurements over a long period, for example 30 years, and calculating the averages.
- Climate depends on several factors, such as distance from the equator, and altitude. So it can vary a lot between different places, even within the same country.
- Earth can be divided into different regions of broadly similar climate.

A students' version of this big picture is given in the *geog.2* students' book opener for Chapter 5.

The chapter outline

Use this, and their chapter opener, to give students a mental roadmap for the chapter.

5 **Weather and climate** The chapter opener in the students' book is an important part of the chapter; see page 11 for notes about using chapter openers

5.1 **It's the weather!** Some very different kinds of weather

5.2 **So what causes weather?** How the Sun drives the weather

5.3 **Measuring the weather** What weather is, how it is measured, and by whom

5.4 **More about rain ... and clouds** The three different kinds of rainfall, and the two main clouds

5.5 **Air pressure** The weather associated with high and low pressure, in summer and winter

5.6 **Why is our weather so changeable?** How air masses make our weather change quickly

5.7 **A winter of storms** About deadly storms that tore across the UK in winter 2013/14

5.8 **From weather to climate** How climate is worked out, some climate data, and climate graphs

5.9 **The factors that influence climate** The climate of a place is the net result of several different factors

5.10 **Climates around the world** The world can be divided into regions of broadly similar climate, thanks to the factors in 5.9

Objectives and outcomes for this chapter

Objectives	Unit	Outcomes
Most students will understand:		Most students will be able to:
● what weather is, and that it has different components, which can be measured	5.1, 5.3	● define *weather*; identify at least five components of weather; say what instruments are used to measure these, and give the units of measurement
● that the Sun is the driving force of weather	5.2	● describe how the Sun produces weather conditions
● that weather can be shown on a weather map	5.3, 5.6, 5.7	● read a simple weather map; identify the symbols for fronts, on a weather map
● that water vapour in rising air leads to rain	5.2	● describe the key steps in the formation of rain
● that we give rainfall different names, depending on what caused the air to rise	5.4	● name convectional, relief, and frontal rainfall, and say how each is formed
● that there are different types of cloud	5.4	● explain what clouds are; name and identify the two basic types: cumulus, stratus
● what air pressure is, and that high and low pressure bring different types of weather	5.5	● explain in simple terms what air pressure is; describe high and low pressure weather, in summer and winter
● what fronts are, and how they bring a change in the weather	5.6	● say that a front is the leading edge of an air mass; explain how it brings a change in the weather
● what depressions are (at a simple level)	5.7	● say that a depression is a cold front chasing a warm one; explain why it can bring stormy weather
● that climate is the average of weather measurements	5.8	● define climate and say how it is worked out; read, and draw, a climate graph
● that climate is the result of different factors	5.9	● give six factors that influence climate
● that the world can be divided into regions of broadly similar climate	5.10	● name and briefly describe at least four of the world's climate regions

These tie in with the outcomes for each unit, in this teacher's handbook, and with 'Your goals for this chapter', in *geog.2* students' book.

Opportunities for assessment

See the formal assessment materials for this chapter on *geog.2 Kerboodle Lessons, Resources, & Assessment*. They include an extended assessment task, an exam-style question, end-of-lesson assessments, and a self-assessment form. See also the notes on pages 14–15 of this book.

Getting ready for this chapter

geog.2 Kerboodle contains plans and presentations for each unit, including interactive activities, animations, and worksheets.

About 'Your chapter starter'

Six months after the photo on page 66 of *geog.2* students' book was taken, it would have been summer, with snow, ice and cold a distant memory. Snow forms in the same way as rain – but if the air is very cold, snow falls instead. This chapter starter could lead on to a discussion about why we have seasons.

The Earth travels non-stop around the Sun and is tilted as it travels. A full orbit takes one year. The tilt is the reason why our climate changes through the year – it gives us our seasons. In June, the Northern Hemisphere is tilted towards the Sun, so we get more heat – it's our summer. By December, it is tilted away from the Sun. We get less heat – it's winter.

It's the weather!

About this unit

This unit uses photographs to introduce students to different kinds of weather.

Key points

◆ There are many different kinds of weather.

◆ Some weather conditions are dangerous.

◆ You can tell a lot about the weather in a place from photographs.

Key vocabulary

(No new vocabulary)

Skills practised in 'Your turn'

◆ Geography skills: q1, analyse and describe photographs; q2, compare and link photographs; q6, define a key term

◆ Literacy skills: q1, write a series of weather descriptions based on photographs

◆ Thinking skills: q2–q4, make photograph selections with explanations; q5, make a decision with supporting examples; q6, compare definitions and make a reasoned selection; q7, explain the role of the Sun in causing different weather conditions

Unit outcomes

By the end of this unit most students should be able to:

◆ give examples of different weather conditions, including dangerous conditions

◆ write a definition of weather

Ideas for a starter

1 Ask: What's the weather like today? What words can you give to describe it? (Write them on the board.) Do people usually look at the sky to tell the weather? Why? Do you think the weather is the same everywhere in the UK today?

2 Ask students to think of a word relating to weather for as many letters in the alphabet as they can. Then they circle the ones that describe today's weather.

3 Ask students to act out words relating to the weather (e.g. icy, wind, cloud, rain, storm, snow, blizzard, hurricane). Others have to guess each word.

4 Play songs relating to weather (e.g. with weather-related titles or lyrics). Ask: What topic do you think we are going to study today?

5 Use 'Your turn' question 1 as a starter activity.

Ideas for plenaries

Plan plenaries at strategic points throughout the lesson, as well as at the end.

Mid-lesson

1 Give students some headlines from newspapers that show how the weather affects our lives, e.g. *Dense Fog Travel Chaos; Bank Holiday Washout; Five Inches of Snow Hits UK; Bush Fires Rage in Scorching Sun*. Ask: How does weather affect our lives? Has the weather affected your life at all this week?

2 Do starter **5** as a plenary, if you have not already used it.

3 In pairs, students sit back to back. One has a word relating to weather (e.g. ice, wind, cloud, rain, snow, hail stones, fog, lightning) and the other has a pencil and piece of paper. The student with the word describes it, without saying the actual word and the partner tries to draw it as accurately as possible.

End-of-lesson

4 Ask: What kinds of jobs might be affected by the weather? Students list as many as they can. Take feedback.

5 Write *WEATHER* on the board vertically. Students use it to create an acrostic: each letter starts a sentence about weather, covering ideas met in the lesson.

6 Students start their own mind map of weather terms and definitions, and add any words that they have learned this lesson (e.g. weather). They can add to this throughout the chapter.

7 Give students two minutes to work with a partner and write down three things they have learned from this lesson and one interesting question about weather that has not been covered. (This could produce a good enquiry question that the class could follow up.)

Further class and homework opportunities

Suggestions 1–4 on page 110 of this book

geog.2 workbook, page 36

geog.2 Kerboodle: lesson presentation, worksheets, end-of-lesson assessment

Answers for 'Your turn'

1 You could use this as a whole-class activity or as a starter.

2 **a** There's no obviously 'right' answer and answers will vary, but A and B, or D and G are candidates.

   b A and C, or C and E, or A and D, or C and I are all possible.

3 **a** and **b** Answers will vary.

4 Students will probably pick out C, E, G, and I. In fact only B and D were definitely taken in the UK:

A, Budapest, Hungary	**C,** South Dakota, USA (drought in 2006)
E, urban USA	**F,** rural USA **G,** Beijing, China
H, not known	**I,** Nassau, the Bahamas (Caribbean)

5 It can be very dangerous. For example, high winds can destroy buildings and overturn vehicles. They can whip up waves, which overturn boats and flood coasts. Rain can lead to severe flooding and people may drown. Lack of rain can lead to drought, so crops may fail, animals die, and people starve. Severe heat can cause heat stroke and cold can cause hypothermia and frostbite. Ice and fog cause road accidents. You could get killed by lightning, or it could cause a fire. And there are many records of people being killed by large hailstones, some as large as a teacup.

6 **a** and **b** Students could present their definitions to the class. This exercise should help them understand the meaning of *weather*.

7 This exercise is a good lead in to the next unit, and Unit 5.9, on factors that influence climate. The Sun is the cause of different types of weather.

So what causes weather?

help at a glance

About this unit

This unit explains the key role played by the Sun in causing different weather conditions, plus where in the atmosphere those conditions tend to occur.

Key points

◆ The Sun is behind all types of weather – in particular, through causing water vapour to form (largely from the oceans) via evaporation.

◆ The Sun heats Earth, which in turn heats the air. Warm air rises and cools as it does so. This cooling causes the water vapour in the air to condense and form clouds of water droplets.

◆ The rising air also leads to low pressure, so air rushes in from colder places to replace it – as wind.

◆ Depending on the temperature at a place (i.e. the strength of the Sun), heavy water droplets may fall from the clouds as rain, hail, sleet or snow. In addition, when it's cold, water vapour may condense much lower down in the atmosphere – giving fog, mist or dew.

◆ Most water vapour is in the lowest level of the atmosphere – the troposphere – where we live. So that is where most weather occurs.

Key vocabulary

atmosphere, clouds, condense / condensation, dew, evaporate / evaporation, fog, hailstones, mist, rain, sleet, snow, the Sun, troposphere, water vapour, wind

Skills practised in 'Your turn'

◆ Geography skills: q2a, q4a, define a key term

◆ Literacy skills: q1, the cloze technique

◆ Thinking skills: q2b, design a test; q3, explain the link between key terms; q4, explain the atmosphere; q5, use common sense and prior knowledge to speculate and reach reasoned conclusions

Unit outcomes

By the end of this unit most students should be able to:

◆ explain the terms given in 'Key vocabulary' above

◆ explain the role of the Sun in causing different weather conditions

◆ state that most weather occurs in the lower part of the atmosphere: the troposphere

Ideas for a starter

1 One or more students pretend to be the teacher. They summarise the last lesson and question the class on what they learned about weather.

2 Students create a spider diagram using all the weather conditions they covered in the previous lesson.

3 Ask: What's the weather like today? Why?

4 Look at photo **A** from page 68 of the students' book. Ask: What caused that rain? What caused that wind? Write students' suggestions on the board, without duplication. Say you'll come back to them later.

Ideas for plenaries

Plan plenaries at strategic points throughout the lesson, as well as at the end.

Mid-lesson

1   If you used starter **3**, repeat the question again.

2   If you used starter **4**, revisit the suggestions on the board and let the class score them.

3   Jumble up the following processes related to the causes of weather and ask students to put them in the correct sequences:

Sun	Water vapour
1 The Sun heats Earth unevenly.	1 The Sun warms the oceans.
2 Earth heats the air.	2 Water from oceans, rivers, and lakes evaporates and becomes water vapour in the atmosphere.
3 Warm air rises.	3 Warm, moist air rises and cools.
4 Colder air (wind) flows in to replace it.	4 The water vapour condenses into tiny water droplets as it cools down.
	5 Clouds are formed.
	6 Tiny water droplets may join to form bigger heavier drops that fall as rain, snow, and sleet.

End-of-lesson

4   Ask students to work in small groups to create dominoes using the following terms: weather, water vapour, evaporate, condense, troposphere, stratosphere, cloud, wind, fog, mist, dew, sleet. They will need to write the definitions. Then they can play dominoes matching the terms and definitions.

5   Students add the key terms covered in Unit 5.2 to the mind map they started in Unit 5.1, and add definitions.

Further class and homework opportunities

Suggestions 5–6 on page 110 of this book

geog.2 workbook, page 37

geog.2 Kerboodle: lesson presentation, worksheets, end-of-lesson assessment

Answers for 'Your turn'

1   This is the completed paragraph:

Places get warm because of the *Sun*. It heats *Earth*, which in turn *warms* the air. The Sun also causes *wind*. That's because the warm air *rises*, so *colder* air rushes in from somewhere else to take its place. As warm air rises it *cools*, and the water vapour *condenses*. That's why we get clouds, and rain.

2   a   It is water in gas form. When sunlight strikes the surface of the ocean (and lakes and rivers) it warms the water. Some of the water evaporates to form a gas.

  b   Leave a glass of water in the freezer for a while. (Make sure the outside of the glass is really dry.) Take it out, leave it on a table, and see if a thin film of water forms on the outside of the glass. It is the result of water vapour in the air condensing.

3   They are all caused by water vapour. Water vapour condenses into clouds of tiny water drops, which fall as rain. If the air is cold they may fall as snow or hailstones. In chilly weather, water vapour may condense in the air as fog or hang in the air as mist.

4   a   The atmosphere is the blanket of gas (that contains the water vapour) that surrounds Earth. It reaches up to 10 000 km. It is made up of layers.

  b   The bottom layer that we live in is called the troposphere.

  c   There is very little water vapour in the stratosphere. This means that there is little condensation, which creates the water droplets that make up rain.

5   All areas would heat more evenly. There would be no significant differences in temperature across Earth. It is the differences in temperature that create the movement of air by wind. There would be no wind.

Measuring the weather

About this unit

This unit explains which aspects of weather are measured – and how it's done.

Key points

- ◆ Weather means the state of the atmosphere in a place.
- ◆ We can tell a lot about the weather by looking and feeling, but to get a clear picture we must take measurements.
- ◆ The five main variables measured, in order to determine the state of the atmosphere at a place, are: temperature, precipitation, air pressure, wind speed, and wind direction. Each variable is measured using a particular standard piece of equipment, for consistency, e.g. an anemometer for wind speed.
- ◆ Weather measurements are taken continually, all around the world, 24 hours a day, at different heights above Earth, using a whole range of sources – from terrestrial weather stations to weather balloons, and even weather satellites which look down on the weather.

Key vocabulary

air pressure, anemometer, barometer, Met Office, rain gauge, precipitation, temperature, thermometer, weather, weather map, weather station, wind direction, wind speed, wind vane / wind sock

Skills practised in 'Your turn'

- ◆ Geography skills: q1, q3a, define key terms; q7, identify and explain key weather map symbols; q8, q9, use a weather map (and a photo for q8) to describe weather conditions at a particular place
- ◆ Literacy skills: q1, write a key definition; q2, write a full weather description for the last week
- ◆ Thinking skills: q3b, explain importance; q5, consider how weather could be measured; q6, provide reasoned examples

Unit outcomes

By the end of this unit most students should be able to:

- ◆ explain the terms given in 'Key vocabulary' above
- ◆ state the main variables which are measured in order to describe the weather at a particular place, and the methods employed to measure each one (including the units used)
- ◆ use a weather map effectively to describe weather conditions in particular places

Ideas for a starter

1 Ask: Why do you think people measure the weather?

2 Ask: What questions would you need to ask to describe the weather fully? What would you need to measure to answer the questions?

3 Show students pictures of instruments used for measuring weather to assess prior knowledge. (You could display the ones from page 72 of the students' book.) Ask: What are these instruments? Do you know what they measure?

4 Write on the board: *Weather means the state of the atmosphere in a place*. Ask: What's the atmosphere? Where is it? Turn to photo **A** on page 72 of the students' book. Ask: Do you think it's warm or cold there? How could you tell *exactly* how warm or cold it is? Elicit that you could measure the temperature. What else could you measure? How?

Ideas for plenaries

Plan plenaries at strategic points throughout the lesson, as well as at the end.

Mid-lesson

1   Give students five sets of cards (one for each weather element), each set containing: 1) images of an instrument used for measuring weather; 2) name of the instrument; 3) what it measures; and 4) the unit of measurement. Turn the cards face down and mix them up. Students turn the cards over and try to match them.

2   Write on the board: *In X it is wetter in winter than in summer.* For X use a local town. Ask: What information would you need to collect to show this? Students access this information online (or be supplied with the data) and create graphs (with titles and labelled axes) to prove the point.

End-of-lesson

3   Write three to six sets of items for 'odd-one-out' on the board. For example:

   –   millimetre; rainfall; °C; millibars

   –   anemometer; wind speed; air pressure; km/h

   Students choose the odd one and explain their choice.

4   Students add the key terms covered in Unit 5.3 to the mind map they started in Unit 5.1, and add definitions.

Further class and homework opportunities

Suggestions 7–12 on page 110 of this book

geog.2 workbook, page 38

geog.2 Kerboodle: lesson presentation, worksheets, end-of-lesson assessment

Answers for 'Your turn'

1   Weather means the state of the atmosphere in a place.

2   Answers will vary depending on time of year and location. Students should be able to describe it in terms of temperature, precipitation, air pressure, and wind direction and strength.

3   a   Air pressure is the force pressing down on us due to the weight of the air.

   b   It can tell us what kind of weather to expect depending on whether the air pressure is rising or falling.

4   a   anemometer   barometer   thermometer   rain gauge

   b and c

Name	What it measures	Units
Anemometer	Wind speed	Miles per hour (mph) or kilometres per hour (kph)
Barometer	Air pressure	Millibars (mb)
Thermometer	Temperature	Degrees Celsius (°C)
Rain gauge	Amount of water that has fallen as precipitation	Millimetres (mm) or centimetres (cm)

5   Answers include: cloud cover and visibility, humidity, amount of sunshine.

6   Students' responses will vary, but they should explain why weather forecasts are essential for their chosen groups.

7   a   Cloudy

   b   Cloudy with sunny spells

   c   Cloudy with light rain

   d   Cloudy with sunny spells and some rain

   e   Heavy cloud and rain

   f   Heavy cloud with sunny spells and some rain

   g   Wind blowing from the south west at a speed of 20 mph

   h   Wind blowing from the south east at a speed of 10 mph

   i   Temperature 16°C

8   b   It appeared to be a dry day at Seaburn when the photo was taken but it was cloudy. The temperature at Seaburn was 16°C. The wind was blowing from the south east onto the coast at a speed of 20 mph and making the sea choppy.

   c   The temperature at Seaburn was 16°C – fairly warm. The temperature figure is given on the weather map.

9   a   X: Thick cloud and heavy rain, but with some sunny spells; SW wind at 20 mph; temperature around 16°C.

   b   Y: Cloudy but dry, with sunny spells; SE wind at 10 mph; temperature around 19°C.

   c   Responses will vary.

More about rain ... and clouds

About this unit

This unit introduces the three different kinds of rainfall, named after what causes the air to rise, as well as two common types of cloud.

Key points

◆ All rain forms in the same way:

- The Sun heats water on Earth's surface and causes some of it to evaporate and form water vapour in the lower atmosphere.

- When air rises, it cools down. Eventually the water vapour in the air condenses to form clouds of water droplets.

- When the water droplets become heavy enough, they fall as rain.

◆ Air rises for different reasons – so we give the rainfall different names:

- Convectional rainfall – air rises because the ground warms it up.

- Relief rainfall – the wind (or air in motion) rises on meeting high ground.

- Frontal rainfall – a warm air mass slides up, or is pushed up, over a cold air mass. (The leading edge of an air mass is called a front.)

◆ Clouds come in different shapes and sizes, depending on many factors (including how fast the air rose). Two common types of clouds are: cumulus and stratus.

Key vocabulary

air masses, convectional rainfall, convection currents, cumulus clouds, frontal rainfall, leeward, relief rainfall, stratus clouds, windward

Skills practised in 'Your turn'

◆ Geography skills: q1, explain a key term; q5a, analyse a photograph

◆ Thinking skills: q3, summarise to show understanding; q4, reasoned explanations to support conclusions; q5b, explain a cloud formation; q6, provide a reasoned explanation, based on a map

Unit outcomes

By the end of this unit most students should be able to:

◆ explain the terms given in 'Key vocabulary' above

◆ give a basic description of how rain forms

◆ list the three types of rainfall and explain how they work

◆ describe two different types of cloud

Ideas for a starter

1 Ask: What is a cloud? Can you remember (from Unit 5.2) how a cloud is formed? Draw a diagram based on the water cycle on the board, like the one on the right. Students write labels in the blanks, and on the arrows, under instructions from the class.

2 Ask: Why does it rain?

3 Show students photos of the main types of clouds and ask them describe them. Ask: What questions would you like to know about clouds? (e.g. Why don't all clouds look the same? Do clouds weigh much?)

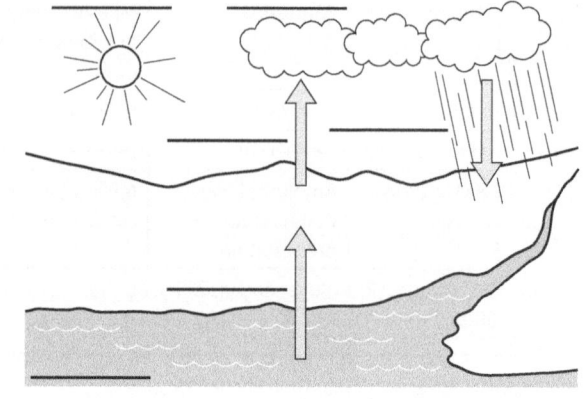

Ideas for plenaries

Plan plenaries at strategic points throughout the lesson, as well as at the end.

Mid-lesson

1 Ask students to decide if the statements below are true or false.

- – Water only evaporates from oceans. (False: Water also evaporates from rivers, lakes, glaciers, etc.)

- – Water vapour forms when water evaporates. It rises, cools and condenses to form water droplets.

- – Evaporation is when water turns from gas to liquid. (False: This is condensation.)

- – Water is evaporating all the time, even though we can't see it.

- – Clouds are made of water vapour. (False: They are made of water droplets.)

2 Divide students into three groups. Each group should create a wall display about one type of rainfall and how it forms.

End-of-lesson

3 Ask rainfall questions about the map on page 139 of the students' book. For example: Which is more likely to get convectional rainfall, Milton Keynes or Aberdeen? Why? Which is more likely to get relief rainfall, Norwich or Swansea? Why?

4 Revisit starter **3**. Students discuss the questions on clouds that they wanted answered. They can also discuss other questions on clouds, for example:

- – Do clouds always give rain? (No. Conditions must be right for the tiny droplets inside them – around 0.1 mm across – to join to form larger drops.)

- – Why don't all clouds look the same? (It depends on many things, including how fast the air rose, and why, and how much water vapour it had in it.)

- – Why do clouds look grey or black when it's going to rain? (When they get thick enough, and the water droplets are large enough, sunlight can't get through.)

- – Do clouds weight much? (Even little ones weigh tonnes.)

5 Students add the key terms covered in Unit 5.4 to the mind map they have been creating, and add definitions.

Further class and homework opportunities

Suggestions 13–15 on page 110 of this book

geog.2 workbook, page 39

geog.2 Kerboodle: lesson presentation, worksheets, end-of-lesson assessment

Answers for 'Your turn'

1 Because it is caused by changes in the height of the ground. When wind (air in motion) meets a hill it is forced to rise. It cools and its water vapour condenses into clouds leading to relief rainfall.

2 Frontal rainfall.

3 Rising air and water vapour.

4 a Yes. Moist wind is forced to rise over hills at any time of day or night; so the air cools and clouds form. Warm air masses can also meet cold ones at any time, day or night, leading to air rising and clouds forming. But the Sun warms the ground only during the day, so clouds that form through convectional heating will form in the daytime.

b No: Not every cloud has rain coming from it. The water droplets in a cloud have to become heavy enough to fall as rain. If the water droplets aren't heavy enough, they won't fall as rain.

Instead they may hang in the air and become mist or condense to give fog.

5 a Cumulus

b The Sun warmed the ground, which in turn warmed the air. The warm air rose in convection currents. As it rose it cooled and the water vapour condensed to form these clouds.

6 The prevailing winds in the British Isles are south west winds. They blow in from the Atlantic laden with water vapour. When they reach the Cambrian Mountains, they are forced to rise sharply. They cool, and the water vapour condenses to clouds. The result is relief rainfall. The Cambrians also get plenty of frontal rainfall since many air masses arrive in from the Atlantic. (Often a cold air mass chases a warm one, giving a weather system called a depression, which can bring plenty of rain. Students will meet depressions in Unit 5.7.)

Air pressure

About this unit

This unit concentrates on air pressure, and the different kinds of weather that high and low pressure bring (depending on the season).

Key points

◆ Air pressure is the force, or pressure, that the air exerts on surfaces. Think of it as the mass of all the gas above us pressing down.

◆ When warm air rises, pressure falls. But rising air causes water vapour to condense, giving clouds and rain. At the same time, air rushes in as wind from other places that are at higher pressure. So low pressure means clouds, rain and wind.

◆ Meanwhile, when warm air rises in one place, cold heavy air sinks somewhere else. Where the cold heavy air sinks, the air pressure rises. This time no clouds form, because the air warms up as it sinks towards Earth – so its water vapour does not condense. Therefore, high pressure means clear skies.

◆ In summer, high pressure means bright sunshine and hot days. However, because there is no cloud to keep the heat in, the evenings can be cool.

◆ In winter, high pressure means bright clear days. Again, because there is no cloud to keep any limited heat in, it gets really cold when the Sun goes down. You get ice and frost.

Key vocabulary

air pressure, barometer, dew, drought, fog, flooding, frost, high pressure, ice, low pressure, thunderstorms

Skills practised in 'Your turn'

◆ Geography skills: q5, explain key terms

◆ Thinking skills: q1, use word selections to demonstrate understanding; q2–q4, apply information to practical examples; q6, consider personal feelings

Unit outcomes

By the end of this unit most students should be able to:

◆ explain the terms given in 'Key vocabulary' above

◆ explain in simple terms what air pressure is

◆ describe high- and low-pressure weather – in summer and winter

Ideas for a starter

1 Ask: Who can remember what air pressure is, and how we measure it?

2 Show a barometer. Explain that changes in air pressure cause the hand to turn to different weather descriptions. Point out that even tiny changes in pressure lead to changes in the weather. And air pressure is changing all the time.

3 Ask: Why do meteorologists keep measuring air pressure? (It helps in forecasting the weather.)

4 Draw a diagram like the one on the right, showing the air above us. Explain: Air weighs down on us, creating air pressure. If the air is sinking, air pressure will rise. If the air is rising, air pressure will fall.

Ask students to stand, then crouch, as if weighed down by the air, to remind them that sinking air means high pressure. Then they stand and stretch as tall as they can to remind them that rising air means low pressure. Say that even tiny changes in pressure lead to changes in the weather. And air pressure is changing all the time.

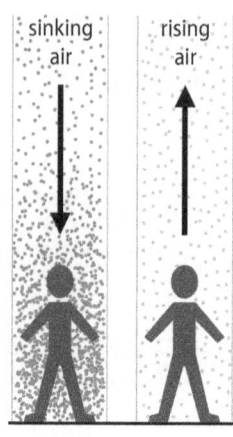

Ideas for plenaries

Plan plenaries at strategic points throughout the lesson, as well as at the end.

Mid-lesson

1   Ask: What kind of air pressure do you think we have today? Why do you think that? How could you find out for certain? (Measure it.)

2   Write the units for air pressure (millibars) on the board. Explain that the average air pressure at sea level is 1013 millibars (mb). 1020 mb and over is counted as high pressure. 1000 mb and under is counted as low pressure. The lower the pressure, the stormier the weather.

3   Show examples of weather maps with isobars. Explain: Isobars are like contour lines, joining places of equal air pressure. If isobars are close together, it means there is a big pressure difference across an area, and this means wind. (Air rushes from high to low pressure as wind).

4   Following on from plenary **3** and using a weather map (e.g. from the Met Office) with a date on (to show the time of year), ask: Where is the highest pressure on the map? Where is the lowest pressure? Where is the windiest place? Why? For different points on the map, ask: What would the weather be like in X?

End-of-lesson

5   Give students cards containing statements relating to high pressure and low pressure weather. For example:
    –   I'll need a waterproof jacket.
    –   You'll be able to see the stars at night.
    –   It will be wet and windy.
    –   Roads could be icy.
    –   I'll need to take sunscreen.
    –   I'll need to take my wellies.

    Write the following headings on the board: *High pressure; Low pressure*. Students sort the cards according to the type of weather.

6   Students add the key terms covered in Unit 5.5 to the mind map they have been creating, and add definitions.

Further class and homework opportunities

Suggestions 16–21 on pages 110–111 of this book

geog.2 workbook, page 40

geog.2 Kerboodle: lesson presentation, worksheets, end-of-lesson assessment

Answers for 'Your turn'

1   Students should choose from each pair: unsettled; stormier; clear; hot; cold.

2   There will be different examples for different seasons:

    In summer: Farming (there may be drought so crops suffer); gardening (drought kills plants); forest rangers (big risk of forest fires); people managing water companies (in times of drought they may need to turn off the water supply at intervals).

    In winter: People who travel for work since the roads may be icy; plane and ferry pilots, since visibility may be low.

3   Examples are: farming (crops can rot from too much rain); tour operators and other people who depend on tourists (bad weather puts visitors off); painters and decorators (can't do external work in wet weather); builders and gardeners (can't do many jobs in wet weather).

4   Students could choose four of: sun block, things to swim in, shorts, T-shirts, light cover-up clothing for when the Sun gets too strong; cream to treat sunburn, sunglasses, water bottles, deodorant, insect repellent.

5   **a**   High pressure in winter.

    b   Fog – water vapour condenses on particles in the air; frost – water vapour condenses and freezes on cold surfaces.

6   Responses will vary.

Why is our weather so changeable?

About this unit

This unit considers why the UK's weather can change so quickly.

Key points

- Air moves around the world in huge 'blocks' – called air masses. (They move because of the temperature differential from the Equator to the Poles.)
- Air masses differ from each other in temperature and moisture content. They can be hot or cold, damp or dry – depending on where they came from.
- Because they have different characteristics, air masses can clash when they meet – leading to rapid changes in the weather.
- The leading edge of an air mass is called a front. Fronts have special symbols on weather maps – red frills for a warm front and blue teeth for a cold one.
- When a warm front meets a cold air mass, it slides up over it (because the warm air is lighter). When a cold front meets a warm air mass, it drives sharply under it – pushing it upwards. Either way, the rising warm air leads to clouds, rain and wind.
- The unsettled weather eases off when the new air mass has taken over.

Key vocabulary

air masses, front, cold front, warm front

Skills practised in 'Your turn'

- Geography skills: q1, q3a, explain key terms; q2, analyse a map and apply geographical information; q3b, draw an annotated diagram
- Thinking skills: q2, apply knowledge of air masses to reach reasoned conclusions

Unit outcomes

By the end of this unit most students should be able to:

- explain the terms given in 'Key vocabulary' above
- explain why different air masses have different characteristics
- explain how the arrival of a front leads to a change in the weather

Ideas for a starter

1 Show some time-lapse images of how weather can change over a relatively short period of time.

2 Ask: What was the weather like last week? The day before yesterday? Yesterday? What's it like today? It can change from day to day. Why do you think this is?

3 Ask: What would air over the Sahara Desert be like? Hot or cold? Damp or dry? If it drifted over the UK, how would it affect our weather? What might air over the Arctic be like? How would that affect our weather if it drifted over the UK? Explain that air masses are always coming our way, causing changes in the weather.

Ideas for plenaries

Plan plenaries at strategic points throughout the lesson, as well as at the end.

Mid-lesson

1   Draw a rough map on the board, like the one at the bottom of page 79 of the students' book. Write *Summer* above it. Then mark in the arrows from that map. These show the five common air masses that affect the UK.

   Ask students to come up and shade in the arrows, red for warm air and blue for cold. Then they write on each arrow *damp* or *dry*. (The world map at the back of their books may help here.)

   Ask the class how each air mass would affect the UK weather in summer. Then cross out *Summer* and write *Winter,* and repeat the exercise.

   Only air mass C changes its characteristics, from warm and dry to cold and dry. (But note: air mass D does not usually come our way in winter.)

2   With books closed, ask students to fill in the gaps to show what happens when a warm air mass arrives in a place where there is a cold one.

   The [one word] air mass slides up over the [one word] air mass. As it [one word], the air pressure [one word] and the weather starts to [two words]. As the [two words] cools, a bank of clouds form. It starts to [one word]. (Words for the gaps (in order are): warm; cold; rises; falls; get windy; rising air; rain.)

   Now ask students to write a similar paragraph, with gaps, to show what happens when a cold air mass arrives in a place where there is a warm one.

End-of-lesson

3   Ask a volunteer to explain in 60 seconds why our weather can change so quickly. Other students can challenge hesitation, deviation, or incorrect information.

4   Students add the key terms covered in Unit 5.6 to the mind map they have been creating, and add definitions.

5   To round off, show a time-lapse video of satellite images of weather for the UK. Elicit that the white areas are clouds. This is a great way to show fronts on the move. (You will see some classic depression patterns; depressions will be met in Unit 5.7.)

Further class and homework opportunities

Suggestions 22–23 on page 111 of this book

geog.2 workbook, page 41

geog.2 Kerboodle: lesson presentation, worksheets, end-of-lesson assessment

Answers for 'Your turn'

1   Air mass: a huge block of air, perhaps thousands of kilometers across, with a particular set of characteristics (e.g. warm and dry, or cold and wet) depending on where it came from

2   **a**   B. It's from the cold Arctic. Because it is very cold it does not take up water vapour from the ocean it passes over.

   b   A and E. They pass over the ocean so take up water vapour. (A is not as cold as B; and E, from the south west, is warmer.)

   c   C. It passes over a huge land mass rather than ocean, so it's dry. Large land masses tend to get very cold in winter and hot in summer so the temperature of this air mass changes accordingly.

   d   D. Since it comes from the tropics (but it does not in fact usually come our way in winter).

3   **a**   **i**   A warm front is the leading edge of a warm air mass.

      ii   A cold front is the leading edge of a cold air mass.

   b   Students' drawings should look something like this:

Symbol for warm front   Symbol for cold front

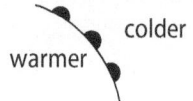
colder
warmer

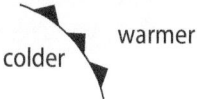
warmer
colder

A winter of storms

About this unit

This unit examines the causes and effects of the UK's winter storms of 2013/14.

Key points

- During the winter of 2013/14, the UK suffered the worst succession of severe storms for decades. They brought heavy winds and rain, as well as coastal storm surges and flooding.

- Because the storms hit the country with very little gap between them, the heavy rain that they brought had no chance to drain away. As a result, large areas of the West Country, in particular, were flooded for weeks on end.

- The storms also brought high winds, which caused extensive structural damage and blew down many power lines – leaving many homes without electricity for long periods.

- There was also extensive travel disruption: flooded roads became impassable for most traffic; flights were cancelled due to the high winds; and the railway line connecting the West Country to the rest of the UK was washed away by the sea.

- These storms were all caused by the clash of warm and cold air masses over the Atlantic, which created a series of depressions – driven eastwards over the UK by the prevailing wind direction and the jet stream in the upper troposphere.

Key vocabulary

depression, jet stream, troposphere

Skills practised in 'Your turn'

- Geography skills: q6, analyse a weather chart
- Thinking skills: q1, explain how clashing air masses generate strong winds; q2, use common sense and prior knowledge to make suggestions; q3, empathise and predict; q4–q5, construct a broad explanation; q6–q7 offer simple explanations

Unit outcomes

By the end of this unit most students should be able to:

- explain the terms given in 'Key vocabulary' above
- describe the effects on the UK of the series of storms which occurred during the winter of 2013/14
- explain what caused the winter storms

Ideas for a starter

1   Show students a video / pictures showing the damage caused by the storms in 2013 / 2014. Ask: What damage did the storms cause? Who was affected? What caused the storms?

2   Ask students to close their eyes and get ready for a mind movie. Then select one or more to read out the account on page 80 of the students' book.

3   One or more students pretend to be the teacher. They summarise the last lesson on air masses and fronts, and question the class about the topic.

4   Ask: Why is it quicker to fly from the USA to the UK than the other way around? Has anyone heard *jet stream* used in weather forecasts? Can anyone say what the jet stream is? How might it affect our weather in the UK?

Ideas for plenaries

Plan plenaries at strategic points throughout the lesson, as well as at the end.

Mid-lesson

1   Put the following steps (listed here in the correct order) in the formation of a depression on cards. Mix them up. Students sort them in the right order.

  – Warm air mass pushes into cold air mass

  – Warm air rises and air pressure drops

  – Cold air rushes into replace warm air – strong winds

  – Warm air rises and cools

  – Water vapour in the warm air condenses

  – Banks of cloud form

  – Rain begins

2   Imagine: It is winter 2013 and the UK has already experienced several storms. One big storm has just passed and another is expected soon. Ask students to write a short, snappy news bulletin on the recent storm and what caused it. They need a catchy headline and should give the public advice on how to stay safe in the next storm.

3   Give students blank copies of the diagrams at the top of page 81 of the students' book showing the formation of a depression from above. Give students a few minutes to study the diagrams in their book. Then, with books closed and working in pairs, they reproduce the diagrams from memory.

End-of-lesson

4   Ask students to read out their answers for 'Your turn' question 7 to the class. Discuss what makes one answer better than another.

5   Ask: Do you think that you'll be able to recognise a depression on a satellite image? Explain that on satellite images, depressions show up as a great swirl of cloud. Show students a satellite image containing a depression(s) and ask them if they can pick it / them out.

6   Students add the key terms covered in Unit 5.7 to the mind map they have been creating, and add definitions.

Further class and homework opportunities

Suggestions 24–27 on page 111 of this book

geog.2 workbook, page 42

geog.2 Kerboodle: lesson presentation, worksheets, end-of-lesson assessment

Answers for 'Your turn'

1   A storm moved across the Atlantic Ocean from west to east. A cold air mass clashed into a warm air mass and pushed it upwards. This caused strong winds.

2   Examples include: trees, homes, shops, farmland, buildings, bridges, cars, trucks, power lines, roads, railways.

3   Answers include: trees / power lines blown down, buildings that have been destroyed, overturned cars / lorries, debris that has been blown around, flooding, roads that have been closed. They might feel: strong and blustery winds, heavy rain; frightened, worried, angry because of the disruption, curious to see large waves.

4   Because cold polar air meets warm tropical air over the UK. A depression forms which causes strong winds and rain.

5   a   Depression

b   The prevailing wind direction in the UK is from the south west and the jet stream also moves from west to east. The depression is dragged from west to east across the UK.

6   X is located in the wedge of warm air between a warm front and a cold front, which are moving from west to east. Y is located west of the cold front, so it is colder there than at X.

7   The explanation could be along these lines:

There's a huge block of warm air moving along. A huge mass of cold air is following it, but going faster. The cold air mass pushes in under the warm one, shoving it upwards. This causes stormy winds and heavy rain. So we get bad weather. But in a while the two blocks of air get mixed together and the weather gets better.

About this unit

This unit explains the difference between weather and climate, provides a summary of how climate varies across the UK, and uses both a climate table and a climate graph for student analysis.

Key points

◆ Weather is the state of the atmosphere at a given place at a given time – it can change very rapidly.

◆ Climate is the *average* weather in a place for a given month.

◆ The British Isles can be divided roughly into four climate zones.

◆ The climate data for a place can be presented either as a table (which has more options, e.g. number of days with gales), or as a climate graph (which displays two variables: average monthly temperature as a red line, and average monthly rainfall as blue bars).

◆ For most purposes, such as planning a holiday, a climate graph provides a good visual indicator of the things that interest most people – average temperature and rainfall.

Key vocabulary

average, climate, climate graph, climate table, weather

Skills practised in 'Your turn'

◆ Geography skills: q1, explain key terms; q3, analyse a climate data table; q5, interpret map data; q6–q7, analyse a climate graph; q9, compare climate graph and climate table data

◆ Numeracy skills: q6, calculate averages; q9, use calculations to assess comparative climate data and reach conclusions

◆ Literacy skills: q5, write four short climate descriptions

◆ Thinking skills: q2, classify statements; q3d, interpret climate data to reach reasoned conclusions; q4, use common sense and prior knowledge to explain circumstances; q8, reach a reasoned conclusion

Unit outcomes

By the end of this unit most students should be able to:

◆ explain the terms given in 'Key vocabulary' above

◆ state the difference between weather and climate

◆ describe the UK's four climate zones

◆ analyse and interpret a climate graph and a climate table

Ideas for a starter

1 Ask: What is weather? Can anyone remind me of the definition of weather?

2 Ask students whether these statement refer to weather or climate.

- November is usually the wettest month in the UK.

- Last Friday it was 19°C and sunny.

- It rained all day yesterday.

- This morning there was fog.

- The rainy season in Mexico lasts from May to September.

- Scotland is wetter than England.

Ideas for plenaries

Plan plenaries at strategic points throughout the lesson, as well as at the end.

Mid-lesson

1   Using the climate data for Plymouth on page 82 of the students' book, students calculate the temperature range, the total annual rainfall, and average annual temperature.

2   Give students cards showing climate graphs for various locations. For each location, prepare a card with a description of the climate (e.g. We have quite hot summers. Most winters I get to build a snowman. There is a fairly high chance of rain throughout the year.). In pairs, students match each graph to the correct description.

3   Students compare one of the climate graphs from plenary **2** to the graph for London on page 83 of the students' book. Ask: How does it vary from London? Which place is hottest? Which place gets most rain?

End-of-lesson

4   Students look at the map on page 82 of the students' book. Ask: Where do you live? Do you agree with what it says about the climate in your region?

5   Students add the key terms covered in Unit 5.8 to the mind map they have been creating, and add definitions.

Further class and homework opportunities

Suggestion 28 on page 111 of this book

geog.2 workbook, page 43

geog.2 Kerboodle: lesson presentation, worksheets, end-of-lesson assessment

Answers for 'Your turn'

1   Weather is the state of the atmosphere in a place at a given time, whereas climate is the 'average' weather in a place. Climate tells you what the weather is usually like, in a given month.

2   **A** Climate   **B** Climate   **C** Weather
    D Climate   **E** Weather   **F** Climate

3   **a**   December   **b** January   **c** July

    d   **i** For fine, dry weather most students will select either June or July. June is the drier of the two, with most hours of sunshine and only a very low chance of gales. July is hotter and calmer but quite a bit wetter and has fewer hours of sunshine (since the longest day has already passed).

    ii Answers will vary but most students will probably select January since it has the most unsettled weather. It is one of the coldest, wettest, and darkest months and has the most chance of gales (so tents could blow away).

4   **a**   Although the Sun's rays are most intense in the middle of the day, it takes a few hours for them to be absorbed into the atmosphere and heat it up.

    b   The Sun heats up the atmosphere. At night the temperature drops once the Sun has gone down and no longer provides heat.

5   **a**   Peterborough's climate is dry all year round. It has warm summers and cold winters.

    b   Belfast has a wet climate with mild summers and mild winters.

    c   Aberdeen has a relatively wet climate with mild summers and cold winters.

    d   Newport has a fairly wet climate with warm summers and mild winters.

6   **a**   Average monthly temperature

    b   **i** July and August   **ii** On average 23°C

    c   **i** December and January   **ii** 8°C

7   **a**   Average monthly rainfall

    b   **i** March   **ii** Approximately 40 mm

    c   **i** October   **ii** Approximately 70 mm

8   The climate graph will give an idea of whether it is likely to be rainy for the month that she is coming but the figures are averages so they don't tell what the weather will be like for a given week. They'd need to check the weather forecast.

9   **a**   London   **b** They are both similarly cold in winter.

    c   Plymouth has the highest rainfall at 950 mm a year compared to approximately 615 mm for London. The total rainfall can be worked out by adding together the average monthly rainfall.

    d   Yes, it does fit with the map on page 82 of the students' book. According to the map, Plymouth has a fairly wet climate and London has a dry climate.

About this unit

This unit explains the main factors that influence climate, starting with latitude – the most important one.

Key points

◆ Climate is the net result of several factors.

◆ The main one is latitude, or distance from the Equator. Overall, as you move away from the Equator, temperatures fall.

◆ The next important one, especially for mid-latitude countries like the UK, is the tilt of Earth's axis as it travels around the Sun. This gives us our distinct seasons.

◆ Other factors also play a part, and can greatly modify the effect of latitude. For example, you will find glaciers up high mountains, even near the Equator.

Key vocabulary

altitude, Equator, latitude, North Atlantic Drift, Northern Hemisphere, ocean currents, prevailing wind, sea breeze, seasons, tilt of Earth's axis

Skills practised in 'Your turn'

◆ Geography skills: q2, q7a, explain key terms; q3, map interpretation

◆ Literacy skills: q1, draw a summary spider diagram

◆ Thinking skills: q3–q5, use map data to produce reasoned explanations; q6, apply knowledge to reach conclusions; q7, produce a reasoned explanation

Unit outcomes

By the end of this unit most students should be able to:

◆ explain the terms given in 'Key vocabulary' above

◆ give six factors that influence climate

◆ explain how these factors affect the climate

Ideas for a starter

1   Ask: Can anyone remind us what latitude is? Write on the board a list of places from around the world, their latitudes, and their average monthly temperatures for a year. Ask: What do you notice about places near the Equator?

2   Illustrate the effect of latitude using a torch (for the Sun) and a globe. With the torch shining on the Equator, ask: Which part of Earth gets the strongest light? Which part gets least light? (This works best in a darkened room.)

3   Show students a photo of Mt Kilimanjaro with snow on the top. Show them a map of its location close to the Equator. Ask: If this mountain is located on the Equator, why does it have snow on top?

4   Give students a few minutes to write down all the things they think might affect the UK climate. They can work in pairs. Then summarise the responses on the board as a tally chart or on a spider diagram.

Ideas for plenaries

Plan plenaries at strategic points throughout the lesson, as well as at the end.

Mid-lesson

1 Show an animation of Earth's orbit around the Sun. Stop at different points to show the effect on the northern and southern hemispheres.

2 Ask students to work in pairs to make up statements about the UK's climate, some true, some false (using the map on page 139 of the students' book). For example:

   – Plymouth is warmer than Milton Keynes in winter. (True: The sea is warmer than the land in winter so Plymouth gets a warm sea breeze.)

   The rest of the class can decide if the statements are true or false, and you can correct any misunderstanding.

End-of-lesson

3 With the use of props (e.g. torch and globe) ask a pair of students to explain and demonstrate how Earth's tilt affects the amount of sunlight reaching places during the year.

4 Briefly outline other things that can affect climate. Did you know that volcanic eruptions and meteorite collisions can affect climate by affecting the amount of sunlight reaching Earth?

5 Students add the key terms covered in Unit 5.9 to the mind map they have been creating, and add definitions.

Further class and homework opportunities

Suggestions 29–32 on page 111 of this book

geog.2 workbook, page 44

geog.2 Kerboodle: lesson presentation, worksheets, end-of-lesson assessment

Answers for 'Your turn'

1 Students' spider maps should contain all six factors given in the unit.

2 a How far north or south of the Equator a place is, measured in degrees.

   b The height of a place above sea level.

   c The direction that the wind blows from most often.

3 a Aberdeen is further north and does not enjoy the warming effect of the North Atlantic Drift, as Plymouth does.

   b Ben Nevis is further north and it rises to a high altitude, whereas Plymouth is at sea level.

4 Tehran is inland and land heats up faster than the sea in summer. It is about 36°N while Lisbon is about 39°N, but that alone can't account for the differences in their climates. Lisbon is on the coast. A sea breeze will keep it cool in summer, and warm in winter. (The average maximum temperature in Tehran is 37°C in summer and 11°C in winter. For Lisbon, it's 27°C in summer and about 14°C in winter.)

5 Students should at least know to look in the northern hemisphere (since it's December), near the Arctic Circle, and inland away from the warming effect of the sea. They should also think about height above sea level.

6 a Why is the temperature of the sea cooler than the temperature of the land in summer? Why are places on the coast cooler in summer?

   b Why is the temperature of the sea warmer than the temperature of the land in winter? Why are places on the coast warmer in the winter?

7 a The wind blows the most often from the south west.

   b Since it is blowing from further south it brings warmth and since it blows over the ocean it brings moisture.

   c The UK would be colder all year round. The south would be drier than it is now because most rain and snow would fall in the mountainous areas in the north.

Climates around the world

help at a glance

About this unit

This unit examines how and why climate varies around the world.

Key points

- ◆ The world can be divided into big regions, each with its own distinctive climate.
- ◆ The climatic differences between these regions are due to the factors given in Unit 5.9.
- ◆ Within a climate region, the climate will vary from place to place. But, overall, it is broadly similar throughout the region.

Key vocabulary

climate regions

Skills practised in 'Your turn'

- ◆ Geography skills: q1–q2, analyse and interpret choropleth map data; q4a, explain a key term; q4, analyse map data; q6–q7 analyse and interpret a climate graph
- ◆ Literacy skills: q6d, write a comparative explanation with data evidence
- ◆ Thinking skills: q2, q4c, q5, provide reasoned explanations; q3, recall

Unit outcomes

By the end of this unit most students should be able to:

- ◆ explain the term given in 'Key vocabulary' above
- ◆ say that the world can be divided into different climate regions, and name and briefly describe at least four of them
- ◆ understand that climate varies to some extent within a climate region

Ideas for a starter

1 One or more students pretend to be the teacher. They summarise the last lesson and question the class on the factors that influence climate. Give them key words to include if scaffolding is needed.

2 In small groups, give students an outline map of the world with space to add other information around it. Students shade in the climate zones using a different colour for each climate and using the map on page 86 of the students' book as a guide. They should add a key and title to their map.

   Ask: What do you notice about the climate zones near the Equator? What do you notice as you move away from the Equator?

3 Show climate graphs for two capital cities in the northern hemisphere with very different climates. Ask: What do the graphs show? Which place gets hottest? Which is coolest? Which is driest?

Ideas for plenaries

Plan plenaries at strategic points throughout the lesson, as well as at the end.

Mid-lesson

1   Give students photos of the different climate regions. Ask what they show. Can they match the photos to the climate regions on the map? Students use the photos to annotate their maps from starter **2** by sticking them around the outside of the map and drawing pointers to an example of the correct climate zone. They should also add a label. Ask: How did they decide where each photo and label should go?

2   Students look at the map of world population distribution on page 20 of the students' book. Compare it with the map of climate regions. Ask: Any connections?

End of lesson

3   Students add the key terms covered in Unit 5.10 to the mind map they have been creating, and add definitions.

Further class and homework opportunities

Suggestion 33 on page 111 of this book

geog.2 workbook, page 45

geog.2 Kerboodle: lesson presentation, worksheets, end-of-lesson assessment

Answers for 'Your turn'

1   **a**   At L: very dry, hot summers, cooler winters.

b   At D: warm summers and cold winters, rain all year.

c   At E: warm and wet all year.

d   At J: hot tropical with rain. It has a dry season.

2   **a**   D is further north. (The further from the Equator, the cooler it gets.)

b   J is nearer to the Equator than F so it is hotter.

3   Other factors include: Earth's tilt; distance from the coast; prevailing wind direction; ocean currents; height above sea level.

4   **a**   An ocean current is like a river of warmer or colder water, flowing within the ocean, in a definite direction.

b   North Atlantic Drift.

c   **i** Any one from: Greenland, Chile, Argentina, Japan, part of north eastern Canada, the west coast of the USA, the west and south coasts of Australia.

ii A cold ocean current will cool the winds that pass over it and these will cool the country (especially if they are prevailing winds). Cool winds will not pick up so much moisture from the ocean and that means less rain.

d   **i** Any one from: South Africa, Mozambique, Papua New Guinea, north eastern Australia.

ii Canada

Point out that this map shows only a selection of prevailing winds.

5   **a**   C is the Himalayas, a high mountain range. The higher a place is, the cooler it is.

b   G is on the west coast of the UK, which is warmed by the North Atlantic Drift, a warm ocean current. But F, in north eastern Canada has a cold ocean current flowing by.

c   K is cooled by a cold ocean current, whereas H is warmed by a warm one.

d   L and I are at the same latitude. But L is inland and dry because winds reaching it will already have lost much of their moisture. Skies over L will usually be clear, so sunlight can get through. I is on the coast. Winds passing over it from most directions will be rich in moisture. Cloudy skies will be common, and clouds help to reflect sunlight.

6   **a**   July and August; **b** May; **c** January to May and October to December (i.e. when it is below freezing).

d   The climate for Frobisher Bay is drier and colder than London's climate. The maximum temperature in London is likely to be about 24°C in August whereas the maximum temperature in Frobisher Bay is likely to be about 9°C in July. Frobisher Bay also has less rainfall than London. The highest average monthly rainfall is approximately 55 mm in Frobisher Bay compared to 70 mm in London. The total annual rainfall is greater in London at 615 mm a year. In Frobisher Bay it is approximately 450 mm a year. North eastern Canada has a cold ocean current flowing by and cold winds pick up less moisture meaning less rain. The UK is warmed by the North Atlantic Drift, a warm ocean current that gives rain.

7   K. It's in Canada.

Many of these suggestions are addressed to your students. Where research or further resources are needed, the internet will almost certainly provide the answer.

The suggestions are graded *,**,*** according to level of difficulty. Some are suitable for all levels, and can be differentiated by outcome.

It's the weather!

1   Weather collage   Collect photos of different weather conditions from magazines or other sources and make them into a collage. Find an interesting way to group them.   *

2   Weather in advertising   A more challenging variation on the activity above. Collect adverts that include different weather conditions. Make a collage with annotations explaining why that image was chosen for the advert.   **

3   Weather words   Collect short interesting descriptions of the weather, from novels, poems or plays (say 1–9 lines). Your English teacher might help. Display them in an exciting way, perhaps around, or on, a photo.   ***

4   Fog   Read the class this poem called *Fog* by American poet Carl Sandburg (1878–1967).

The fog comes
on little cat feet.
It sits looking
over harbor and city
on silent haunches
and then moves on.

Inspired by this, ask students to write a short poem for another aspect of weather. If they are very short of words, they could try a cinquain. (For cinquains, see suggestion 19 on page 87 of this book.)   */**/***

So what causes weather?

5   Walter the water molecule   There you are, sitting on the surface of the Atlantic Ocean – and the next thing you know… Write a story or draw a strip cartoon about a week in your life, where you get to play a part in the weather! Perhaps you end up in snow or fog, or in a hailstone? Or on an umbrella?   *

6   It's the Sun   The Sun is the main driver of our weather. But what is it? What goes on in the Sun? How far away is it? Will it last forever? Do your research, and present your findings in a very exciting form.   ***

Measuring the weather

7   Wind vane   Come up with a design for a wind vane, using recycled materials. There may be a prize for the best design! And an even better prize for the best completed wind vane that works?   **/***

8   Record the weather   Working with a group, record the weather for a week, for your area: temperature, precipitation, wind speed and direction. Take measurements using the school weather centre, or look up reports. Show the data in tables, then use it to draw graphs. See if you can learn how to draw a simple wind rose.   **/***

9   Europe's weather today   Mark Europe's capital cities on a large outline political map of Europe. Now mark in today's weather information, from a newspaper or the internet. (You can share the job of collecting information). Try to explain the differences you find.   **/***

10   Weather around the world today   This is a variation on the previous activity. This time use a map of the world, and mark in three or four cities on each continent and today's weather information. Try to explain the differences you find. Is there a big difference between the northern and southern hemispheres?   **/***

11   How hot is hot?   It can be hard to know what a temperature 'feels' like. Draw a long thermometer, the length of an A4 page, or longer. Mark in a scale from −20°C to 100°C. Then mark in and label a range of temperatures. For example, body temperature, the temperature of ice lollies and boiling water, a comfortable bath temperature, a comfortable room temperature in winter, the temperature on a hot summer day in the UK, the maximum daytime temperature in the Sahara. Try to think of others to add.   **

12   The Beaufort Scale   Wind speed is often expressed using the Beaufort Scale. Find out what this is, and show it in an interesting way with wind speeds in kilometres per hour.   **

More about rain…and clouds

13   The water cycle   Clouds and rain are part of the water cycle. Draw a colourful diagram of the water cycle (if you don't remember look back at page 82 of *geog.1* students' book or a science book). You could make it a large diagram, and incorporate photos.   **

14   Cloud album   There are two common types of cloud. They can be subdivided into different types depending how high in the sky they are, and whether they will give rain. For example *cumulonimbus, altostratus*.

The names are based on Latin words: *cumulus, nimbus, alto, stratus*.

Find out what these words mean. Then make a cloud photo album showing the two common types of cloud, and their subtypes. Add text captions to the photos.   ***

15   Thunder and lightning   Closely linked to clouds! What causes them? Find out! Then either prepare a presentation about them for the class, using PowerPoint, drawings on the board or some other method, *or* prepare a double-page spread, like the units in *geog.2* students' book.   ***

Air pressure

16   Aide memoire   Find a way to help yourself remember that low pressure brings wind and rain, and high pressure means clear skies.   *

17   Barometer   Find out how a barometer works, and tell the class. You could do a PowerPoint presentation, or a stand-up presentation at the board.   ***

18   All about isobars   Hint! Isobars are to do with air pressure. Download a weather chart showing isobars, from the

internet. Your job is to annotate it, to help someone else understand about isobars and what they show. So you will need to add notes explaining:
- what an isobar is
- the kind of weather you get when isobars are close together
- what counts as low pressure
- what counts as high pressure
- what wind is, and which way it will blow. ***

19 Wind and pressure Find a simple way to demonstrate that air rushes from high pressure to low, as wind. Okay, you can use a balloon. **

20 The wind in a frolic Read the poem *The wind in a frolic*, by William Howitt, to the class. You can easily find it on the internet. *

21 Celebrate the wind! Do a drawing or write a poem to celebrate the rush of air from high to low pressure. The poem could be a cinquain. (For more on cinquains see suggestion 19 on page 87 of this book.) */**/***

Why is our weather so changeable?

22 Frontal attack Cut out a newspaper weather map that shows warm and cold fronts. (You may need a national broadsheet for this). Stick it on a piece of paper and annotate it to show where the air is warm, where it's cold, and where there is likely to be wind and rain. *

23 Weather wise? There are many old weather sayings – but are they wise? Choose one of these (or all three):
- Rain before 7, dry before 11.
- When dew is on the grass, rain won't come to pass.
- Rain on St Swithin's day (15 July) brings rain for 40 days following.

Decide whether there could be any truth in the saying, and explain why you think that. **

A winter of storms

24 A depressing challenge? A depression is a weather system made up of a cold front chasing a warm one. The cold front travels faster. Eventually it catches up with the warm front (the leading edge of the warm air mass) giving an occluded front.

Tell the story of a depression in the form of a cartoon strip, giving views from above at different stages. ***

25 Interpret a satellite image Satellite images of the Earth help with weather forecasting because they show cloud. Search the internet for a satellite image of a depression over the UK. Use the map of the UK on page 81 of the students' book as a guide – you are looking for an image that shows cloud in the same shape as the cold and warm fronts. Annotate your image with the positions of the warm and cold fronts and what you think the weather will be like in different places (use page 79 of the students' book to help you). ***

26 The shipping forecast 1 Record the UK shipping forecast and play it to the class, or go online and find the BBC weather shipping forecast and read part of it to the class. Show them a map of the sea areas mentioned in the forecast. Ask students who the forecast is for, and why they need it. **

27 The shipping forecast 2 Provide students with a map of the sea areas used for the shipping forecast and ask them to write their own forecast for sea areas to the north (or east, west etc) of the UK. They need to include wind, sea state, weather and visibility in the forecast. ***

From weather to climate

28 Draw a climate graph Use the figures in the table below to draw a climate graph for Aberdeen. Check the graph for London on page 83 of the students' book to make sure you know what goes on the axes.

	Jan	Feb	Mar	Apr	May	Jun	Jul	Aug	Sep	Oct	Nov	Dec
Rainfall mm	71	52	54	51	55	53	64	70	68	76	77	71
Maximum Temperature °C	6	6	9	11	13	17	18	18	16	13	9	7

Then compare your graph with that for London. How is the climate for the two places similar? How is it different?

Then compare the data in the table with the data for Plymouth on page 82 of the students' book.

Which did you find easier to use – the graph or the table? Why? ***

The factors that influence climate

29 Great UK climate maps Go to the Met Office website. In the search box type *UK mapped averages,* then select the first item in the list. At the choice bars, select *annual,* then *mean temperature.* Choose a year and click backwards and forwards through the years to look at the mean temperatures. Describe the patterns. Try *rainfall amount* too. Enjoy! ***

30 The four seasons Play students extracts from Vivaldi's *The Four Seasons*. They could close their eyes. Can they guess which extract relates to which season? */**

31 Some extreme climates Find out where the hottest and coldest places are on Earth. Then compare climate graphs for them (try *Google images*). Write a paragraph comparing the climates – and then explain the differences. Don't forget a map to show where they are. **/***

32 Heat islands The local climate can also depend on how built-up a place is. Big cities form heat islands. Find out what these are and why they form. Tell the class. ***

Climates around the world

33 World travel Collect travel brochures for places with different climates. Try for one for each of the eight climate regions on the map on page 86 of the students' book. Cut out sample holidays/images for your selected places. Display them around a map of the world's climate regions. **

Our warming planet

chapter overview

About this chapter

Addressing the KS3 Programme of Study

◆ Understand the processes that give rise to global warming, and how they bring spatial variation and change over time.

◆ Understand how human processes influence and change environments and the climate, and how human activity relies on effective functioning of natural systems.

About the content

◆ This chapter starts by explaining that Earth's temperatures have always risen and fallen.

◆ It goes on to explain how global warming is currently creating climate change, why it is happening, and its effects around the world.

◆ Finally, it explores what governments, scientists, and individuals can do to reduce carbon dioxide emissions.

The big picture

These are the key ideas in this chapter.

◆ Earth's temperatures have cooled down and warmed up ever since it was formed.

◆ Global warming is the process of temperatures rising around the world.

◆ Some scientists say global warming is a natural change, but most say it's due mainly to carbon dioxide (the gas that forms when we burn fossil fuels) and, to a less extent, methane.

◆ Rising temperatures bring changes in rainfall, wind patterns, and ocean currents – in other words, climate change, including in the UK.

◆ Climates are changing around the world already, affecting humans and other species.

◆ Climate change will affect people in poor countries most.

◆ We can't stop global warming, but we can take action to limit it, especially by reducing the amount of carbon dioxide we produce.

A students' version of this big picture is given in the *geog.2* students' book opener for Chapter 6.

The chapter outline

Use this, and their chapter opener, to give students a mental roadmap for the chapter.

6 Our warming planet The chapter opener in the students' book is an important part of the chapter; see page 11 for notes about using chapter openers

6.1 Earth's temperatures through the ages How and when Earth has cooled down and warmed up, and how scientists know about temperatures before records began

6.2 Global warming Some different reasons for the causes, and a closer look at greenhouse gases

6.3 Climate change As air temperatures rise, patterns of rainfall, wind, ocean currents, and therefore climates will change, and a wide range of consequences are predicted, some disastrous

6.4 It's happening already! Example impacts of global warming on places, people, plants, and animals in eight places around the world

6.5 Who will suffer most? Why the poorest people in the world will suffer most, and carbon dioxide production around the world

6.6 So what can we do? Why we can't stop global warming, and measures we can take to limit it

Objectives and outcomes for this chapter

Objectives	Unit	Outcomes
Most students will understand:		Most students will be able to:
• that Earth's temperature has always been subject to change	6.1	• describe how Earth's temperature has changed through history, referring to a graph
• that greenhouse gases, and carbon dioxide in particular, are considered by many scientists to be the main cause of global warming	6.2	• explain what greenhouse gases are, name the two main ones, and explain how they cause global warming; say that carbon dioxide is produced when we burn fossil fuels and wood
• that humans are causing greenhouse gases	6.2	• identify carbon dioxide as the greenhouse gas we add to the air most; give at least two examples of where we burn fuels that produce it
• that climate change will have positive and negative consequences	6.3	• give at least two positive and two negative examples of the predicted consequences of climate change
• that climate change will affect humans, places, plants, and other species	6.4	• explain at least three impacts of climate change
• that local actions have global effects	6.5	• identify countries that produce most carbon dioxide; say how burning fossil fuels locally can affect people around the world
• that we can't stop global warming, but we can limit it	6.6	• evaluate and explain the rise in emissions; evaluate various responses to global warming; list action we can take to reduce emissions

These tie in with the outcomes for each unit, in this teacher's handbook, and with 'Your goals for this chapter', in *geog.2* students' book.

Opportunities for assessment

See the formal assessment materials for this chapter on *geog.2 Kerboodle Lessons, Resources, & Assessment*. They include an extended assessment task, an exam-style question, end-of-lesson assessments, and a self-assessment form. See also the notes on pages 14–15 of this book.

Getting ready for this chapter

geog.2 Kerboodle contains plans and presentations for each unit, including interactive activities, animations, and worksheets.

About 'Your chapter starter'

The people dressed as polar bears in the photo on page 88 of *geog.2* students' book are protesting about climate change. The protest was part of the *I Count* campaign (run by *Stop Climate Chaos*, a coalition of environmental and international development NGOs). Supporters of *I Count* were visiting Downing Street to hand in a petition demanding the UK act on climate change in order to keep average global temperature increases to under 2°C.

Why dress as polar bears? In the Arctic Ocean, more sea ice is melting each year, and it is melting earlier. Polar bears use the sea ice as a platform for hunting seals. A reduction in sea ice means they must swim further for their food, or starve.

Earth's temperatures through the ages

help at a glance

About this unit

This unit provides an overview of how Earth's temperature has constantly changed since its formation 4.5 billion years ago – up to and including today.

Key points

◆ Since its formation 4.5 billion years ago, Earth has ranged from being a molten ball to a snowball! However, for most of this period, Earth was completely ice-free, e.g. during the time of the dinosaurs.

◆ There have, however, been a number of ice ages during Earth's existence. The last major ice age began 110 000 years ago and lasted 100 000 years. During this time, 30% of Earth was covered in ice, whereas only about 10% is covered in ice today.

◆ Humans were around during the last ice age, and, like many species, were forced to abandon Britain and head further south.

◆ Since the end of the last ice age, 10 000 years ago, average temperatures have continued to fluctuate globally – with both warm periods and mini ice ages. We are currently in quite a warm period, but not the warmest.

Key vocabulary

evolution, ice age, ice cores, Northern Hemisphere, sediment, tree rings, tundra

Skills practised in 'Your turn'

◆ Geography skills: q2, interpret a temperature graph

◆ Numeracy skills: q2c, calculate a temperature range

◆ Literacy skills: q1, write correct statements

◆ Thinking skills: q1, assess a statement's accuracy

Unit outcomes

By the end of this unit most students should be able to:

◆ explain the terms given in 'Key vocabulary' above

◆ summarise how Earth's temperature has changed since its formation 4.5 billion years ago

◆ explain what effects the changes in Earth's temperature have had on humans, e.g. growing grapes in Britain and settling Greenland during warm periods, and abandoning Britain during the last major ice age

Ideas for a starter

1 Ask: Can anyone remind us what the difference between weather and climate is? Recap the factors that influence climate.

2 Ask: How did dinosaurs become extinct? Show students pictures of a dinosaur and other things that may have caused them to become extinct (e.g. asteroid impact, erupting volcano, a large ice mass). What does each picture show? How might it have caused dinosaurs to become extinct?

3 Show students the graph on page 91 of the students' book. Ask: What is it showing? Give it a title.

Ideas for plenaries

Plan plenaries at strategic points throughout the lesson, as well as at the end.

Mid-lesson

1   Explain how sediment from ocean / lake floors, ice from within ice sheets, and tree rings can be used to give historical information about temperatures.

2   Give students pictures / illustrations showing cross sections of trees (i.e. the rings) and information about when the tree was cut down. They could try to work out the age of the tree and, from the widths of the rings, in which years it might have grown more or less. Ask: What might have caused the tree to grow more or less?

3   Following on from plenary **2**, ask: Why is it important to gather information about past climate?

End-of-lesson

4   Use 'Your turn' question 1 as a plenary.

5   Give students some scenarios that might affect Earth's temperature and ask: What if …? What if the amount of Sun reaching Earth changed? What if a huge volcano erupted or an asteroid hit Earth and created a giant dust cloud? Students describe how these might affect Earth's climate.

6   In pairs, students share their new knowledge by talking to their partner about the two most interesting pieces of information they have learned in this lesson.

Further class and homework opportunities

Suggestions 1–3 on page 126 of this book

geog.2 workbook, page 47

geog.2 Kerboodle: lesson presentation, worksheets, end-of-lesson assessment

Answers for 'Your turn'

1   **A**   False. 650 million years ago, at the time of Snowball Earth, Earth was completely covered in ice. At the peak of the last ice age, which began 110 000 years ago, ice sheets only covered 30% of Earth, so they did not reach the Equator.

B   False. There was no ice on Earth when the dinosaurs lived.

C   True

D   False. Temperatures on the whole planet, and therefore the UK, were extremely hot when it first formed 4.5 billion years ago. Since then the planet and the UK have warmed up and cooled down many times. During Snowball Earth the whole planet was covered in ice. During the last ice age, which began 110 000 years ago, the north of the UK was covered in ice and the southern part became tundra so the temperature was much colder than now. More recently, about 11 000 years ago the temperature in the UK was about 4°C colder than it is today. Temperatures in the northern hemisphere and the UK rose rapidly between 11 000 and 10 000 years ago and since then there have been fluctuations with warmer periods and colder periods.

2   **a**   11 000 years ago. The ice age is coming to an end so the ice is melting. People who had migrated to warmer parts of Europe are returning to the UK.

b   Yes, the graph shows that it was about half a degree warmer approximately 6 500 years ago and 4 500 years ago.

c   Approximately 5.6°C. 11 000 years ago the temperature was approximately 10.5°C and at its maximum around 6 500 years ago it was approximately 16.1°C.

Global warming

About this unit

This unit brings the story of Earth's average temperature up to the present day, and introduces the theory of global warming.

Key points

◆ Earth is currently experiencing a warm period, which many scientists believe is being enhanced by human actions. They call this global warming – and they believe that the main cause is the release of additional greenhouse gases into the atmosphere, due to human actions.

◆ Some of those actions are direct (such as burning fossil fuels), and some are more indirect (such as cutting down forests, which act as carbon dioxide sinks).

◆ Global temperatures are also affected by changes in Earth's tilt and orbit around the Sun, and changes in the amount of energy that the Sun gives out – both of which are cyclical.

Key vocabulary

atmosphere, carbon dioxide, global warming, greenhouse gases, methane

Skills practised in 'Your turn'

◆ Geography skills: q1a, define a key term

◆ Literacy skills: q2, complete statements

◆ Thinking skills: q1c, explain (with examples) how humans may be causing global warming; q3, use common sense and prior knowledge to explain the effect on carbon dioxide levels of the Industrial Revolution; q4, respond appropriately to stated opinions with arguments against them

Unit outcomes

By the end of this unit most students should be able to:

◆ explain the terms given in 'Key vocabulary' above

◆ explain three factors which affect Earth's average temperature over time

◆ explain what most scientists believe is causing global warming today

◆ explain how greenhouse gases work and describe two of them

Ideas for a starter

1 Write *Global warming* on the board. Ask students to list all the words they associate with global warming. Create a mind map of words on the board, which can be added to / amended throughout the lesson. From their list of words, students try to come up with a definition of global warming.

2 Hold up a globe. Ask: Why does Earth get warm? (Sunlight strikes the surface and is converted to heat.) Look at the graph on page 92 of the students' book. What general trend does it show? Why might that be? Write students' suggestions on the board, around a glowing Earth. Say you'll come back to them later.

3 Show a short video on global warming, at an appropriate level for your class.

4 Show pictures of different types of human activities (e.g. driving a car / an aeroplane / a bus, watching TV, washing clothes, cooking a meal, making a fire). Ask: Which of these activities relates to global warming?

Ideas for plenaries

Plan plenaries at strategic points throughout the lesson, as well as at the end.

Mid-lesson

1 Ask: What are the main gases in the atmosphere? Which ones are greenhouse gases? Why are they called greenhouse gases?

2 Revisit starter **4** and ask: Which of these activities creates the most greenhouse gases? Students rank the activities. For each activity, what could you do to reduce the amount of greenhouse gases created?

3 Students draw a diagram showing the causes of climate change, adding a title and labels to explain it.

End-of-lesson

4 Discuss: Why have developed countries been blamed for the increase in carbon dioxide in the atmosphere?

5 Students write down three questions that today's lesson has inspired them to think of.

Further class and homework opportunities

Suggestions 4–9 on page 126 of this book

geog.2 workbook, page 48

geog.2 Kerboodle: lesson presentation, worksheets, end-of-lesson assessment

Answers for 'Your turn'

1 a Global warming refers to the rise in average temperatures around the world.

b Any two of the following: changes in Earth's tilt (which affects the amount of solar rays received) and Earth's path around the Sun (which can become more elliptical and affect the amount of solar rays received) changes in the amount of energy the Sun gives out; volcanic eruptions; meteorite impact.

c Humans add two main greenhouse gases to the air – carbon dioxide and methane.

Carbon dioxide is produced when we burn coal, oil, gas, and petrol. It is taken in by trees and plants. We are producing more carbon dioxide than is being absorbed by trees and plants, and we are also cutting down trees. The excess carbon dioxide remains in the atmosphere.

Methane is produced by animals, such as cows, sheep, and goats, and is also given off from swamps, paddy fields, and landfill sites. The amount of methane is on the increase too.

The molecules in the greenhouse gases absorb the heat given out by Earth and so the average temperatures rise.

2 a We'd die without greenhouse gases, because otherwise all the heat would escape from Earth and we'd freeze.

b Greenhouse gases can harm us because they are leading to an increase in global warming (with the attendant issues).

c The two main greenhouse gases are carbon dioxide (CO_2) and methane (CH_4).

3 The Industrial Revolution saw huge changes in the manufacture of products, transport, and communication. Machines were introduced to increase production of goods and factories were built to house the new machines. Roads, railways, and canals were built to transport goods. Towns and cities grew as people moved from rural areas for work. Steam engines were introduced to power the new machines, and replaced water and horsepower. Steam was generated by burning coal. In the centuries following the Industrial Revolution we have become dependent on other fossil fuels (e.g. oil and natural gas for electricity / heating) and petrol / diesel (for running cars). Burning coal and other fossil fuels releases carbon dioxide into the atmosphere.

4 a Cars burn petrol and diesel, which produce carbon dioxide. This is one of the two main greenhouse gases and its levels are continuing to rise.

b There are a few ways in which eating less meat will help to reduce the level of greenhouse gases:

– Large areas of trees have been cleared for land to rear cattle and other animals. Trees absorb carbon dioxide and by cutting them down less carbon dioxide is absorbed from the atmosphere.

– Also, cows and other animals such as goats belch out methane and contribute to greenhouse gases.

– Meat often comes from other parts of the world. Transporting it by air or road burns fuel, which produces carbon dioxide.

Climate change

About this unit

This unit examines the effects of global warming on Earth's climates, including that of the UK.

Key points

◆ Earth's average temperature today is only about 4.5°C higher than it was in the last ice age. Therefore, a rise of just a few degrees globally may have catastrophic effects.

◆ As the temperature rises, the patterns of rainfall, wind, and ocean currents (i.e. climates) will change too. This will affect everyone:

   – Extreme weather events, such as hurricanes, will be more common.

   – Sea levels will rise, due to melting polar ice sheets and glaciers. This will cause low-lying coastal areas, even entire countries (like the Maldives, Singapore, Bangladesh, and many Pacific islands), to flood. Many of the world's major cities, such as London, Mumbai, New York and Sydney would also be at risk.

   – As rainfall patterns change, droughts will occur in some areas and floods in others, which will affect global food production at a time of rapid population growth.

   – Diseases such as malaria will spread to new regions, as places become hotter and wetter and more suitable for mosquitoes.

   – The number of environmental refugees will soar as large areas of the planet become uninhabitable.

Key vocabulary

climate, extreme weather events, ice sheets, sea levels

Skills practised in 'Your turn'

◆ Geography skills: q1, analyse a global climate change map

◆ Numeracy skills: q1, specify temperature changes

◆ Thinking skills: q2, q4, consider and evaluate some consequences of climate change to reach a reasoned conclusion; q3, evaluate statements

Unit outcomes

By the end of this unit most students should be able to:

◆ explain the terms given in 'Key vocabulary' above

◆ explain the possible implications of global warming and climate change for people around the world

◆ describe what may happen to the UK's climate if global warming continues

Ideas for a starter

1 Show students some headlines where you have removed *climate change* (e.g. _____ _____ behind extreme weather; _____ _____ threatens food supply in South Asia). Ask them to guess the missing words.

2 Display the climate graph for Frobisher Bay on page 87 of the students' book. Elicit facts about its climate from the graph. Then ask questions such as: In what months is the ground thawed out? How will a temperature rise of 5°C affect thawing? How might it affect plants? How might it affect animals?

3 Ask: What if Earth heats up? Create a mind map of students' ideas, which can be revisited and amended throughout the lesson.

Ideas for plenaries

Plan plenaries at strategic points throughout the lesson, as well as at the end.

Mid-lesson

1   Look at the map on page 94 of the students' book. Ask: Which parts of the world will be hottest / coldest in 2050? Does the class agree? (This is a trick question to make sure students understand that the map shows temperature *rise,* not *actual* temperature.) In which hemisphere / continents / countries will the temperature rise most? Least? Encourage students to use the map on pages 140–141 of the students' book to answer.

2   If you did starter **2**, ask: By how much will the temperature in Frobisher Bay rise? (Use the map on page 94 of the students' book to answer.)

3   Use 'Your turn' question 4 as a plenary.

4   Fast forward to 2050. Ask students to write a diary entry explaining what it is like living with the effects of global warming. How has the climate changed? What effect does the climate have on your day-to-day life? How do you feel about living in 2050? Is it better than now? Is it worse?

End-of-lesson

5   Ask: Can we be sure that the map on page 94 of the students' book is correct? (No. It is based on predictions. Temperature rises could be less or more.)

6   Ask: How might climate change affect the following people in the UK: company offering holidays in the UK; people living on the Norfolk coast; a skier in the Scottish Highlands?

7   Ask: What are the three most important things you've learned about climate change now and in the future?

Further class and homework opportunities

Suggestions 10–15 on pages 126–127 of this book

geog.2 workbook, page 49

geog.2 Kerboodle: lesson presentation, worksheets, end-of-lesson assessment

Answers for 'Your turn'

1   **a**   Answers will depend on students' ages.

   b   Temperature will vary across Earth. It will rise more in the northern hemisphere than the southern hemisphere.

   c   The Arctic

   d   Between 2.5 and 3°C warmer

2   Answers will vary. Ask students how they arrived at their decisions.

3   **A**   True. It may bring some benefits, such as warmer winters, but heat waves will make life unbearable in places. Millions may be forced to flee, as refugees, from disasters such as severe floods, drought, and famine. Wars over water and other resources are likely, as is the spread of disease.

   B   False. It costs a lot to cope with disasters, look after refugees, and treat diseases. People's livelihoods will be affected if crops fail or tourists stay away from places they used to visit that are now too hot. The cost of many foodstuffs, water, and other essentials is likely to rise as patterns of production and supply change. But new opportunities will open up for some people.

   C   False. Some people will feel their local climate has improved. They may be able to grow new crops where it was once too

cold. New tourist resorts will open up. Companies working on 'green energy' will flourish. So will companies selling things like fans, air conditioning, and umbrellas!

   D   False. All seas around the world are joined. So sea levels will rise everywhere. Low-lying coastal areas around the UK are at risk of being drowned.

4   **a**   **i**   More hot summer days; summer will last longer; fewer very cold winter days; summers will be drier; we will be able to grow new crops (e.g. peaches, kiwi fruit, sweetcorn); some places will attract more tourists; new breeds of birds (such as the hoopoe) are likely to breed in the UK.

   ii   Low-lying coastal areas are at risk of flooding; more extreme weather events, such as heat waves, droughts, gales, and storms; heavy downpours may cause flash floods; rivers are more likely to flood due to extreme weather events; animals and plants will have to adapt or will die out.

   b   Answers will vary. Ask students how they arrived at their decisions.

It's happening already!

help at a glance

About this unit

This unit describes some changes that are already happening as a result of global warming and climate change.

Key points

◆ Climate change is not simply some theoretical future doomsday scenario – it is happening right now (although the worst implications are yet to come).

◆ In the Arctic, which is expected to experience the highest average temperature rise by 2050 (an increase of up to 5°C), the sea ice is already melting earlier and more extensively than before. Glaciers in the Andes and the Himalayas are also melting rapidly, which has implications for the rivers they feed. These changes are already putting species like polar bears under stress, as well as causing problems for humans as agriculture and drinking water supplies are affected.

◆ Thawing permafrost in the warming Arctic region is releasing stores of methane, which adds to the level of greenhouse gases in the atmosphere and increases the rate of global warming.

◆ Droughts and floods across the world are increasing in frequency and severity. This has major implications for agriculture, which may become impossible in some areas – or require a change in the crops grown to allow for shifting rainfall patterns, e.g. growing rice (a major food crop which requires a lot of water) may no longer be possible in some countries if the monsoon rains change.

Key vocabulary

glacier, permafrost, sea ice, tundra

Skills practised in 'Your turn'

◆ Geography skills: q1, identify places and name continents; q2a, define a key term

◆ Literacy skills: q3, write a newspaper report; q4, empathise and express feelings in writing; q5, summarise key ideas in a spider diagram

◆ Thinking skills: q2b, use prior knowledge to consider and explain the implications of thawing permafrost

Unit outcomes

By the end of this unit most students should be able to:

◆ explain the terms given in 'Key vocabulary' above

◆ describe some of the changes which are currently happening as a result of climate change – and explain their implications

Ideas for a starter

1 Ask: Why is the polar bear in photo **A** on page 96 of the students' book getting better at swimming?

2 Show students two photos of a retreating glacier (perhaps one from 20 years ago and one from the last few years). Ask: What has happened? Why? What effects might this have?

3 Ask: How do we know that climate change is already happening? Show students evidence in the form of illustrations and video clips (e.g. shrinking ice sheets, extreme events, photos **B** and **C** on page 96 of the students' book). Is it happening nearer to home?

4 Ask students to write down the questions they would like answered about the effects of climate change that are already happening.

Ideas for plenaries

Plan plenaries at strategic points throughout the lesson, as well as at the end.

Mid-lesson

1   Ask students to write a newspaper caption to accompany photo **A** on page 96 of the students' book that sums up the effects of climate change on wildlife.

2   Ask: Are there any benefits to the ice melting in the Arctic (e.g. tourism, access to natural resources)?

3   Students write a song or tweet (maximum 140 characters) about the effects of global warming.

4   With books closed, ask: What things have we already seen happening to prove that climate change is real? Students answer the question as a list of bullet points based on the information from the lesson. Then they write out the bullet list again but with key words in each bullet point missing. They swap and complete the bullet points.

5   Students write an email to the United Nations explaining why we need to tackle climate change. They need to explain how climate change is affecting glaciers, ice, and sea levels, with facts and figures, and who is being affected and why.

End-of-lesson

6   Read out some newspaper headlines about the current effects of global warming, some containing facts and others opinions. Ask students to raise their left hand if a headline contains facts, right hand for opinions. Explain the difference between fact and opinion. Ask: Why is this important to geographers when looking at the effects of climate change?

7   Use 'Your turn' question 5 as a plenary activity.

8   Give students 30 seconds to draw a picture that summarises today's lesson.

9   Ask: What new facts have you learned today? Are there any facts that have stuck in your head?

Further class and homework opportunities

Suggestions 16–19 on page 127 of this book

geog.2 workbook, page 50

geog.2 Kerboodle: lesson presentation, worksheets, end-of-lesson assessment

Answers for 'Your turn'

1   **A, B and C** North America; **D** South America; **E** Africa; **F** Asia; **G** Oceania; **H** Europe

2   **a**   Where the ground under the surface is permanently frozen in regions of tundra.

    b   Methane, which is a greenhouse gas, is trapped inside permafrost. As the permafrost melts the methane will be released into the atmosphere.

3   Answers will vary.

4   **a** and **b**   Answers will vary, but may include: polar bear (worried about starving; tired or fitter because they are having to swim further for food); Brown Argus butterfly (excited to be living in a new area; nervous about finding possible new sources of food).

5   Answers may include:

On people: loss of property and possessions due to flooding; drought leading to water shortages; famine leading to death; increased risk of disease; increasing food prices; new types of food to eat; more refugees.

On wildlife; loss of habitats for breeding and feeding; changing seasonal patterns with things hatching / flowering at different times; adaptation of species; extinction of certain species; new species of plants and animals in different places.

On the physical world; changing rainfall patterns; more extreme weather events (heat waves, droughts, storms, flooding); desertification; melting ice sheets and glaciers; melting permafrost and release of methane; changing seasons; changing temperatures.

Who will suffer most?

About this unit

This unit explores who is most to blame for the global-warming problem, and who will suffer the most.

Key points

- The world's richest countries, particularly in Europe and North America, have released the most greenhouse gases into the atmosphere since the Industrial Revolution began. This is because those countries are the ones which industrialised first.

- In recent decades, developing countries like China have begun to industrialise rapidly, which has greatly increased their greenhouse gas emissions. However, these countries argue that they should be allowed to industrialise and develop, just as Europe and the USA did in the nineteenth century, and not have to pay the penalty for others' actions in the past.

- The difficulty is that those countries that will suffer the most from the climate change caused by global warming are the poorer countries of Africa and Asia – those that are least able to deal with the fallout, both in terms of finance and infrastructure. And these countries have had very little to do with causing the problem, because they generate low amounts of greenhouse gases per person.

Key vocabulary

the term 'local actions, global effects'

Skills practised in 'Your turn'

- Geography skills: q3, analyse a bar graph
- Numeracy skills: q3, make calculations based on graph data
- Literacy skills: q4, complete written explanations
- Thinking skills: q1–q2 consider personal responsibility for global warming; q3, use common sense and prior knowledge to provide reasoned explanations

Unit outcomes

By the end of this unit most students should be able to:

- explain the term given in 'Key vocabulary' above
- explain why and how the world's richer countries have had the most to do with causing global warming
- explain why the world's poorer countries will suffer the most from climate change

Ideas for a starter

1. Ask students to draw a room in their house from memory. They should include everything in the room that uses energy. Ask: How many things in the room use energy? What are they? Collate this information for the whole class. Who uses the most energy? Who uses the least energy?

2. Write *carbon footprint* on the board. Ask: Does anyone know what this means? Students calculate their carbon footprint using an online calculator. Is it likely to be greater or less than a person from a less-developed country? Why?

3. Divide the class into two groups. One group draws some of the consequences of climate change. The other group has to guess what they are drawing.

Ideas for plenaries

Plan plenaries at strategic points throughout the lesson, as well as at the end.

Mid-lesson

1   Ask: Do you think there is a link between the wealth of a country and the amount of carbon dioxide it produces per person? Take a show of hands.

Show a world map of GDP per capita on the whiteboard. Students work in pairs or small groups to compare the map with the chart on page 98 of the students' book. They report back their findings, and try to explain them.

2   Write on the board: *'The poorest countries will suffer earliest and most, even though they have contributed least to the causes of climate change.'* (from Sir Nicholas Stern, 2007) Ask: What do you think this means? Why do you think that less developed countries will suffer the most?

3   Students make a 60-second news bulletin about 'local actions, global effects'. Encourage them to use different headlines (e.g. factual / informative, sensational / attention grabbing). They sketch a storyboard for the content / ideas that they will cover.

End-of-lesson

4   Students create a comic strip summarising a key idea / concept they have learned in today's lesson. The comic strip should contain speech bubbles.

5   Ask: What really made you think in today's lesson? Which fact / statistic challenged your thinking? Was there anything that you struggled to make sense of?

6   Say: We have now looked at the causes and effects of global warming and who will be affected the most. What do you think we will look at next lesson?

Further class and homework opportunities

Suggestions 20–25 on page 127 of this book

geog.2 workbook, page 51

geog.2 Kerboodle: lesson presentation, worksheets, end-of-lesson assessment

Answers for 'Your turn'

1 a Answers will vary.

   b Make sure students have looked carefully at the diagram on page 98 of the students' book before they do this.

   c Make sure they understand that fossil fuel is burned on the spot for some things (e.g. in a gas cooker, in a car engine), but it is burned in a power station to produce energy.

2 Students will probably decide that they depend quite heavily on fossil fuels.

3 a The USA. This is one of the world's top ten wealthiest countries and is highly developed. It has many power stations, factories, and a huge number of cars. Homes have many electrical goods (freezers, dishwashers, tumble dryers, air conditioners, TVs, computers, etc.) so electricity consumption is high. There's also gas central heating. So, overall a huge amount of carbon dioxide is produced, giving a high average per person.

   b Ghana. It is a poor country compared with the USA. There are not many factories or power stations. Car ownership is very low. Millions of people don't have electricity and depend on firewood for cooking. Most homes have few or no mod cons so the total amount of carbon dioxide produced is low, giving a low average per person.

   c About eight times as much. (India produced nearly 1 tonne per person and the UK 8 tonnes per person.)

   d i About 9450 million tonnes (or 9.45 billion).

     ii About 512 million tonnes.

4 a 'Local actions, global effects' means that things we do locally can affect people all over the world.

   b The burning of fossil fuels is an example of 'Local actions, global effects' because the carbon dioxide generated from burning fossil fuels in one place leads to climate change everywhere.

So what can we do?

About this unit

This unit explains that global warming cannot be stopped – but it could be limited. It then goes on to consider several options.

Key points

◆ Global warming cannot be stopped – whether it's completely naturally occurring, or due to human actions that are leading to increased levels of greenhouse gases in the atmosphere. Even if we stopped generating carbon dioxide today, the amount of extra carbon dioxide already in the atmosphere will last for at least 100 years.

◆ However, if we can't stop it, we could at least limit future temperature rises by cutting back on greenhouse gas emissions from now on. Plus also work out ways to adapt effectively to the climate change already happening.

◆ The problem is the reluctance from many national governments – all the way down to individual citizens – to accept the urgency of the problem and the need to do anything tangible about it. Governments are reluctant to annoy their electorates by imposing restrictions on them in terms of greenhouse gas emissions, or raising prices by adding green taxes.

Key vocabulary

emissions

Skills practised in 'Your turn'

◆ Geography skills: q1, define a key term; q1, analyse an emissions graph

◆ Literacy skills: q3, write reasons; q6, write an action list

◆ Thinking skills: q1, evaluate the accuracy of statements, with evidence; q2, give a reasoned explanation; q3, evaluate options and reach reasoned conclusions; q4, explain a statement; q5, sort and assess possible actions

Unit outcomes

By the end of this unit most students should be able to:

◆ explain the term given in 'Key vocabulary' above

◆ explain what could and could not be done to address global warming

◆ explain the problems involved in agreeing effective action

Ideas for a starter

1 Display pictures of the causes of climate change (e.g. cars, lights, a landfill site, a power station). Ask: What do these pictures show? Can you suggest any other causes? Ask students to think of an alternative for each picture / cause that has less impact on climate change.

2 Show students a set of images of things that burn fuel (e.g. cars, buses, a Formula One race, a power station, a factory chimney, a person cooking on a gas stove, a person cooking with firewood). Add in a couple of photos of things that don't burn fuel / use renewable energy (e.g. a wind-up radio, a solar panel, a bicycle). Ask: Which is / are the odd one(s) out? Why?

3 With books closed, display the upper left photo from page 101 of the students' book. Ask students what they think it's about. What are emissions?

4 One or more students read(s) out the report on page 100 of the students' book.

Ideas for plenaries

Plan plenaries at strategic points throughout the lesson, as well as at the end.

Mid-lesson

1   Ask: How can we reduce our carbon dioxide emissions? Students draw a spider diagram with these legs: saving energy; renewable energy; recycling; individual people; governments. Students should add ideas to each leg, e.g.: cutting down on flights; reducing packaging.

2   Split the class into groups. For one of the following categories, each group thinks of ideas of how they can adapt to combat climate change: home; school; travel and holidays; other activities. Each group presents their ideas to the rest of the class. Take a vote on which are the most important.

End-of-lesson

3   Students think of an object that they use on a daily basis. Working in pairs, they decide how they might redesign it to reduce the impact on global warming.

4   Read out the following statement: Climate has changed between warmer and colder phases throughout the history of Earth. It will continue to do so. Ask: Do we need to worry about levels of carbon dioxide emissions if the climate is going to change anyway? Why? Discuss as a whole class.

Further class and homework opportunities

Suggestions 26–33 on page 127 of this book

geog.2 workbook, page 52

geog.2 Kerboodle: lesson presentation, worksheets, end-of-lesson assessment

Answers for 'Your turn'

1   a   Waste gases and particles emitted from power stations, car exhausts, and so on.

   b   i True. The line on the graph is rising steeply.

   ii True. They have been rising more steeply than ever since 2000.

   iii False. Seven times more carbon dioxide was emitted in 2010 than in 1950. In 1950 just over 5 billion tonnes were emitted and in 2010 it was just over 35 tonnes.

2   All three contribute to the rise in emissions, as explained below.

   a   More people means more fuel used (including electricity) for cooking, washing, pumping water, lighting homes, and transport. More power is used in factories to make goods.

   b   As poor countries develop and get wealthier, people want to buy things like cars, washing machines, fridge freezers. So, more fossil fuels are burned in producing and using the extra goods. The total amount of carbon dioxide the country produces rises.

   c   When flights get cheaper, more people fly off on holiday, including short breaks, so the number of flights increases. Aviation fuel (kerosene) produces carbon dioxide when it burns so total carbon dioxide emissions from air travel increase.

3   Answers will vary. Encourage class discussion for **3 c ii**.

4   Governments want to remain popular with people and businesses to retain their vote. If they restrict the use of fuel they will make people who live there and businesses unhappy. Restricting fuel use will mean that people can't heat their houses as much, use their washing machines (for example) as much, or travel when they want / need to. Restricting fuel use for business will mean that businesses can't produce as much and it won't be as easy to transport goods to customers. This would not only affect the profits of the company but also the economy of the country (e.g. through less tax paid to the government).

5   a   Option A: no action for this option

       Option B: 2, 8, 12

       Option C: 1, 3, 4, 5, 7, 10

       Option D: 11

       Option E: 6, 9

   b   i 2, 6, 8, 11; ii 1, 4, 5, 7, 8, 9, 10, 11, 12 (If a method of burying carbon dioxide was developed, putting it into practice would need government permission. Planning laws would need to be put into place stating that all new homes need to be built in a way to keep out floods. Putting giant mirrors into space would need international agreement as would paying countries to protect their rainforests.)

   c   Answers will vary, but 3 and 5 are good candidates.

   d   Responses will vary.

6   Students could work together to agree a class list for this.

Many of these suggestions are addressed to your students. Where research or further resources are needed, the internet will almost certainly provide the answer.

The suggestions are graded *,**,*** according to level of difficulty. Some are suitable for all levels, and can be differentiated by outcome.

Earth's temperatures through the ages

1 **Earth's temperature timeline** Create a timeline to show how Earth's temperature has changed. Put these dates and events in the correct place on the timeline.

Time (years ago)	Event
4.5 billion	Earth was formed
650 million	Snowball Earth
65 million	Dinosaurs became extinct
110 000	Last ice age began/People left Britain for warmer parts of Europe
20 000	Peak of last ice age
11 000	People returned to Britain
10 000	Ice age ended
2000	Warm period during the Roman Empire
1000	Medieval Warm Period
0 (today)	Temperature is rising

/*

2 **Past temperatures** Scientists can tell a lot about past temperatures by studying things like:
   – sediment from deep in the floors of oceans and lakes
   – ice from deep in the ice sheets of Antarctica and Greenland
   – tree rings in the wood of ancient trees.

   Choose one method. How can it be used to tell us about past temperatures? You might need to do some research. Create a bright, interesting poster to explain to a non-scientist how we can learn about past temperatures. **

3 **Imagine** Instead of the temperature warming, imagine that it is cooling, and that we are heading for another ice age. What does that mean? How cold will it get? How far will the ice reach? Will we still be able to live in the UK? Write an online news article telling people what to expect. */**

Global warming

4 **Good greenhouse gases** We could not survive without greenhouse gases. Without them the Earth would be about 33°C cooler, with the average temperature about −18°C instead of around 15°C. Write a story set in a world where the level of greenhouses gases is falling very fast. **/***

5 **Greenhouse gas display** Create a wall display about greenhouse gases and how they work. Add notes giving the names of the main greenhouse gases, and where they come from. Don't forget how they help us (see above) */**/***

6 **Greenhouse gases – animated** Do an internet search for *greenhouse gas animation*. Select an animation that's an appropriate level for your class, and show it. Or you could let students review them and choose the one they think is clearest. */**/***

7 **Global warming causes** Work in a small group. Some people think that global warming is due to natural causes and others think humans are to blame. Write the headings *Natural* and *Human* on a large sheet of paper. In your group add ideas below each heading. Then take a vote. Do most people think global warming is natural, or do most think that human actions are to blame? */**

8 **Global warming survey** Design a questionnaire – at least five questions – to find out about people's attitudes to global warming. For example, you could enquire how much they think they know about it, whether they believe we humans cause it, and what they are prepared to do about it, if anything. Would it be best to ask people of different ages? Would it be useful to records their ages?

   Carry out the survey. The class groups the results, finds an interesting way to display them, and presents their overall conclusions. Are these surprising? Discuss. */**/***

9 **Dissension** Some scientists still think that global warming is mostly natural. Find out more about the possible natural causes mentioned on page 92 of the students' book (changes in the Earth's tilt and its path around the Sun, changes in the amount of energy the Sun gives out). Do a presentation to the class, or write a double-page spread like the units in the students' book. Work in groups? ***

Climate change

10 **Spring comes early** One sign of climate change in the UK is that spring is already coming earlier. Find out more and tell the class. ***

11 **Today's climate news** What are they saying about climate change around the world today? Working in groups, students access a range of major newspaper websites. (One or two per group?) For example, The Times, Guardian or Independent, Times of India, China Daily. They look for news items about climate change, choose one, and present it to the class in an appropriate form, e.g. reading it aloud. **

12 **Heat wave** It's predicted that there will be more heat waves, as a consequence of global warming. Good news? Research the heat wave in France in 2003 when nearly 15 000 people died. Write a report *in your own words*. */**/***

13 **Wars over water** Wars over water are predicted, thanks to a combination of population growth and global warming. The trouble spots will be where countries share a river. It's estimated that 40% of the world's population lives in shared river basins. Over 200 rivers around the world are shared by two or more countries. And 50% of Africa's land is in shared river basins.

   Using atlases students identify say, five big rivers that are shared by countries. They mark in and label the rivers, and shade and label the countries, on an outline world map. Around the map they add information about each country:

its population, its population growth rate, its wealth in terms of GDP per capita, a description of its climate today (from the atlas or the map of world climate regions on page 86 of the students' book), and the predicted temperature rise by 2050 (from the map on page 94 of the students' book).

In which one of those places might conflict be most likely? Students should give reasons for their choice. ***

14 **Forest fires** When places get hot and dry, forest fires are a big risk. Research a recent forest fire – in Australia for example, and create an illustrated page about it or a PowerPoint presentation. Don't forget a map. And note: *you must use your own words* and *create your own map*. **

15 **An enquiry** Working in a group, choose one predicted consequence of global warming from page 94 of the students' book. Agree on an enquiry question about it, and carry out the enquiry. Each group should choose a different prediction. **/***

It's happening already!

16 **Tuvalu under water** It's the year 2100, and the water is rising. Soon Tuvalu will have disappeared under the waves. Most of the islanders have left and you are one of the last residents remaining. What are your thoughts and feelings? What has caused this disaster and who is to blame? Write a poem or a song to express your views. */**

17 **More change?** The examples included in the students' book on pages 96–97 are just a fraction of the changes already talking place around the world as a result of climate change. What else is happening? Find out. Produce a poster or a presentation of your findings. Aim to shock the world into taking action to combat climate change with your poster or presentation. **/***

18 **The polar bear's story** Imagine you are the polar bear in the photo on page 96 of the students' book. You are losing weight and are in pretty bad shape. What is happening to the ice? Why is that important? Where is your next meal coming from? Tell us your story. **

19 **Methane** You live in Alaska, in the tundra (check the map on page 96 of the students' book – it's location B). The permafrost is thawing. And as it does it is releasing methane. Why does that matter? Explain. ***

Who will suffer most?

20 **Fossil fuels** They are the main fuels used around the world today. So what are fossil fuels? How were they formed? Find out and present your answers as strips of labelled drawings, with text below. **

21 **It's electric!** Most of our electricity in the UK comes from burning fossil fuels. Find out how it is generated, using fossil fuels, and tell the rest of the class. **

22 **Dependent on …** fossil fuels. Take photos to show how dependent you, or your local area is on fossil fuels. Create a display, with a caption for each photo. (Remember: most electricity is generated by burning fossil fuels.) **

23 **In the grip of fossil fuels** The first settlers in Britain depended on wood for fuel. Now we depend mainly on fossil fuels. Find a low aerial shot of a British town (*Google images?*), stick it on a larger sheet of paper, and annotate it to show how dependent our settlements are on burning fossil fuels directly (for transport, oil and gas heating, gas cooking) and indirectly (for electricity). **

24 **A link between carbon dioxide production and GDP per capita?** Challenge students to find a way to use maps and map overlays (or GIS) to check for a link between the carbon dioxide production per capita of different countries, and their GDP per capita – and explain their findings. Students might find suitable maps in their atlases or on the internet. (Any maps they use must match in terms of projection and scale). ***

25 **It's not fair** Richer countries produce by far the most carbon dioxide per capita. The resulting global warming affects poorer countries who may find it hard to cope. Draw a satirical cartoon for a magazine to show how unfair this is. ***

So what can we do?

26 **Saved by giant plants** The world is taken over by giant plants, that scientists developed to gobble up carbon dioxide. So, no more global warming! But there is a terrible price to pay! Tell us the story. */**/***

27 **A low energy home** Working in small groups, design an energy-efficient house. Display the results on the wall. **/***

28 **Saving energy at school** Working in small groups, do an energy audit of your school. Is energy being wasted? Where? What can be done about it? The class prepares a report and action plan. */**/***

29 **A 'save energy' campaign** Working in groups, brainstorm ideas for a campaign to get everyone in school to save energy. Think about slogans and logos too. The class pools ideas, selects the best, and works in groups to develop a display. Show it in a prominent place in the school? */**/***

30 **Prepare an assembly …** based on the work in the activity above to present to the rest of the school. ***

31 **Letter from your great-great-granddaughter** Write a letter from the future to you, as if from your great-great-granddaughter. She tells you about life in a warmer world, and asks why you people did not do more to tackle global warming while there was still time. */**/***

32 **So what can we do to get ready?** What can we do to get ready for global warming? How could we help poorer countries get ready? Brainstorm ideas. **/***

33 **Where have the politicians got to?** Governments must work together to tackle global warming. Why? How far have they got? Find out (from TV, newspapers, the internet?) and tell us. ***

About this chapter

Addressing the KS3 Programme of Study

◆ Develop knowledge of Asia, and its physical and human characteristics.

◆ Interpret maps, graphs and photos.

◆ Communicate geographical information, including through writing at length.

About the content

◆ This chapter opens with a unit on the continents, with the main focus on Asia. This helps to set Asia in its world context, before moving on to its countries and main regions.

◆ Unit 7.3 outlines Asia's history up to independence from colonisation, as useful background to its human geography today.

◆ Later units explore Asia's physical features, population density, and biomes through atlas-style maps.

The big picture

These are the key ideas in this chapter.

◆ Asia is the world's biggest continent, by both area and population.

◆ It is home to 60% of the world's population (4.3 billion people).

◆ It sits on the same landmass as Europe; five countries lie partly in Asia and partly in Europe, including Russia.

◆ Asia has 49 countries.

◆ China and India have 2.7 billion people between them!

A students' version of this big picture is given in the *geog.2* students' book opener for Chapter 7.

The chapter outline

Use this, and their chapter opener, to give students a mental roadmap for the chapter.

7   Asia The chapter opener in the students' book is an important part of the chapter; see page 11 for notes about using chapter openers

7.1 What and where is Asia? Compares Asia with other continents (area and population) and establishes its global position

7.2 Asia's countries and regions Identifies Asia's regions, countries, and their capital cities

7.3 A little history The history of Asia, and links and conflicts with Europe and Britain, from trade to colonisation to independence

7.4 What's Asia like? The range of peoples, cultures, levels of affluence, and economies of modern Asia

7.5 Asia's physical features The locations of Asia's key physical features, using a map and satellite image

7.6 Asia's population Population densities across Asia, using a map and bar chart

7.7 Asia's biomes Characteristics and locations of eight biomes across Asia, introducing the idea that biomes are affected by humans

Objectives and outcomes for this chapter

Objectives	Unit	Outcomes
Most students will understand:		Most students will be able to:
• that Asia is one of the world's seven continents, and where it is located	7.1	• describe the location and relative size of Asia; compare its population with other continents
• what physical features form the border between Asia and Europe, and that some countries straddle the border	7.1, 7.2	• describe the physical features along the border between Asia and Europe; identify two countries that straddle the border
• the difference between a continent and a country	7.1	• explain the difference between a continent and a country
• that Asia has 49 countries in 6 main regions	7.1, 7.2	• name and locate Asian countries and regions; locate various capital cities in Asia
• that Asia has a long history of great empires and civilisations	7.3	• recall key information about Asia's history
• that Asia's past was linked with Europe, through religion, trade, and colonisation	7.3	• explain why European traders traded with Asia; identify various countries in Asia colonised by European countries
• that Asia has more peoples, cultures, climates, and human environments than any other continent	7.4	• identify a range of different physical and human characteristics across Asia
• how GDP (PPP) is used to measure and compare economies	7.4	• compare the GDP per person (PPP) of various Asian countries
• where Asia's major physical features are located	7.5	• name, identify the location of, and describe major plateaus, rivers, mountain ranges, surface waters, and deserts in Asia
• that population density varies across Asia	7.6	• describe and compare the distribution of population across Asia
• that Asia has a wide range of biomes	7.7	• explain why Asia has a range of biomes; identify eight biomes in Asia and countries within each

These tie in with the outcomes for each unit, in this teacher's handbook, and with 'Your goals for this chapter', in *geog.2* students' book.

Opportunities for assessment

See the formal assessment materials for this chapter on *geog.2 Kerboodle Lessons, Resources, & Assessment*. They include an extended assessment task, an exam-style question, end-of-lesson assessments, and a self-assessment form. See also the notes on pages 14–15 of this book.

Getting ready for this chapter

geog.2 Kerboodle contains plans and presentations for each unit, including interactive activities, animations, and worksheets.

About 'Your chapter starter'

The satellite image on page 102 of *geog.2* students' book, dramatically shows those areas of Asia with sufficient rainfall to support vegetation (the green areas) and those which are either too dry, or too cold, or high, to support much vegetation (the sand-coloured areas). The dark curve in the middle of the image is the world's highest mountain range – the Himalayas – home to Mt Everest, the world's highest mountain (8848 m).

Try to ensure students can locate and name the Arctic, Pacific and Indian Oceans, and some of the seas which surround Asia – check the map on p112 of the students' book.

Although the image shows Asia, it also shows much of Europe, part of Oceania and Africa, and even North America.

What and where is Asia?

About this unit

This unit uses two maps to introduce students to the location and boundaries of Asia, before comparing it with the other six continents.

Key points

- The world has seven continents, of which Asia is one.

- Asia has land borders with three other continents: Europe, Africa and Oceania.

- Asia is the world's largest continent by both land area and population. It holds over 60% of the world's population in just 30% of the land area. The two most populous countries on Earth are both in Asia – China (1.36 billion) and India (1.24 billion).

Key vocabulary

border, continent, country, Eurasia

Skills practised in 'Your turn'

- Geography skills: q3, analyse map data; q6, explain key terms

- Numeracy skills: q1, q2, interpret bar and pie charts

- Literacy skills: q4, q5, write a short description (paragraph); q7 compile a spider diagram to summarise

- Thinking skills: q3c, apply understanding to make and explain choices; q4b, interpret map information to reach a conclusion

Unit outcomes

By the end of this unit most students should be able to:

- explain the terms given in 'Key vocabulary' above

- state that Asia is one of the world's seven continents

- describe where Asia is, relative to the other continents, and point it out on a world map

- discuss and explain Asia's borders with other continents

- state that Asia is the world's largest continent by both land area and population

Ideas for a starter

1 With books closed, ask: How many continents can you name?

2 With books closed, give each student an outline map of the world with Asia marked on it. Ask them to write or draw anything they already know about Asia on their map, add their name, and hand it in. Students may have a variety of views about the continent. Use this knowledge to help you broaden their perceptions as the units progress. Repeat the exercise at the very end of the chapter and compare the results.

3 On the board, write *Asia*. Ask students what they already know about Asia in terms of its location, places, people, climates, landscapes, animals, and so on.

4 Discuss: Where in the world is Asia?

5 Ask: What is the capital of Asia? Draw out what is wrong with this question. If necessary, explain that Asia is not a country but a continent of many countries. Ask: Which countries in Asia do you know of? Make a list.

Ideas for plenaries

Plan plenaries for strategic points throughout the lesson, as well as at the end.

Mid-lesson

1 Ask: How much of Asia is north of the Equator? How much of it is north of the Arctic Circle? Which continent is Asia furthest from?

2 Look at map B on p104 of the students' book. Ask students to describe the route of the border between Europe and Asia. Does it seem strange that part of Russia is in Europe, but most of it is in Asia?

End-of-lesson

3 Give students an outline map of the world. Ask them to shade in Asia, and mark in the Equator, the Tropics of Cancer and Capricorn, and the oceans.

4 Ask: What would you like to know about Asia?

5 Ask: How many times do you think the British Isles would fit into the continent of Asia? Have a guess! (Answer = 148.7 times.)

6 Display a range of photos of different places in one Asian country that may not match stereotypes. Ask: Which photos are from your chosen country? Explain that they all are. Explore which images surprised students, and why. Recap on the meaning of *stereotype*. Ask: How can you ensure that your views of other parts of the world are not based on stereotypes?

Further class and homework opportunities

Suggestions 1–6 on page 144 of this book

geog.2 workbook, page 54

geog.2 Kerboodle: lesson presentation, worksheets, end-of-lesson assessment

Answers to 'Your turn'

1 A True; B True; C False (Asia is over four times the size of Europe.)

2 A True; B True; C False (There are seven and a half times more people in Asia than in North America.)

3 a Yes

b Yes: Arctic Circle, Tropic of Cancer

c i P. It lies north of the Arctic Circle and is the place furthest from the Equator, so it will be very cold. It will have little or no daylight in winter, due to its latitude.

ii R. It's almost on the Equator and so will have an equatorial type climate – hot and wet all year. Tropical rainforests grow in this type of climate.

4 a Students' paragraphs should mention that the Arctic Ocean lies off Asia's north coast, the Pacific Ocean lies to the east, and the Indian Ocean lies to the south of Asia. Students must include the names of the oceans and also *coast, north, south*, and *east*.

b The west coast of North America.

5 Students' paragraphs should describe the route of the border between Asia and Europe from the *Arctic Ocean* in the north, south to the *Caspian Sea*, following the *Ural Mountains*. The border between the continents also links the Caspian Sea and the *Black Sea*. The Bosporus forms part of the border between Europe and Asia, connecting the Black Sea and the *Mediterranean Sea*. Students should include the words in italics in their paragraphs.

6 a A continent is a large landmass, plus its associated islands. A continent is divided up into political entities called countries. (Antarctica is an exception: although seven countries lay claim to it, it is not officially divided up.)

b Students could check their list of countries against the map on page 106 in the students' book. You could ask who came up with the most countries.

7 Spider map headings should include: Population, Size and location, Countries, Physical features, Biomes. Encourage students to use their prior knowledge to add notes.

About this unit

This unit explores Asia's countries, capital cities and regions.

Key points

- There are 49 countries in Asia today.
- Asia consists of six regions: West (usually called the Middle East), Central, North, East, South, and Southeast Asia.
- Asia extends from above the Arctic Circle to below the Equator.
- The largest countries in Asia are Russia and China. Russia's land area is 17 098 242 sq km (but that includes European Russia). It is the largest country in the world. China is the fourth largest country in the world, at 9 984 670 sq km, but it has the largest population.
- The smallest country in Asia is the Maldives (at just 298 sq km).
- Asia borders three oceans: Arctic, Pacific, and Indian.

Key vocabulary

(No new vocabulary)

Skills practised in 'Your turn'

- Geography skills: q1–q5, q7–q8, analyse maps
- Thinking skills: q6, reach a conclusion and explain the reasoning

Unit outcomes

By the end of this unit most students should be able to:

- name at least 12 Asian countries and their capitals, and say roughly where in Asia they are (e.g. in Southeast Asia)
- name the six Asian regions
- name and locate on a map the largest and smallest countries in Asia

Ideas for a starter

1 With books closed, ask: How many Asian countries can you name? List them on the board. When no one can think of any others, say: Now turn to page 106 of the students' book.

2 With books closed, write up the names of some Asian countries – but all jumbled up. Who will be the first to unjumble them?

3 Display photographs or play film clips from several Asian countries to give an overview of their diversity (e.g. search online for *'7 billion others'* – interviews with people from around the world).

Ideas for plenaries

Plan plenaries for strategic points throughout the lesson, as well as at the end.

Mid-lesson

1   Display the outline of several Asian countries. Ask students to identify them from the shape, or locate them on the map. Ask: What are the neighbouring countries? How many landlocked countries are there on the Asian continent?

2   Ask: Why are countries in Asia such different sizes? Is it to do with physical or human factors? Do countries change in size, for example for political reasons? Can students come up with any recent examples of countries changing in size?

End-of-lesson

3   Ask: Which country in Asia would you most like to visit and why?

4   Ask students to complete these sentences about this unit:

–   The most interesting thing I found out was …

–   I was surprised to learn that …

–   I would like to know more about …

Further class and homework opportunities

Suggestions 7–14 on page 144 of this book

geog.2 workbook, page 55

geog.2 Kerboodle: lesson presentation, worksheets, end-of-lesson assessment

Answers to 'Your turn'

1   a   Mongolia

  b   Japan

  c   Russia

  d   India

  e   Indonesia

  f   Myanmar

  g   Singapore

  h   North Korea and South Korea

  i   Iraq

2   a   M: Mongolia, Maldives, Myanmar, Malaysia

  b   P: Pakistan, The Philippines

  c   I: Iran, Iraq, India, Indonesia, Israel

  d   T: Thailand, Turkmenistan, Tajikistan, Turkey, Taiwan, (East) Timor

3   a   Riyadh (Saudi Arabia)

  b   Jakarta (Indonesia)

  c   New Delhi (India)

  d   Kabul (Afghanistan)

  e   Hanoi (Vietnam)

  f   Beijing (China)

  g   Pyongyang (North Korea)

  h   Kuala Lumpur (Malaysia)

  i   Moscow (Russia)

  j   Manila (The Philippines)

  k   Islamabad (Pakistan)

  l   Ulan Bator (Mongolia)

4   a   The ten most obvious countries are: Russia, China, India, Saudi Arabia, Indonesia, Kazakhstan, Iran, Pakistan, Mongolia, Turkey.

  b   Ten possible suggestions from across the continent are: Singapore, Maldives, Sri Lanka, South Korea, Brunei, Taiwan, Bhutan, Qatar, Israel, Armenia.

5   a   Five from: Kazakhstan, Afghanistan, Uzbekistan, Tajikistan, Kyrgyzstan, Turkmenistan.

  b   Four from: India, Pakistan, Sri Lanka, Maldives, Bangladesh, Bhutan, Nepal.

  c   Russia

  d   Five from: Turkey, Georgia, Armenia, Azerbaijan, Lebanon, Syria, Israel, Iraq, Iran, Kuwait, Bahrain, Qatar, Saudi Arabia, Yemen Republic, Oman, United Arab Emirates, Jordan.

  e   Five from: China, Mongolia, North Korea, South Korea, Taiwan, Japan.

  f   Five from: Myanmar, Laos, Thailand, Cambodia, Vietnam, Malaysia, Indonesia, Singapore, East Timor, Brunei, The Philippines.

6   Answers will vary.

7   Two from: Russia, Kazakhstan, Turkey.

8   a   Russia

  b   Yemen, Maldives, Sri Lanka, Thailand, Laos, Vietnam, Cambodia, Malaysia, Singapore, Indonesia, Brunei, The Philippines, East Timor

A little history

About this unit

This unit provides some basic information about Asian history, with an emphasis on historical and trading contacts between Asia and Europe.

Key points

◆ Asia has a long history of great civilisations and empires.

◆ It played a crucial role in the birth of all of the world's major religions.

◆ Connections between Asia and Europe were founded on trade and its control.

◆ The Silk Road was the first route by which Asian goods, such as silk and spices, reached Europe.

◆ After trade via the Silk Road ended, trade by sea took over and led eventually to (mostly European) colonisation of much of southern Asia.

◆ As in Africa, the Asian colonies mostly gained independence after the end of the Second World War, because their colonisers were left too economically and militarily weak to maintain control over such huge areas and large populations on the other side of the world, once demands for independence began to grow.

◆ Now it is the countries of Asia, particularly China and India, that control much of the world's trade. China is expected to take over from the USA as the world's most powerful economy within 20 years (China's economic growth rate was 7.7% in 2013) and India is growing rapidly too.

Key vocabulary

colonisation, colony, empire, independence, trade

Skills practised in 'Your turn'

◆ Geography skills: q4a, define a key term; q1b, q4b–q4d, analyse a map

◆ Thinking skills: q2a, empathy and imagination; q2b, q3, explain and reason

Unit outcomes

By the end of this unit most students should be able to:

◆ explain the terms given in 'Key vocabulary' above

◆ name and roughly locate at least one ancient Asian civilisation or empire

◆ explain the place of Asia in major world religions

◆ describe what the Silk Road was

◆ state that a number of (mostly European) countries colonised much of southern Asia – plus name several colonised countries and the country / countries that colonised them

◆ explain the link between colonisation and trade

Ideas for a starter

1 Recap on Asia's vital statistics. See if students can remember key facts about Asia, such as: it's the largest continent, by both population and area; it has 49 countries; it is divided into 6 regions.

2 Ask: Who has heard of Genghis Khan? Where was he from? When did he live? Why was he famous? Tease out information, giving students clues if necessary.

3 Show students the image of people making silk in China from p108 of the students' book. Ask: Which country is shown in the image? What are these people doing? What will happen to the product they are making?

Ideas for plenaries

Plan plenaries for strategic points throughout the lesson, as well as at the end.

Mid-lesson

1 Create a labelled timeline of Asia's history.

2 Explore the map of the Mongol Empire at its peak. Ask students to describe the size and extent of the empire. Why would the Mongols want to protect the Silk Road?

3 Use 'Your turn' question 3 as a mid-lesson plenary. Why wouldn't China want other countries to make silk?

4 Ask: Why does Genghis Khan's portrait still appear on Mongolian banknotes, nearly 800 years after his death?

End-of-lesson

5 Use 'Your turn' question 4 as a plenary. Prompt forward thinking: What consequences or results of colonisation might still be apparent in these Asian countries today?

6 Ask: Does any one country have a right to colonise another?

7 Write a set of statements on the board in a jumbled up order, giving events in Asia's history. Include, for example: *The rise and decline of the Indus Valley civilisation, The start of trade along the Silk Road, The first Portuguese traders arrive.* Ask students to arrange them in chronological order.

Further class and homework opportunities

Suggestions 15–18 on page 144 of this book

geog.2 workbook, page 56

geog.2 Kerboodle: lesson presentation, worksheets, end-of-lesson assessment

Answers to 'Your turn'

1 a Genghis Khan was the founder of the Mongol Empire. It grew to cover a large area of Asia. It lasted for about 160 years from 1206–1368.

  b Three from: China, Mongolia, North and South Korea, Iran, Iraq, Afghanistan, Turkmenistan, Tajikistan, Kyrgyzstan, Uzbekistan, Kazakhstan, Armenia, Georgia, Azerbaijan, Pakistan, Russia, Turkey.

2 a Answers will vary, but may include: extreme climatic conditions, both in winter (cold and snow) and summer (heat and drought); difficult terrain from deserts to mountains; bandits and robbers; local rulers demanding bribes and 'taxes' to allow free passage; damage to fragile goods, such as porcelain; illness and disease experienced by both traders and pack animals; the massive distances involved and the time it took to travel by pack animal from China to the Mediterranean.

  b The Silk Road provided a source of luxury goods, such as silk and spices, which were otherwise unavailable in Europe. These goods were desirable in Europe as symbols of wealth and status.

3 China wanted to maintain a monopoly over the lucrative silk trade. If other countries got hold of silkworms and began producing the cloth too, then as well as China losing trade and wealth, the fact that more silk was being produced elsewhere would make it more common and less valuable.

4 a A colony is a country or area which is partly or completely under the political control of another country and is occupied by settlers from that country.

  b Three from: India, Pakistan, Sri Lanka, Myanmar, Bangladesh, Malaysia, Singapore, Brunei.

  c Vietnam, Laos, Cambodia.

  d The Philippines.

What's Asia like?

About this unit

This unit gives an overview of Asia and its people today.

Key points

◆ Asia is the largest and most diverse continent on Earth.

◆ Overall it contains over 60% of the world's population, but their distribution across the continent varies dramatically. More than half (2.7 billion) live in China and India, whereas Saudi Arabia (the world's 13th largest country) only has a population of 27 million (less than half that of the UK). By contrast, India (the world's 7th largest country) has a population of 1.24 billion!

◆ Asia contains a huge variety of ethnic groups, who speak thousands of different languages and practise a variety of religions (in particular Islam, Hinduism and Buddhism, which all started in Asia).

◆ About 58% of the Asian population still lives in rural areas, but the rate of urbanisation is increasing rapidly in some countries. In China the rate of urbanisation is 2.85% and over 50% now live in urban areas. By contrast, the rate of urbanisation in Kazakhstan is just 0.87% and in Cambodia 80% still live in rural areas.

◆ There is also a huge diversity in wealth and economic development, both between and within Asian countries and regions. India has the fourth largest GDP in the world, but 30% of its people still live below the poverty line. Southeast Asia remains a mainly agricultural region, whereas East Asia has become a global industrial powerhouse.

Key vocabulary

diverse, diversity, ethnic groups, exports, GDP per person (PPP)

Skills practised in 'Your turn'

◆ Numeracy skills: q4, interpret GDP per person data

◆ Literacy skills: q7, write a short summary (a paragraph)

◆ Thinking skills: q2, make choices

Unit outcomes

By the end of this unit most students should be able to:

◆ explain the terms given in 'Key vocabulary' above

◆ explain population data for Asia, including distribution, diversity of cultures, urbanisation and wealth

◆ describe the economic diversity between Asia's regions

Ideas for a starter

1 Recap previous lessons. Write on the board: *Size and location* and *History*. Students to give you five facts for each heading. Ask: What else would you like to know about Asia?

2 Ask: Has anyone ever been to Asia? Where did you go? Using an outline map, ask students to label the areas they have been to. Can you tell us about your visit? Does anyone have family that lives in Asia? Where do they live (country, city, region)? What do they do for a job? What language do they speak? What religion are they?

3 Take in a variety of foods or other products imported from Asia and help students to find out where they came from. Ask students to find those places on the map of Asia.

4 Ask: Can you think of any stories about Asia that have been in the news recently? What were they about?

Ideas for plenaries

Plan plenaries for strategic points throughout the lesson, as well as at the end.

Mid-lesson

1   Asia is rich in natural resources. Ask: What does that mean? Is it a good thing or a bad thing? Does all of Asia benefit from the wealth of natural resources? Explain.

2   **a**   For a number of contrasting countries in Asia (including in the Middle East), provide students with some different development indicators (e.g. GDP, life expectancy, literacy rate). Ask them to rank and compare the countries.

    b   Ask students to present their results as a graph / chart. Explain how development indicators can hide the real picture on wealth distribution.

3   Following on from plenary **2**, ask students to write a diary entry for the day in the life of two people from two countries. Ask them to include their views about any inequalities.

4   Use 'Your turn' question 7 to further explore the inequalities of wealth.

End-of-lesson

5   Use 'Your turn' question 2.

6   Ask: Would you like to visit Asia? Why?

7   Ask students to note down about the lesson: something that has made you think; something you have felt; something you did not find interesting and something you will remember and take away.

Further class and homework opportunities

Suggestions 19–23 on page 145 of this book

geog.2 workbook, page 57

geog.2 Kerboodle: lesson presentation, worksheets, end-of-lesson assessment

Answers to 'Your turn'

1   China and India.

2   Answers will vary.

3   **a**   East Asia

    b   The Middle East

    c   South Asia

4   **a**   GDP is the total amount that the population of a country earns in a year. GDP per person, is the GDP divided by the population. PPP stands for Purchasing Power Parity and is where the GDP per person is adjusted to take into account that things cost more in some places than in others.

    b   **i**   Qatar

        ii   Qatar has large oil and gas reserves, which make it very wealthy. It also has a small population (2.1 million in 2014), so the wealth is divided between fewer people, making the GDP per person higher.

        iii Two and a half times.

5   Yemen

6   Japan

7   Students could discuss: huge differences in wealth, both within and between Asian countries; the varied economies of the different Asian regions, e.g. the industrial strength of East Asia versus the traditional agricultural economies of Southeast Asia; that Asia contains many of the world's megacities, e.g. Shanghai and Mumbai, but 58% of Asia's population are still farmers.

Asia's physical features

help at a glance

About this unit

This unit looks at Asia's key physical features and their locations.

Key points

- As the world's largest continent, stretching from above the Arctic Circle to below the Equator, Asia has a huge variety of physical features.

- These features include:

    - the Himalayas – the world's highest mountain range, home to Mount Everest – the world's highest mountain (8848 m)

    - the Gobi Desert – a cold desert, where temperatures in winter can drop to minus 40°C

    - the Arabian Desert – a hot desert where temperatures in the summer can reach as high as 50°C

    - the Plateau of Tibet – the world's highest plateau, which is the source of the following major rivers: Indus, Mekong, Brahmaputra, Yangtze, Huang He (Yellow River)

    - the Bay of Bengal – the world's largest bay, into which the Ganges and Brahmaputra rivers flow

    - many active volcanoes in East and Southeast Asia (part of the Pacific Ring of Fire).

Key vocabulary

bay, desert, mountain range, ocean, peak, peninsula, plateau, sea

Skills practised in 'Your turn'

- Geography skills: q1, q9, define key terms; q1–q11, analyse and interpret maps, including obtaining information by comparing two maps; q11, study a satellite image

Unit outcomes

By the end of this unit most students should be able to:

- explain the terms given in 'Key vocabulary' above

- analyse and interpret a choropleth map showing relief and main physical features

- say, at least roughly, where these physical features are in Asia:

    - The Himalayas

    - The Mekong, Indus, and Ganges rivers

    - The Plateau of Tibet

    - The Gobi and Thar deserts

    - The Bay of Bengal

Ideas for a starter

1 Ask: What do we mean when we say *physical features*? Can you name any of the physical features in Asia (e.g. Himalayas, Gobi desert, Yangtze River)?

2 Using the maps on pages 106 and 112 of the students' book, give students clues about Asia and its physical features and ask them to work out where you are, e.g.:

- I am a range of mountains found in Nepal, Bhutan and China. I contain the world's highest mountain, which is 8848 m tall.

- I am a range of mountains in Russia that form the border between Asia and Europe.

- I am the highest mountain in Japan and am an active volcano.

Ideas for plenaries

Plan plenaries for strategic points throughout the lesson, as well as at the end.

Mid-lesson

1 Explore the map on page 112 of the students' book. Ask: Can you name five major rivers in Asia? Where is the source of most of the major rivers in Asia? Which are the highest places? Which is the lowest place?

2 On a blank outline map of Asia and with the use of the map on page 112 and atlases, ask students to colour code the different physical features of Asia – cold plateaus, mountainous areas, deserts, tropical regions. They should also label the main oceans and the Tropic of Cancer and the Equator. They will return to these maps for 7.6 starter **2**.

3 After completing 'Your turn' question 3, ask students to write a short descriptive paragraph about the Plateau of Tibet.

End-of-lesson

4 Ask a student to talk for a minute on Asia's physical geography with no pausing, repetition or incorrect information. Other students put up their hands if there is any hesitation, repetition or incorrect information.

5 Ask students to justify this statement: Asia is a continent of geographical contrasts.

Further class and homework opportunities

Suggestions 24–25 on page 145 of this book

geog.2 workbook, page 58

geog.2 Kerboodle: lesson presentation, worksheets, end-of-lesson assessment

Answers to 'Your turn'

1 a A plateau is an area of fairly flat high land.

  b China

2 a The Deccan

  b Anatolian Plateau

  c Central Siberian Plateau

3 a Indus (Arabian Sea); Bramaputra (Bay of Bengal); Ganges (Bay of Bengal); Huang He (Yellow Sea); Yangtze (East China Sea); Salween (Andaman Sea); Irrawaddy (Andaman Sea); Mekong (South China Sea)

  b **i** Yangtze (3900 miles long); **ii** Ganges; **iii** Indus; **iv** Mekong

4 a The Himalayas

  b China, India, Bhutan, Nepal

  c Everest (8848 metres high)

  d K2 (8611 metres high)

  e The Plateau of Tibet

5 a **i** Tien Shan and Kunlan Shan; **ii** Zagros and Elburz

  b China, Mongolia, Russia, Kazakhstan

6 a Caspian Sea

  b Russia, Kazakhstan, Turkmenistan, Iran, and Azerbaijan

  c The Volga

7 a Arctic, Pacific, Indian

  b Seas are smaller than oceans and are usually located where the land and ocean meet. Typically, seas are partially enclosed by land.

  c **i** Bering Sea; **ii** South China Sea; **iii** Arabian Sea

8 a Three from: India, Bangladesh, Myanmar, Sri Lanka.

  b A bay is usually smaller than a sea. Most bays are a body of coastal water bounded by a smooth curve of coast between two headlands. The Bay of Bengal is the largest bay in the world, so isn't typical of most bays.

9 a A peninsula is land that juts out into the sea and is almost surrounded by water.

  b Arabian Peninsula. Three from: Saudi Arabia, Yemen, Oman, United Arab Emirates, Kuwait, Qatar, Bahrain.

  c Malay Peninsula

10 a The Gobi Desert is cold rather than hot because of its altitude (over 1000m above sea level) and its latitude.

  b Mongolia and China

11 a Thar Desert

  b Indus

  c The Himalayas

About this unit

This unit uses a choropleth map to study population density in Asia.

Key points

- Population density is the number of people living in a place, per sq km.
- Asia is the world's most populous continent; it contains about 4.3 billion of the 7 billion people on Earth – over 60% of the total.
- The largest Asian populations, in terms of both population density and total numbers, are in China (1.36 billion) and India (1.24 billion). Japan also has a very high population density, with 127 million people in a much smaller area.
- As of 2014, there were 30 megacities in the world (metropolitan areas with populations of over 10 million) – 11 of which had populations of over 20 million – and 8 of these 'super megacities' were in Asia. Tokyo is the largest metropolitan area / urban agglomeration by population (37.8 million), with Delhi second (27 million), and Shanghai is the largest city proper (24.75 million).
- The population density in Asia is highest away from mountains, deserts (and the Arctic). Particularly high concentrations of people occur along coastlines and rivers, where many of the megacities are located.

Key vocabulary

population density, populous

Skills practised in 'Your turn'

- Geography skills: q1, define a key term; q2–q3, analyse and interpret a choropleth map
- Numeracy skills: q4–q5, analyse a bar graph; q6, calculate population density
- Thinking skills: q6b, q7, apply knowledge to reach conclusions

Unit outcomes

By the end of this unit most students should be able to:

- explain the terms given in 'Key vocabulary' above
- interpret and analyse a choropleth map showing population density
- describe the pattern of population density across Asia
- give at least two factors that influence that pattern, such as physical features (e.g. mountains) and climate (particularly extremes of heat and cold)

Ideas for a starter

1   Ask: Who can remember what *population density* is? Is the population in Asia likely to be spread equally across the continent? Why / Why not?

2   Use the maps students created in 7.5 plenary **2**. Ask students to label areas where they think people are most, and least, likely to live.

Show students a climate map of Asia – and ask them again to label areas on their maps where they think people are most, and least likely to live.

Finally, students compare their maps with the population distribution map on page 114 of the students' book. How good were their predictions?

3   Explore the map of Asia's population density as a class.

Ideas for plenaries

Plan plenaries for strategic points throughout the lesson, as well as at the end.

Mid-lesson

1 Ask questions about the map on page 114 of the students' book to check that students can interpret it. Ask: What are the deep red areas? What are the palest areas? What are the yellow squares? What are the black dots?

2 Russia has a population of 146 million but the map on page 114 of the students' book, shows vast areas with a population of under one person per sq km. Ask: Can you explain this? Also draw out that in the areas of low density, the density increases slightly along the length of the major rivers.

End-of-lesson

3 Working in small groups, students write a paragraph summarising what they've learned about Asia's population and its distribution. Ask some to read theirs out. Discuss what makes a good summary, in geography. Students could rewrite their paragraphs in response.

4 Ask students to note down something from this lesson that they will remember and take away.

Further class and homework opportunities

Suggestions 26–28 on page 145 of this book

geog.2 workbook, page 59

geog.2 Kerboodle: lesson presentation, worksheets, end-of-lesson assessment

Answers to 'Your turn'

1 Population density is the average number of people living in a place, per sq km.

2 a True

  b False. Most people live in the southern half of Asia.

  c False. Overall, China is more densely populated than Russia.

  d False. Overall, the European part of Russia is more densely populated than the Asian part.

  e True

  f False. Most of China's cities are in eastern China.

3 a There are fewer people around W than around X, because W is located in the Arctic, with its harsh climate (particularly in winter), whereas X is located in the tropics, with an equatorial climate all year round.

  b The population density at Y is over 100 people per sq km.

  c The population density at Z is under one person per sq km. This is because Z is located in the Gobi Desert, a cold desert with very low rainfall and very extreme temperatures.

  d W (Russia); X (Myanmar); Y (China); Z (Mongolia)

4 a India and China

  b China

  c i 1350 million; ii 1.35 billion

  d Thailand, Iran, Vietnam (and the UK)

5 a About 21 times more

  b About 7 times more

6 a About 7714 people per sq km

  b Students' suggestions for possible problems might include: pressure on housing availability and cost, together with pressure on educational and healthcare facilities; the availability of sufficient jobs; the need to import food and other resources to meet the needs of such a large population; where to put all the waste that these people generate; how to generate sufficient energy to meet the population's needs; pressure on transport infrastructure; pollution.

7 a Students' suggestions for potential problems might include: the difficulties experienced in feeding, housing, employing, educating and keeping healthy 1.35 billion people; having such a large population reduces the GDP per capita, despite China's strong economy; the pressure of supporting such a large population has resulted in economic decisions, such as rapid industrialisation, urbanisation and huge dam-building projects, which have caused massive problems of waste, pollution and environmental damage; much of western China consists of deserts and mountains, so most of the population is concentrated in the east, leading to high population density and the particular problems that brings (as specified for Singapore).

  b A big population provides a large workforce of young people to support China's growing economy, both creating the goods and services in the first place and then providing a domestic market for them. Having a large population also gives China political and economic clout on the world stage.

help at a glance

About this unit

This unit examines Asia's wide range of biomes.

Key points

◆ A biome is a large region with its own distinct climate, plants and animals.

◆ Asia has a wide range of biomes – from tundra to tropical rainforest.

◆ This wide range is caused by the huge variation in climatic conditions occurring in a continent that extends from the Arctic to the Equator.

◆ Human actions have had, and are still having, a huge effect on Asia's biomes.

    – Within Asia itself, deforestation (particularly of the rainforests) has led to the loss of 50% of the original forest. For example, large areas of the island of Borneo have been deforested to provide timber for sale and to create space for massive oil palm plantations (according to WWF – using satellite studies – 56% of the natural forest in Kalimantan was cut down between 1985 and 2001). This deforestation has led to a huge loss of biodiversity across Southeast Asia.

    – More globally, climate change due to human actions has had an effect on the Arctic region and its biomes in particular. Rising sea levels also affect mangrove swamps.

Key vocabulary

biome, climate zone, coniferous, deciduous, cold desert, hot desert, mangrove swamp, steppe, taiga, temperate forest, tropical rainforest, tundra, warm moist forest

Skills practised in 'Your turn'

◆ Geography skills: q1, q4, define key terms; q5, analyse and interpret maps

◆ Literacy skills: q4, write short definitions of key terms

◆ Thinking skills: q2, q6, provide an explanation; q3, analyse data and apply knowledge to reach a conclusion

Unit outcomes

By the end of this unit most students should be able to:

◆ explain the terms given in 'Key vocabulary' above

◆ describe the range of biomes present across Asia and the climatic circumstances which cause them

◆ roughly locate the biomes on a map of Asia

◆ describe the impact of people on Asia's biomes

Ideas for a starter

1 Write *biome* on the board. Ask: Can you remember what this means?

2 Display photos of different biomes in Asia (e.g. the photos on pages 116–117 of the students' book). In groups, allocate students a couple of photos. For each photo, groups to give three adjectives that sum it up. They should imagine that they are there and think about what they would see, hear, smell and feel.

3 Ask: Why do each of the biomes in the photos on pages 116–117 of the students' book look different? What factors might affect biomes?

Ideas for plenaries

Plan plenaries for strategic points throughout the lesson, as well as at the end.

Mid-lesson

1   Students to create a poster showing Asia's eight different biomes using pictures and a map, and annotating it with information about the biomes.

2   Ask: Do you think you could live in the Arctic tundra? What kind of lifestyle would you have? What challenges might you face? Create a spider diagram showing students' ideas.

3   Show a video on rainforest destruction in Indonesia. Ask: If all of Indonesia's rainforest is cleared to grow palm oil, do you think that Asia will still have a rainforest biome?

4   Following on from plenary **3**, ask: What can people in the rainforest in Indonesia do to protect the tropical rainforest? What can we in the UK do to protect it?

End-of-lesson

5   Where am I? Read out clues for biomes – students guess where you are, e.g.

   ◆   Summers are hot and winters are very cold. You will find camels here and I am located south of the steppes. (Cold desert)

   ◆   I am located in the north with long, very cold winters. Spruce and fir trees can be found here. (Taiga)

6   In small groups, give students eight sticky notes. From memory, students try to write each type of biome on a note. Once they have done this, each group should place their notes in an appropriate place on an outline map of Asia on the board. Discuss and recap the locations and types of biomes.

Further class and homework opportunities

Suggestions 29–32 on page 145 of this book

geog.2 workbook, page 60

geog.2 Kerboodle: lesson presentation, worksheets, end-of-lesson assessment

Answers to 'Your turn'

1   A biome is a very large area with a similar climate, plants, and animals.

2   Asia is a huge continent, which stretches from above the Arctic Circle to below the Equator. It has a variety of different climates resulting in a wide range of biomes.

3   **a**   Tundra

   b   Steppe

4   **a**   Temperate – relating to a mild climate: not hot, not too cold (temperate forest).

   b   Tree line – the line or altitude above which it's too cold for trees to grow (mountain).

   c   Coniferous – describes trees that bear cones, such as pine trees (taiga).

   d   Mangroves – trees that grow in salty swamps along the coast (mangrove swamp).

   e   Permafrost – the ground under the surface that is permanently frozen (tundra).

   f   Deciduous – describes trees that lose their leaves in winter (temperate forest).

5   **a**   Russia

   b   Russia

   c   Three from: Saudi Arabia, Yemen, Oman, United Arab Emirates, Kuwait, Qatar, Iraq, Iran, Jordan, Israel, China, Pakistan, Uzbekistan, Turkmenistan.

   d   Two from: China, Mongolia, Kazakhstan, Kyrgyzstan, Uzbekistan, Tajikistan.

   e   Two from: India, Sri Lanka, Bangladesh, Myanmar, Thailand, Laos, Cambodia, Vietnam, China, The Philippines, Indonesia, Malaysia, Brunei, Taiwan, Papua New Guinea.

   f   Three from: Saudi Arabia, Oman, United Arab Emirates, Qatar, Kuwait, Iran, Pakistan, India, Sri Lanka, Bangladesh, Myanmar, Thailand, Malaysia, Indonesia, Brunei, The Philippines, Papua New Guinea, Taiwan, China, Cambodia, Vietnam.

6   X is located in the Gobi Desert, which is a cold desert with very low rainfall and extremes of temperature – very hot in the summer and very cold in the winter. Thus, it is extremely difficult for humans to sustain themselves in large numbers here. Those who do live here tend to be nomadic, rather than living in permanent year-round settlements, so the population density is very low.

Many of these suggestions are addressed to your students. Where research or further resources are needed, the internet will almost certainly provide the answer.

The suggestions are graded *,**,*** according to level of difficulty. Some are suitable for all levels, and can be differentiated by outcome.

What and where is Asia?

1 **World wordsearch** Create a wordsearch on the continents and oceans. Swap and do your partner's. */**

2 **Continent bingo** Create a bingo sheet with seven rows of squares (or six rows, if you don't want to include Antarctica), say five or six squares in a row. Label each row with the name of a continent. Give a sheet to each small team of students. At regular (short) intervals, call out a number and then a name, for example, the name of a country, capital city, famous tourist attraction, continent-specific animal (such as penguin, Indian tiger), international football team, or a continent-specific phrase, such as *South Pole*. Students write the numbers in the appropriate rows, one in each square, while you also keep track. The first group to fill all the rows correctly wins. */**/***

3 **Ocean bingo** Do the same as 2 above for the oceans. You could call out the names of countries or cities that border them. Let students work with atlases to find the answers, perhaps allowing more time. ***

4 **Did you see?** A student takes the hot seat, chooses a continent, and says he or she has visited everywhere there. Other students open their atlases and fire 'Did you visit X?' questions at the target student, where X is a country on that continent, or not. After say ten questions, or three wrong answers, the student is replaced. When the student gives a wrong answer, the questioner must explain why it is wrong. For example: Vietnam is in Asia, not Africa. (Russia and Turkey may cause problems, since they straddle continents.) ***

5 **Old maps of the world** The map of the world was not always like the one on page 104 of the students' book. Find some images of old maps, and display them. ***

6 **Google Earth** Explore the continents on Google Earth, without any labels turned on, and then with the lowest level of labelling. Turn Earth this way and that! */**/***

Asia's countries and regions

7 **Adopt an Asian country** You are a geography detective. What geographical questions would you ask about a country you have never been to? Agree a set of questions with the class, and a way to present the answers. Then choose an Asian country, or your teacher will allocate one. To your answers, add two very interesting or unusual facts you discovered about the country. */**/***

8 **Asia in the news** Make a note of all the references to Asian countries in the news this week, in a newspaper or on TV. Find a way to display the references (perhaps as speech bubbles linked to a blank political map of Asia, with the country shaded). Overall, is the news positive? */**/***

9 **Asia wordsearch** Make up a wordsearch for the names of Asian countries. See how many you can fit in. The put it with an outline political map of Asia (with the country boundaries marked on). Give it to a partner. The partner has to find each name, then shade and label that country on the map (preferably without looking at a reference map – or else use the map on page 106 of the students' book). */**/***

10 **Colour me quick** Give out outline political maps of Asia. A student calls out a country name. Everyone else shades and labels it on their outline maps (with help from the map on page 106 of the students' book). Allow only a short time for this. Then another student calls out a country name. This continues until all the countries are shaded and labelled. If a student calls out a name that was used already, he or she forfeits that turn. */**/***

11 **Place quiz** Choose a country or city in Asia. Without naming it, write down five facts about it to tell the rest of the class. The class has to identify the country or city. (This could be a game. Students take turn to present their facts. Award 1 point to the student who identifies a place first, and 1 to any student whose place is not identified. At the end of each turn, the 'winner' marks the place on a large outline map of Asia.) **/***

12 **A hard snap** Make a pack of cards, with the names of Asian countries on half the cards, and their capitals on the other half. Devise a way to play Snap! **/***

13 **Fiendish anagrams** Make up a set of anagrams of say five or six Asian countries (or use an anagram generator on the internet). See how long it takes for the class to work them out. **/***

14 **The Heart of Asia Monument** When was it built? How are the countries of Asia represented? What else can you find out about it? */**

A little history

15 **Marco Polo – merchant and traveller** Marco Polo travelled extensively in Asia in the thirteenth century. When and where did he go? What was the name of the book he wrote about his travels? **

16 **Genghis Khan** Who was he? When did he live? Where was he from? Why is he famous? Why is his portrait still found on Mongolian banknotes? Produce a poster about this famous leader. */**

17 **The Silk Road** The Silk Road followed different routes. It had a Northern, a Southern and a Southwestern Route. Draw a map to show the different routes. Annotate it to show what was traded on the different routes, and who traded along them. You'll need to do some research. **/***

18 **Independence** Several Asian countries were colonised by Europeans and the Americans, but they did win their freedom. Find out which countries were colonised, by whom and when they gained independence (use the map on page 109 of the students' book as a starting point). Then think up

an interesting way to show the timeline for independence. Perhaps hang cards from a string across the classroom, with the country names, flags and date of independence. It could be colour coded by coloniser. Agree a format, and do one or two cards each, then put them all in order. **/***

What's Asia like?

19 **Asia wall display** Collect as many interesting and varied images of Asia as you can. Find a way to group them, for example, by physical features, people, towns and cities, wild animals. *

20 **Draw a pie chart...** showing the percentage of the world population in each continent. You could draw it by hand or in Excel. But first of all you need to find out the numbers or percentages in each continent. **/***

21 **Asian connections** Think about your connections with Asia. Have you been there? Do you have relatives in Asia? Or friends from there? Do you eat anything grown in Asia? See how many connections you can come up with. Find a way to display them (perhaps around a drawing of you.) */**/***

22 **A famous Asian** Choose a famous Asian, alive or dead. Create a display on an A4 sheet about him or her, or prepare a piece for a website. See if you can choose someone different from everyone else in the class. Make your choice interesting! Write at least 100 words! */**/***

23 **GDP per capita** This gives you an idea of how well off people in a place are, *on average*. Here are some figures for 2010, for the continents.

Continent	GDP per capita
Oceania	39 000
North America	32 000
Europe	25 000
South America	9000
Asia	2900
Africa	1600

Use Excel or a similar program to draw a bar chart for this data. Then add notes to explain what it shows. What can you say about Asia compared with other continents? How many times better off are people in Europe than people in Asia, on average? Do these figures mean that all countries in Asia are poor, or that everyone in Asia is poor? **/***

Asia's physical features

24 **Google maps** Open Google maps, and tour around Asia. Try it with labels and photos off and on. Follow the Yangtze on its journey through China. Explore other features named on the map on page 112 of the students' book. */**/***

25 **Choose a physical feature** From the map on page 112 of the students' book, pick the physical feature you'd most like to visit. Write a set of geographical questions about it. Then find the answers. And next, find a really good way to present them (perhaps a strip cartoon, an annotated map and photos, a movie, a web page). */**/***

Asia's population

26 **Population densities** Fill in the missing population densities in the table below from the list in italics. Use the map on page 114 to help.

Country	Population density (people per square km)
Saudi Arabia	
India	
China	
UK	265

Population densities 145, 13, 421

What can you say about the population density of the UK compared to the three Asian countries? Write at least 50 words. */**

27 **Work it out** The map on page 114 of the students' book is fairly simplified, with the deepest shade representing any number over 100 people per square kilometre. Draw up a table with four columns and these headings: *Country, Population, Area, Population density*. Choose six countries from the map. List their names in the first column, in order of what you *think* is their population density. Look up their populations and area on the internet and complete the second and third columns. Work out their population densities, and write these in the last column. Does your table give a better picture of population density than the map? Did you put the countries in the correct order? If yes, give yourself a gold star! **/***

28 **Population density** Based on what you already know, what factors are likely to influence population density in Asia? Create a spider diagram with three legs for physical, economic and social factors. Give examples for each of the factors, eg climate, relief (physical), jobs (economic) etc. Then colour code the examples to indicate how it affects population density as either low or high. Finally add examples of an area or place in Asia to the factors on your spider diagram, eg, Gobi Desert (for climate and low population density), Shanghai (for jobs and high population density) etc. ***

Asia's biomes

29 **Hot deserts on Google maps** Using the map on page 117 of the students' book to guide you, explore Asia's hot deserts on Google Maps. Look for signs of habitation. What else can you find? */**/***

30 **Other biomes on Google Maps** Repeat the above for other biomes on the map on page 117. */**/***

31 **Giant pandas** The giant panda is an endangered species and there are only 1000–2000 left in the wild. Find out why this is, and plan a visit to a place where you could see them. */**/***

32 **Sum it all up** Get a large sheet of paper and create a mind map for all you have learned about Asia. */**/***

About this chapter

Addressing the KS3 Programme of Study

◆ Develop knowledge of the world's countries, and a region within Asia, including physical and human features.

◆ Understand the processes that give rise to development in Southwest China and how these bring change over time.

◆ Understand how human and physical processes interact to influence and change landscapes and environments.

About the content

◆ This chapter starts with a broad look at the geography of China and the challenges it faces.

◆ Southwest China is a manageable size to study and students will find its physical features, biodiversity, and ethnic mix interesting.

◆ Units also focus more closely on Chongqing, a good example of a city that's developing very quickly, and Tibet, an area where development is more difficult.

The big picture

These are the key ideas in this chapter.

◆ China, one of the world's most important countries, is continuing to change quickly.

◆ Southwest China is over ten times the size of the UK, with over three times as many people.

◆ Much of it is mountainous, and several great rivers flow through it.

◆ It is not a wealthy region, but it has been earmarked for development and is changing fast.

◆ It is one of the world's most biodiverse regions, but needs to tackle deforestation and the endangering of animal species.

◆ There are many dams in Southwest China; many more are planned, despite controversy.

A students' version of this big picture is given in the *geog.2* students' book opener for Chapter 8.

The chapter outline

Use this, and their chapter opener, to give students a mental roadmap for the chapter.

8 Southwest China The chapter opener in the students' book is an important part of the chapter; see page 11 for notes about using chapter openers

8.1 China: an overview China's key features: physical, climate, and population distribution

8.2 The rise of China Changes over the past 40 years, including the effects of private enterprise, global trade, and population policies, and resulting challenges

8.3 China's Southwest region Five different areas in the Southwest, comparing population statistics, economic resources, and GDP

8.4 Chongqing Chongqing – the world's fastest growing urban area

8.5 Life in Chongqing How various types of people make a living in Chongqing, the benefits and disadvantages, and their hopes for the future

8.6 Tops for biodiversity! Measures in the Southwest to reduce the dangers of animal extinction and deforestation, and the problem of rubber plantations for wildlife

8.7 Tibet Its climate and physical features, its people and how they earn a living

8.8 All change in Tibet The history of Tibet since 1950, how it is being developed, and how life has changed for nomadic people

8.9 The rivers and dams The rivers in the Southwest and the benefits and disadvantages of China's dam building

Objectives and outcomes for this chapter

Objectives	Unit	Outcomes
Most students will understand:		Most students will be able to:
that China is one of the world's most important and diverse countries	8.1	give at least four facts to show China's importance; describe China's location, physical features, climates, and population densities
that China has changed and is continuing to change	8.2	identify recent changes that have contributed to China's success, and some of its challenges
that Southwest China has a range of physical features	8.3	identify the five areas of Southwest China and their physical characteristics; describe karst landscape
that most of China's major rivers flow through Southwest China, where many dams have been built and others are planned	8.3, 8.9	identify the major rivers in Southwest China; explain how hydroelectricity will help China's economy and how dams will affect the environment
that Southwest China is not a wealthy region, but is developing fast	8.3, 8.4, 8.5	compare GDP per person (PPP) of the areas of Southwest China; explain why Chongqing is a good candidate for development; describe life in Chongqing for a range of people; explain reform of the hukou system
that Southwest China is one of the most biodiverse regions in the world	8.3, 8.6	Define *biodiversity* and *endangered*; explain why Southwest China has rainforest, why rubber plantations have little/no wildlife, and why it's important to protect animal species
that development in Tibet is progressing but encounters difficulties	8.7, 8.8	identify physical and human features that make Tibet difficult to develop; identify changes in Tibet and explain their contribution to its development

These tie in with the outcomes for each unit, in this teacher's handbook, and with 'Your goals for this chapter', in *geog.2* students' book.

Opportunities for assessment

See the formal assessment materials for this chapter on *geog.2 Kerboodle Lessons, Resources, & Assessment*. They include an extended assessment task, an exam-style question, end-of-lesson assessments, and a self-assessment form. See also the notes on pages 14–15 of this book.

Getting ready for this chapter

geog.2 Kerboodle contains plans and presentations for each unit, including interactive activities, animations, and worksheets.

About 'Your chapter starter'

The photos on page 118 of *geog.2* students' book show just a little of what Southwest China is like, with its many contrasts. The photos on the right show Chongqing city at night (the world's fastest growing urban area), Tibetan Buddhist monks and novices at the Labrang Monastery in Xiahe, Gansu Province, and factory workers in Chengdu city, Sichuan.

The photos on the left show the incredible karst scenery in Guizhou (also found in Yunnan), a woman during a funeral procession in Yunnan – where there are many ethnic groups, and a dam and reservoir on the Dadu River, Sichuan.

The photos aim to give students a flavour of Southwest China – its landscape and people, its customs and its future.

China: an overview

help at a glance

About this unit

This unit introduces the physical features, different climates and population distribution of China as a whole.

Key points

◆ China is the world's fourth largest country by area, and it has the second largest economy (behind the USA) and the largest population (1.37 billion).

◆ About two-thirds of China is mountainous, especially in the south and west – where it forms part of the Himalayas. There are also extensive cold deserts in the northwest.

◆ The western half of China is very dry and cold, whilst the eastern half receives monsoon rains off the sea and is much warmer.

◆ China's population distribution reflects its relief and different climates. Therefore, the bulk of China's huge population is located in the east of the country – in particular in the central belt between Beijing and Shanghai. This flat, central plain is also fed by the Yellow and Yangtze rivers, so it's very fertile.

Key vocabulary

cold deserts, monsoon rains, monsoon winds, physical features, relief

Skills practised in 'Your turn'

◆ Geography skills: q1, use a map scale; q2, describe patterns of relief q3, q5, analyse and compare maps; q6, define a key term

◆ Numeracy skills: q1, calculate distances

◆ Literacy skills: q2, write a description

◆ Thinking skills: q5, q7, use common sense and prior knowledge, as well as map analysis, to give reasoned explanations

Unit outcomes

By the end of this unit most students should be able to:

◆ explain the terms given in 'Key vocabulary' above

◆ state some key facts about China – population size, area, economy

◆ give an overview of China's relief and physical features, including being able to roughly locate the main features on a blank map

◆ describe China's different climates in broad terms

◆ describe China's population distribution in broad terms

Ideas for a starter

1 With books closed, give students an outline map of Asia. From prior knowledge (Chapter 7), ask: Where is China located? Students colour it in on the map.

2 Following on from starter **1**, ask: Can you remember anything about China from Chapter 7 – history, economy, biomes? Students create a mind map.

3 Show students a range of pictures of and / or facts about China starting with the more obscure images (e.g. satellite image of China, terracotta army, dragon, Great Wall of China, Chinese flag, Chinese writing, eating with chopsticks). Ask: Can you guess what we're learning about today?

4 Establish student's prior knowledge about China. Write *China* on the board and explain that they are going to explore the country China. In pairs, students write down five words / images that come to mind. They share their ideas with another pair.

Ideas for plenaries

Plan plenaries at strategic points throughout the lesson, as well as at the end.

Mid-lesson

1 Revisit starter **1**. Using the students' book (page 120 and Chapter 7), atlases and different coloured pens, ask students to add China's main cities, physical features, and climatic zones on an outline map. Ask: What countries does China have borders with?

2 Students create a big spider diagram / mind map about China. They mark in facts they already know, trying to group them under headings (for population, physical features, size, location, culture, food, places of interest, history, etc.). They can add to their spider diagram throughout the chapter.

End-of-lesson

3 Students decide if the following statements are true or false, correcting any false ones.

◆ Ice cream was invented here around 2000 BC.

◆ 25% of the world's population is Chinese. (False: One in five or 20% is Chinese.)

◆ China is the fourth largest country in the world by area.

◆ The longest river in China is the Yellow River. (False: It's the Yangtze.)

◆ China is the world's top exporter of goods.

◆ The deserts in north west China are hot deserts. (False: They are cold deserts.)

4 Ask: Are you looking forward to learning more about China? Why / Why not? Write one question about China that you would really like to know the answer to.

Further class and homework opportunities

Suggestions 1–4 on page 166 of this book

geog.2 workbook, page 62

geog.2 Kerboodle: lesson presentation, worksheets, end-of-lesson assessment

Answers for 'Your turn'

1 **a** About 4000 km
 b About 4500 km

2 The west and southwest of China is largely mountainous. The north west consists of several low-lying deserts. The east and north east is mainly low-lying plains.

3 **a** Beijing is located on a flat plain in the north east of China, relatively close to the East China Sea. It is China's capital city and has a population density of over 100 people per sq km. Beijing is also located on the junction between two of China's climate zones, with dry conditions to the west and cold, quite wet conditions to the east.

 b The Gobi Desert is located in the northern region of China, on roughly the same latitude as Beijing further east. As a desert, it experiences very dry conditions, due to its inland position north of the Himalayas and the Plateau of Tibet, both of which prevent cloud formation and rainfall arriving from the south. The Gobi Desert has a very low population density of less than 1 person per sq km.

4 Most of China's population is located on the flat plains to the east of the country, where the climate tends to be mild and wet. Large areas of the east have a population density of over 100 people per sq km.

5 **a** X and Z have a population density of less than 1 person per sq km, whereas Y has a population density of over 100 people per sq km.

 b Y is located on the coast close to Shanghai and also the mouth of the River Yangtze. This location helps to provide opportunities for employment, which draw people to it. It also has a mild wet climate. X is located on the Plateau of Tibet and Z in the Gobi Desert, both of which are very cold and dry and provide few opportunities for employment. Life in these regions has traditionally been nomadic, due to the extreme climatic conditions, especially in winter.

6 Monsoon rains fall in summer in some regions, when moist winds are drawn in from over the ocean.

7 The monsoon rains do not reach the Taklimakan Desert, because the Himalayas intercept any moisture arriving from the south, which falls as relief rainfall on the southern side of the mountains. The Taklimakan Desert is situated on the leeward side, so is in a rain shadow. It is also located approximately 4000 km from China's east coast, so very little rainfall reaches it from that direction either.

8 Mongolia, Russia, North Korea, Kazakhstan, Kyrgyzstan, Tajikistan, Afghanistan, Pakistan, India, Nepal, Bhutan, Myanmar, Laos, Vietnam.

About this unit

This unit continues the overview of China as a whole, by describing what has happened to the country in the last 40 years.

Key points

- Before 1979, China was an isolationist communist country – with strict state control over all aspects of the economy. The result was a stagnating economy and widespread poverty (compounded by a rapidly growing population). In 1979, state control over the economy was relaxed and private enterprise was permitted once again. This was coupled with an opening up of trade with the outside world.

- The result of these economic reforms is that China is now the world's second largest economy, and the world's largest exporter of manufactured goods. The number of Chinese living in poverty has now dropped from 85% in 1981 to 7% in 2014.

- However, China's economic success story has had social, demographic and environmental consequences. The most famous social and demographic change has been China's one-child policy, which has prevented around 400 million births. There has also been mass urbanisation – with over 50% of the Chinese population living in urban areas by 2011.

- But the economic and demographic changes have come with a large environmental cost – severe pollution.

Key vocabulary

exports, GDP per person, one-child policy

Skills practised in 'Your turn'

- Geography skills: q5a, explain key terms; q5b, analyse a choropleth map

- Thinking skills: q1, explain a title; q3, explain the thinking behind the one-child policy; q4, summarise changes; q5c, use common sense and prior knowledge to produce a reasoned explanation; q6, analyse information to reach a conclusion

Unit outcomes

By the end of this unit most students should be able to:

- explain the terms given in 'Key vocabulary' above

- describe how China has changed economically since 1979

- explain the social and demographic effects of China's reforms after 1979

- explain the challenges which China still faces – and what the government is doing to address them

Ideas for a starter

1   Ask: Who can give me a fact about China?

2   Show students the photo of pollution in Harbin from page 123 of the students' book. Ask: What does it show? Why is it like this?

3   Ask: Who has heard of China's one-child policy? Why do you think China introduced it? Do you think it is right to limit the number of children people have?

Ideas for plenaries

Plan plenaries at strategic points throughout the lesson, as well as at the end.

Mid-lesson

1   In groups, give students a range of newspaper headlines / articles about China (e.g. on urban and industrial growth, pollution). Ask: What are the articles about? What changes are taking place? What is the effect on China? What might be the effects in the future? Link to sustainable development and the impact on the environment.

2   Say: Foreign companies have been able to set up in China. Why might they want to (e.g. because of lower wages, large workforce, large market)?

3   Looking at the maps on pages 120–121 of the students' book, explain why there may be inequalities / a division of wealth between the East and West.

End-of-lesson

4   Discuss the advantages and disadvantages of growth to China.

5   Students show how each of these random words might link to this lesson: trainers; seafood, cars, refrigerators, toys (goods manufactured in China); Marks and Spencer, Jaguar Land Rover, KFC, Nokia (foreign companies in China); air pollution, smog, climate change, power stations (challenges facing China).

6   Students add information that they have learned in this lesson about the changes taking place in China, to the spider diagram started in Unit 8.1.

7   Ask students to write down three things they would like to know about China.

Further class and homework opportunities

Suggestions 5–8 on page 166 of this book

geog.2 workbook, page 63

geog.2 Kerboodle: lesson presentation, worksheets, end-of-lesson assessment

Answers for 'Your turn'

1   China does not have a king, queen, or emperor (a hereditary monarch), so it is called a republic.

2   Mao Zedong was the man who made China a communist country and ruled it from 1949 until his death in 1976.

3   a   China's rapidly growing population put a strain on resources such as food, as well as access to education and health care (all of which were provided free to all by the communist government). There was also extensive poverty in China (in 1981, 85% of Chinese were living in poverty). A rapidly increasing population would only make this situation worse, and might cause political and social unrest, which the government wished to avoid.

    b   China introduced the radical one-child policy to artificially reduce the birth rate. Each couple was only allowed to have one child. This extreme policy has recently been relaxed a little, but it prevented around 400 million births.

4   Students may mention that: the poverty level in China has plummeted to just 7% since 1978; the state no longer controls all factories, businesses, and farms, and private enterprise is now allowed; China has now reversed it's previous isolationist policy and has engaged with the world so much that it is now the world's top exporter of manufactured goods and has the second largest economy in the world after the USA; China's rapid economic expansion, particularly in manufacturing, has led to massive urbanisation since 1978, which in turn has led to severe levels of pollution.

5   a   i Things a country sells to other countries. ii The total GDP divided by the population.

    b   The pattern of wealth in China closely matches the population distribution of the country. The industrialised east, where most of the population lives, has a much higher GDP per person than the rural west.

    c   The factories are in the east because that's where most of the workforce is; the east is close to the coast and its ports, so exports (China's major economic driver) are easier to dispatch around the world by huge container ship; the land in the east is much flatter than the mountainous west, so there is more suitable land for building factories and transport infrastructure, as well as homes for the workers.

6   Basically, it's the profits from selling its exports. It's cheap to manufacture goods in China. These goods are then sold overseas for huge profits, which can be invested in development projects.

China's Southwest region

About this unit

This unit, and the remaining units in this chapter, focus on China's Southwest region, which includes Tibet.

Key points

◆ The Southwest China region is split into five smaller areas: Tibet, Sichuan, Chongqing, Guizhou, and Yunnan. The region as a whole is ten times larger than the UK, and has a population of 195 million.

◆ The five areas which make up the Southwest region are very varied in terms of:

- population size (from 3 million in Tibet, to 81 million in Sichuan)

- ethnicity, with a huge variety of ethnic minorities (particularly in Yunnan and Guizhou)

- physical geography (from the high Himalayas and Plateau of Tibet in the west, to low flat river valleys in the east)

- climate (from the dry cold of Tibet, to the warm moist tropical climate of Yunnan)

- economy (from the industry of Chongqing to the agriculture and tourism of Yunnan and Guizhou)

Key vocabulary

ethnic groups, karst, metal ores

Skills practised in 'Your turn'

◆ Geography skills: q2, analyse a relief map; q3–q4 analyse population and economic data; q5, define a key term

◆ Literacy skills: q6, begin a spider diagram to summarise

Unit outcomes

By the end of this unit most students should be able to:

◆ explain the terms given in 'Key vocabulary' above

◆ name the five areas which make up the Southwest region of China

◆ describe similarities and differences between the five areas

Ideas for a starter

1 Use 'Your turn' question 1 as a starter.

2 In small groups, students create graphs from the information in table B on page 124 of the students' book. Each group takes one column. They should give the graphs a title, decide on a scale and label the axes. Each group presents their graph and describe what it shows. Ask: How does the data vary from one area to another? How does the data compare with the UK?

3 Look back to pages 120–121 of the students' book. Ask students to give three facts about Southwest China's physical features, population, and climate. Link this to the information in table B and/or the graphs created in starter **2**.

Ideas for plenaries

Plan plenaries at strategic points throughout the lesson, as well as at the end.

Mid-lesson

1   Use 'Your turn' question 6 to add to the spider diagram students have been creating.

2   Imagine: You work for the Chinese government's tourism department. You are putting together a travel information pack on Southwest China for tourists and business people. Using the students' book and other sources of information (e.g. the internet), write a short paragraph about one of the five areas for people who will travel there. Students can refer back to previous units for information on climate and physical features, and can include pictures.

3   Ask: Why is Southwest China an interesting region? Students give three facts that make it interesting.

End-of-lesson

4   Using the information in table B on page 124 of the students' book, create 'top trumps' cards for each region. In pairs, students compare their cards to try to trump and win their opponent's card. They need to decide whether the highest value is always favourable and should win.

5   Ask: Out of the five regions in China we have looked at, where would you most like to live? Explain your answer.

6   Display the map from page 124 of the students' book on the board along with the table of population data. Say: I am going on a tour of Southwest China. Read out statements relating to the different regions and students have to guess where you are.

7   Ask: What did you enjoy about today's lesson? What didn't you enjoy about today's lesson?

Further class and homework opportunities

Suggestions 9–12 on page 166 of this book

geog.2 workbook, page 64

geog.2 Kerboodle: lesson presentation, worksheets, end-of-lesson assessment

Answers for 'Your turn'

1   Tibet, Sichuan, Yunnan, Guizhou, Chongqing

2   Tibet

3   a   Tibet

   b   Sichuan

   c   Chongqing

4   a   i Chongqing; ii Guizhou

   b   People in the UK are roughly 3.7 times better off, on average, than people in Chongqing.

5   Karst landscapes are formed when rock such as limestone is attacked by acidic rain.

6   Ensure that students begin their spider diagrams on large sheets of paper, to allow for all the extra information they will add throughout this chapter.

About this unit

This unit, and the next, focus on the Chongqing area of Southwest China – with an emphasis on Chongqing city.

Key points

◆ Although most of Chongqing is currently rural, it has the fastest growing urban area on the planet – predicted to become the world's largest megalopolis.

◆ As a result of Chinese government policies to develop the west of China and increase urbanisation (to improve people's living standards), Chongqing has been selected as a hub for the new developments.

◆ Careful forward planning by the government – in order to build plenty of workers' accommodation and encourage the creation of lots of new jobs – has meant that new arrivals into the city from rural areas (1300 people a day) have been able to settle down quickly without creating the slums present in many other rapidly growing world cities.

◆ A variety of industries have set up in Chongqing, making everything from cars to textiles – mostly for China's rapidly growing domestic market. Government incentives have made it attractive for companies to start up there (cheap land, cheap labour and less government interference).

Key vocabulary

confluence, megalopolis, slum

Skills practised in 'Your turn'

◆ Geography skills: q1, locate a geographical area; q2a, q6a define key terms; q3, analyse photographs

◆ Thinking skills: q4, q5, use common sense and prior knowledge to produce reasoned explanations

Unit outcomes

By the end of this unit most students should be able to:

◆ explain the terms given in 'Key vocabulary' above

◆ describe Chongqing's main features

◆ explain why Chongqing has been chosen as a development hub by the Chinese government

◆ explain why the world's fastest growing urban area has no slums

Ideas for a starter

1 Say: Today we will begin studying Chonqing. What questions would you like answered?

2 Give students clues relating to Chongqing and ask: Where am I? For example:

  - The Yangtze River flows through me.

  - I border Sichuan and Guizhou.

  - I am a mostly rural area but I have a number of towns and cities. I have a population of 30 million.

  - My population density is more than the UK's.

  - You will find the most well off people in Southwest China here.

  - My major city is a port and has the same name as the area.

Ideas for plenaries

Plan plenaries at strategic points throughout the lesson, as well as at the end.

Mid-lesson

1 Imagine: You work for the Chinese government. You have been asked to create a poster to encourage companies to relocate to Chongqing. What information would they want to know? What are the benefits of locating in Chongqing?

2 Use 'Your turn' question 5 as a plenary.

3 Ask: Why are there no slums in Chongqing? Explain that although newcomers to the city live in the flats that have been built, they still face challenges (e.g. low wages).

4 Look at Google Earth images of Chongqing city over time. Ask: What is happening to the land on the edge of Chongqing? Imagine: You are a farmer just outside Chongqing city and your land is going to be built on. How do you feel?

End-of-lesson

5 Students create a spider diagram about the reasons why Chongqing is the world's fastest growing urban area.

6 Ask students to summarise today's lesson in five sentences, then reduce that to five words, and, finally, reduce it to one word.

Further class and homework opportunities

Suggestions 13–17 on page 166 of this book

geog.2 workbook, page 65

geog.2 Kerboodle: lesson presentation, worksheets, end-of-lesson assessment

Answers for 'Your turn'

1 Southwest China

2 a A confluence is where two rivers join.

 b The Yangtze and the Jialing

 c The Yangtze (the world's third longest river)

 d Tributary

3 Answers will vary, but students should mention that Chongqing city is experiencing a building boom (vertically) to accommodate as many people as possible.

4 Chongqing is located right on the Yangtze, which allows large ships to travel right to the city from the coast at Shanghai. This means that raw materials can be brought to the city and finished goods can be easily transported back to the east for domestic sale or for export.

5 Wages in factories, like the car factory in **C**, are much higher than the amount that could be earned through agriculture (and they are regular and reliable). Therefore, workers moving from the countryside to work in a factory will be better off and will have more disposable income. Some of this income will be used to help support family members who remain in the countryside, whilst some of the remainder will be spent in the city, which will boost businesses in the local economy there. Finally, the cars produced in the factory are mostly intended for domestic sale, so owning a car will help to improve a family's status and living standard.

6 a A megalopolis is a very large urban area, consisting of a chain of built-up areas.

 b There are examples of megalopolises in most continents. One early example is the urban area in the north eastern USA from Boston down to Washington DC (including New York, Baltimore, and Philadelphia).

Life in Chongqing

About this unit

This unit continues the focus on Chongqing, by describing life there for a variety of different people.

Key points

◆ Chinese people have a different status, or hukou, depending on whether they are considered to be urban or rural. Those with rural hukou have fewer rights to things like state-provided education or healthcare in a city than those with urban hukou. Simply moving from a rural area into a city does not automatically confer urban hukou on an individual, although this is slowly changing.

◆ Thus, the lives of those who migrate from the countryside into Chongqing city to work are affected by their perceived hukou, and, therefore, the rights to which they are entitled. This is why many migrants leave their children behind in their villages, because they would not be entitled to a full education or good healthcare in the city.

Key vocabulary

bang-bang man, left-behind, urban and rural hukou

Skills practised in 'Your turn'

◆ Geography skills: q3, q7a, define key terms

◆ Thinking skills: q1, q2, q4, q5, analyse text and use common sense to reach a reasoned conclusion; q6, consider and explain the effects on the economy of reforming the hukou system; q7b, use empathy, common sense and text analysis to present conclusions from different points of view

Unit outcomes

By the end of this unit most students should be able to:

◆ explain the terms given in 'Key vocabulary' above

◆ explain why rural migrants choose to come to Chongqing, and what life there is like

◆ describe the feelings of those left behind in rural areas, and explain why they have been left behind

Ideas for a starter

1 One student pretends to be the teacher. They summarise the last lesson on Chongqing region and ask the rest of the class questions on what they learned.

2 Show students pictures of rural China and pictures of Chongqing city. They describe and compare the pictures.

3 Ask a student to read out one of the stories of the people who live in Chongqing from pages 128–129 of the students' book. Ask the rest of the class what are the three main facts that stand out for them. Does the class agree?

Ideas for plenaries

Plan plenaries at strategic points throughout the lesson, as well as at the end.

Mid-lesson

1 Show students a video of people who have moved to the city (e.g. BBC Learning Zone China Stories – Liu Hong Liang). Ask: Why might people (like Liang and the others in Unit 8.5) want to move from the rural areas to Chongqing city?

2 Discuss: What are the effects of large numbers of people moving from rural areas to Chongqing – economic, environmental, social?

3 Imagine: You are one of the people in pictures A–C on pages 128–129 of the students' book. Write a paragraph about how you feel about your life in Chongqing.

4 Reinforce the concept / idea of hukou. Discuss: Why might people with rural hukou not bring their children to Chongqing with them? Explain that the hukou system is being reformed (as reported in various news articles in 2014). How might this help the people who have moved from rural areas to Chongqing? Will it really help rural migrants (the reforms are limited)?

End-of-lesson

5 Use 'Your turn' question 1 as a plenary.

6 Students choose three new words they have learned whilst studying China, and write dictionary definitions. Share words and definitions as a class.

7 Ask: Has anything from today's lesson surprised you? Has anything made you feel angry / annoyed? What has stuck in your head from today's lesson?

Further class and homework opportunities

Suggestions 18–21 on pages 166–167 of this book

geog.2 workbook, page 66

geog.2 Kerboodle: lesson presentation, worksheets, end-of-lesson assessment

Answers for 'Your turn'

1 Answers will vary, depending on students' points of view, but Jian has a more physically demanding job than Hua (outdoors in all weathers), and he also has to share a room with three others.

2 Jian can earn far more money in Chongqing than he could on the family farm, and he has a wife and son to support.

3 In China, you have rural or urban hukou (status), depending on where you were born. If your hukou is rural, you don't have full rights in the city.

4 Wu Shan

5 She is separated from her child, because her rural hukou means that she does not have full rights in the city and, therefore, her son would not receive a good education or proper health care if he lived with her.

6 a Because it will make urban areas even more attractive to rural people and easier for them to move there, which will mean more workers for employers. Further, if the children of these people can go to good schools, in time China will have a better-educated workforce, which will ultimately help the economy.

b By reforming the hukou system slowly, China is trying to keep the pace of change under control. If they don't do it slowly, it's likely that too many people will move to the cities too quickly, and this would put pressure on things like housing, health care, and schools in urban areas.

7 a Because they were left behind when their parents migrated to the city to work.

b i The parents miss their children and don't see them growing up. However, if the children stay in the village, they will be entitled to the education and health care provided for those with rural hukou, which they wouldn't receive if they went to live in the city. Also, the parents live in very cramped shared accommodation in the city, which would be worse if their children lived with them too.

ii The children miss seeing their parents, but the parents' earnings from working in the city mean that the children receive a better standard of living.

About this unit

This unit considers ecological and environmental issues in Southwest China.

Key points

◆ The Southwest is China's most biodiverse region, due to the wide range of ecosystems and climates present there – from the rugged mountains of Tibet to the rainforests of Yunnan.

◆ However, this biodiversity is under threat – mainly from deforestation caused by human demands for more land for settlement and agriculture.

◆ China's rapid economic expansion has also had an environmental impact – not just in the heavily polluted cities of the east, but also in the rainforests of Yunnan. There, many rainforest trees are being cut down to make way for rubber plantations, which cannot sustain the natural wildlife. Why is this related to economic expansion? Well, one of the by-products of China's growing wealth is that more and more Chinese are buying cars – and cars need tyres (made from rubber). China had just 5.54 million vehicles on the road in 1990; 62 million by 2009; and it's estimated that it will have over 200 million by 2020. In 2013, alone, 22 million new vehicles were sold in China. That's a lot of rubber tyres!

Key vocabulary

biodiversity (biodiverse), deforestation, endangered species, rubber

Skills practised in 'Your turn'

◆ Geography skills: q1, explain key terms; q5, analyse a photograph to produce an explanation

◆ Thinking skills: q3, use common sense and general knowledge to reach a reasoned conclusion; q4, use prior knowledge to offer an explanation; q6, construct a reasoned argument

Unit outcomes

By the end of this unit most students should be able to:

◆ explain the terms given in 'Key vocabulary' above

◆ describe what is happening to biodiversity in the Southwest region

◆ explain why biodiversity there is under threat

Ideas for a starter

1 Show students pictures of the different species under threat from pages 130–131 of the students' book. Ask: What do the pictures show? Where do these species live?

2 Show students pictures of reasons why China's biodiversity is under threat (e.g. deforestation, a Chinese city, rubber tyres, a bamboo chopping board / chopsticks). Ask: What links these images? Explain that this lesson will show how they are linked to a growing population.

3 Ask for a volunteer to try and define what is meant by biodiversity.

Ideas for plenaries

Plan plenaries at strategic points throughout the lesson, as well as at the end.

Mid-lesson

1 Use 'Your turn' question 1 as a plenary.

2 Ask students to draw a map of southwest China to show where the endangered species mentioned in this Unit are found. They should add the special area for biodiversity.

3 Following on from plenary **2**, students annotate and / or label their maps with facts about the species (e.g. a picture, the size of the current population, why they are under threat, what is being done to protect them).

4 Say: Protecting endangered species costs millions and takes years to be successful. Use 'Your turn' question 6 as a plenary discussion activity.

End-of-lesson

5 Students create a spider diagram showing the factors that have led to loss of biodiversity in Southwest China.

6 Revisit the pictures and questions in starter **2**. Ask: What is the connection with a growing population?

7 Ask students to write down three new facts they learned today, two things that really made them think and one question they'd like to ask. Share responses, in pairs.

Further class and homework opportunities

Suggestions 22–25 on page 167 of this book

geog.2 workbook, page 67

geog.2 Kerboodle: lesson presentation, worksheets, end-of-lesson assessment

Answers for 'Your turn'

1 Biodiversity means that a location supports many different species of plants and animals. Endangered means that so few of a species are left that it's in danger of extinction.

2 Deforestation

3 They don't want the panda cubs to become too used to humans. They want them to avoid humans in the wild and to associate with their own species, which will increase both their security and also the possibility of breeding more of this endangered species.

4 Yunnan is located right in the southernmost part of the Southwest region and is bisected by the Tropic of Cancer. As a result, it has a hot, wet equatorial climate, which is able to support rainforest.

5 There is no ground cover to hide small animals and little diversity in terms of plant species to feed different wildlife. The constant presence of humans tapping the rubber trees also deters wildlife.

6 Answers will vary, depending on different points of view about the viability and desirability of protecting endangered species.

About this unit

This unit introduces the physical geography and people of Tibet.

Key points

◆ Tibet is located on the Plateau of Tibet, the highest plateau in the world, which is why it's called the Roof of the World. It also shares the world's highest mountain, Mount Everest, with Nepal.

◆ Most of it is tundra, although the Himalayas begin in the south and there are also some fertile river valleys. It has thousands of lakes and glaciers, and most of Asia's largest rivers begin there (fed by melting glaciers).

◆ Tibet's annual temperature varies from cool to freezing – and it's very windy. It's also very dry, due to the shelter of the Himalayas.

◆ Tibet is the least densely populated area of China, with only 3 million people (mostly ethnic Tibetans). Most Tibetans are farmers in the fertile river valleys or, until recently, were nomadic herders. Tibetans are Buddhists and religion is very important to them.

Key vocabulary

nomads, plateau, Roof of the World, tundra

Skills practised in 'Your turn'

◆ Geography skills: q1, q3, define key terms

◆ Literacy skills: q6, write a detailed explanation (a paragraph); q9, add to summary spider diagram from Unit 8.3

◆ Thinking skills: q2, use common sense to reach a conclusion; q4, q5, q7, q8, use common sense and prior knowledge to produce a reasoned explanation

Unit outcomes

By the end of this unit most students should be able to:

◆ explain the terms given in 'Key vocabulary' above

◆ describe what Tibet is like in terms of physical geography and climate

◆ describe how the Tibetan people live their lives

Ideas for a starter

1 Ask: Have you heard of Tibet? If so, what do you know about it? What would you like to know about it?

2 Show students pictures of Tibet. Ask: What do you think it is like living there – relief, climate, biome, etc.?

3 Tibet is described as being the 'Roof of the World'. Ask: What do you think this means? Why might it be referred to as the 'Roof of the World'? Students could look back at the map on page 120 of the students' book for help.

Ideas for plenaries

Plan plenaries at strategic points throughout the lesson, as well as at the end.

Mid-lesson

1   Ask students to shade in, and label, Tibet, on a blank map of China. Ask them to annotate the map with information about Tibet's climate and people.

2   Use 'Your turn' question 6 as a plenary.

End-of-lesson

3   Students work out what the questions are for the following answers:

Answer	Question
South-west	In which part of China is Tibet located?
Lhasa	What is the capital of Tibet?
India, Nepal, Bhutan	Which countries border Tibet?
Himalayas	Which mountain range borders Tibet?
3 million	How many people live in Tibet?
Buddhist	What religion are people in Tibet?
Farming	What is the main economic activity in Tibet?
9 months	How long is the dry season in Tibet every year?

4   Students write glossary definitions for these terms: nomad, plateau, tundra, altitude sickness.

5   Students complete the following sentences: Before this lesson I did not know that … I want to find out …

Further class and homework opportunities

Suggestions 26–29 on page 167 of this book

geog.2 workbook, page 68

geog.2 Kerboodle: lesson presentation, worksheets, end-of-lesson assessment

Answers for 'Your turn'

1   A plateau is an area of fairly flat high land.

2   Satellite imagery or aerial photography.

3   Tundra is a cold region where the ground is deeply frozen; only the surface thaws in summer, allowing small plants to grow.

4   The Plateau of Tibet is the highest plateau in the world. As such, it is a very cold, dry, wind-swept place – just like the Arctic – and has a similar biome.

5   Students might find this difficult. Lakes are fed by melting glaciers; permafrost means that water does not soak into the ground; the climate means that very little water is lost to evaporation.

6   Students should mention: the hostile climate, particularly in winter; the remoteness of Tibet (bordered to the south by the Himalayas and to the north by deserts) and the lack of employment opportunities other than subsistence farming and yak herding.

7   The air at high altitudes has less oxygen. It contains fewer gas molecules, including oxygen, because they are pulled down by gravity and concentrated at lower levels.

8   Students' answers could include: Tibet is a very remote region with an extreme climate, limited transport infrastructure, and a small population (mostly from one ethnic group). Therefore, opportunities to develop Tibet by bringing in more people from other regions of China who are not ethnic Tibetans might be resented by the local population. Also, opportunities to industrialise and urbanise the region might be hampered by its remoteness (making the transportation of raw materials and finished goods difficult), its extreme climate, and the fact that most Tibetans do not traditionally live in towns or cities, but live a rural or nomadic lifestyle, and may not wish to live in organised settlements and work in factories or mines.

9   Students should continue their summary spider diagrams about China's Southwest region.

All change in Tibet

About this unit

This unit describes the changes which are taking place in Tibet.

Key points

◆ Tibet only became a formal part of China in 1959. Many Tibetans would like to regain their independence.

◆ As a way of strengthening its control over Tibet, developing tourism further – and exploiting its natural resources of minerals and water – China has been improving Tibet's transport infrastructure, e.g. constructing a railway that links Lhasa directly to Beijing.

◆ As an integral part of its development of the area, China has also forced all of Tibet's traditional nomadic yak herders into resettlement villages, where state control can be more easily maintained, e.g. through providing formal education for their children. Many Han Chinese are also being relocated to Tibet to help with its development and industrialisation, and the exploitation of its resources.

◆ Climate change has also started to have an effect on Tibet. Global warming is melting the glaciers on the plateau, and the permafrost on the tundra is starting to thaw out – which is one of the reasons given for the forced relocation of the nomads.

Key vocabulary

Dalai Lama, glacier, infrastructure, nomads, permafrost, resettlement, yak

Skills practised in 'Your turn'

◆ Geography skills: q2a, define a key term

◆ Literacy skills: q7, write an advert

◆ Thinking skills: q1, q2b, q6, use common sense and prior knowledge to provide a reasoned explanation; q3, q4 evaluate information to reach a conclusion; q5, consider a personal point of view

Unit outcomes

By the end of this unit most students should be able to:

◆ explain the terms given in 'Key vocabulary' above

◆ explain how and why China plans to develop Tibet

◆ explain what this development has meant for Tibet's nomadic yak herders

Ideas for a starter

1 Show students the following newspaper headline from *The Telegraph*, 26 July 2012: Tibet is a better place than it used to be. Ask: What do you think the headline means? Explain that the lesson will explore the development of Tibet.

2 Show a picture of the Dalai Lama and ask questions to assess understanding of who he is, his role and his connection to Tibet. For example: Who is this man? What does he do? Where does he live? What prize did he win?

3 Using the clues, students unscramble the following words relating to Tibet:

   – Sahal – the capital of Tibet

   – Rundat – a cold region where the ground is deeply frozen

   – Odsman – a person who rears animals and travels with them to find grazing

   – Lapetua – an area of fairly high flat land

   – Asky – reared for milk, meat, leather, hair, and transport

Ideas for plenaries

Plan plenaries at strategic points throughout the lesson, as well as at the end.

Mid-lesson

1   Use 'Your turn' question 7 as a plenary.

2   Use 'Your turn' question 5 as a plenary.

3   Write the following headings on the board: *Benefits* and *Disadvantages*. Students give examples of how development will benefit Tibet, and disadvantages of developing Tibet. They can summarise this information as a spider diagram.

End-of-lesson

4   Students write words associated with Tibet that they have learned over the last two lessons and stick them on a word wall. Ask: Can you group the words?

5   Revisit the headline starter **1**: Tibet is a better place than it used to be. Lead scaffolded discussion about this statement using the information from the students' book. Explain: the article was written by the Chinese ambassador to Britain. Ask: What effect do you think this might have on the article?

Further class and homework opportunities

Suggestions 30–32 on page 167 of this book

geog.2 workbook, page 69

geog.2 Kerboodle: lesson presentation, worksheets, end-of-lesson assessment

Answers for 'Your turn'

1   The Plateau of Tibet is very high and mountainous. It is also covered in thousands of lakes and the climate there is extreme (cold, dry, and windy). In addition, it has less oxygen than in the lowlands, so altitude sickness amongst non-Tibetans is common. Therefore, the workers who built the railway linking Lhasa to Golmud had to contend with significant challenges and problems.

2   **a**   Permafrost, found in the tundra biome, is where the ground under the surface is permanently frozen, apart from a shallow layer at the top, which thaws during the short summer to allow some vegetation to grow.

   b   The land on the plateau mostly consists of tundra, with permafrost that partially thaws in the summer. This could destabilise the railway track unless it is built on strong foundations or raised up on supports (as shown in the photograph on page 134 of the students' book). However, with global warming, the permafrost is now thawing to a greater depth, which further destabilises the railway track's supports and may lead to their collapse unless they are strengthened and deepened significantly. In addition, when permafrost thaws, methane (a greenhouse gas) is released.

3   The most useful change is the construction of two additional airports by 2020 (to add to the existing four). This will enable tourists from overseas to reach Tibet more easily. Many tourists may also be attracted by the idea of travelling by the new train all the way from Beijing to Lhasa, which would allow a certain amount of acclimatisation that isn't possible if you fly directly into Tibet.

4   China is a big country so new railways, roads, and airports will help to link and unify different parts of the country. This will help China function and develop socially and economically.

5   Answers will vary, depending on students' points of view.

6   They will receive a formal education in state-provided schools and health care in state-provided health facilities. They are also more likely to get formal jobs, maybe in one of the new government-sponsored development projects being built in Tibet.

7   Students should include the following topics: Tibet's natural rugged beauty; the Tibetan people and their culture (including their strong religious beliefs); improvements to transport infrastructure to enable tourists to reach Tibet more easily.

The rivers and dams

About this unit

This unit discusses China's dam-building plans, and why they are so controversial.

Key points

- All of Asia's major rivers originate in the Plateau of Tibet, e.g. Yangtze, Huang He, Mekong, and Brahmaputra. They are fed by melting glaciers.

- China has already built dams on all of the above rivers, and has plans to build many more – most of which are in the Southwest region.

- However, these proposed dams are controversial, because of the effects they have and the threats they face:

  - Constructing a dam floods a large area of land, which means that many people have to be relocated; much valuable agricultural land is lost; and many wildlife habitats are destroyed.

  - Building dams reduces the water flow downstream. Because many of these rivers are shared with other countries, they are worried that their water supplies will be affected, e.g. on the Mekong and Brahmaputra. This concern is being compounded by global warming, which is reducing the size of the rivers' feeder glaciers and will eventually reduce their water flow anyway.

  - Southwest China is in a major earthquake zone, caused by the Indian and Eurasian tectonic plates colliding and driving upwards to form the Himalayas. Large earthquakes occur regularly in this zone, which threaten to destroy dams and cause massive flooding. For example, in 2008, an earthquake measuring 7.8 on the Richter Scale struck Sichuan, damaging 391 dams and threatening to completely destroy the Tulong dam.

Key vocabulary

dam, hydroelectricity, transnational

Skills practised in 'Your turn'

- Geography skills: q2, q3a, understand key terms
- Literacy skills: q6, update summary spider diagram
- Thinking skills: q3b, q4, explain; q5, assess and order importance

Unit outcomes

By the end of this unit most students should be able to:

- explain the terms given in 'Key vocabulary' above
- explain why China's dam-building plans are controversial

Ideas for a starter

1. Show students aerial photos of a river before and after a dam was built. Ask: What can you see? What are the differences between the two photos?

2. Ask: What is a dam? In small groups, students design and build their own dams in a shallow tray of water. Provide a range of materials for building a dam (twigs, leaves, gravel, sand, modelling clay). Test the dams by pouring water into one side of the tray. The dam that holds back the most water for the longest period of time is the winner.

3. Using the maps on pages 136–137 of the students' book and geographical language, students write a sentence explaining where all the existing dams (or dams under construction) in China are located. Ask: Where is the Three Gorges Dam located?

Ideas for plenaries

Plan plenaries at strategic points throughout the lesson, as well as at the end.

Mid-lesson

1   Do 'Your turn' question 4 as a plenary.

2   Say: Moving house is one of the most stressful events in a person's life. Around 1.3 million people were moved to build the Three Gorges Dam. How would you have felt if you were one of those people having to leave your home? Is it fair that the Chinese government has made these people move?

3   Recap the concept of sustainability. Following on from plenary 1 discuss: Are the dams that China is building sustainable? How could the Chinese government make them more sustainable (reduce the impact on people and the environment)? Are there other options to dam-building?

4   Students debate: Dams in China: beneficial or not?

End-of-lesson

5   Show students a diagram showing Personal, Learning and Thinking Skills (PLTS). Ask them which skills they have used today. For one of the skills, they should explain how they have used it and how they might use it more effectively in future.

6   Ask: What new facts have you learned today? Has anything from today's lesson shocked you? Has anything upset you / made you feel angry? Has anything impressed you?

Further class and homework opportunities

Suggestions 33–37 on page 167 of this book

geog.2 workbook, page 70

geog.2 Kerboodle: lesson presentation, worksheets, end-of-lesson assessment

Answers for 'Your turn'

1   a   Indus, Brahmaputra, Mekong, Salween, Yangtze, Huang He (Yellow River)

   b   Yangtze, Huang He (Yellow River)

2   Brahmaputra (China, India, Bangladesh); Mekong (China, Myanmar, Thailand, Laos, Cambodia, Vietnam)

3   a   Hydroelectricity is electricity generated when flowing water spins a turbine at a dam.

   b   The dams will provide cheap electricity to power China's industry, which in turn will produce exports to improve China's economy. The electricity will also power the homes of the workers that China needs for its economic expansion.

4   a   They will not produce any greenhouse gas emissions, unlike coal-fired power stations.

   b   Constructing the dams will flood large areas of land, destroying many valuable wildlife habitats.

   c   Many people living in the areas of the new dams are forced to relocate, because their homes and valuable agricultural land are flooded by the lakes produced by the dams. The dams also reduce the water supply further downstream, which may affect people in other countries who lose access to the dammed water. Finally, if any of the new dams are destroyed by an earthquake (common in this region), many people may be killed by the resulting flood.

5   Answers will vary.

6   Students should complete their summary spider diagrams.

Many of these suggestions are addressed to your students. Where research or further resources are needed, the internet will almost certainly provide the answer.

The suggestions are graded *,**,*** according to level of difficulty. Some are suitable for all levels, and can be differentiated by outcome.

China: an overview

1   **Colour in**   On a blank map of China, colour in and label China's regions. Mark and label Beijing, Shanghai, Hong Kong and Chongqing. Mark and label the Tropic of Cancer, the East China Sea and the South China Sea. Add the Chinese flag, a scale bar and a North Point.   */**

2   **Google Maps**   Explore China on Google Maps. Pick out some of its key physical features from the map on page 120 of the students' book. What is your overall impression?   */**

3   **How big?**   Write these on the board as a list: UK 243 610 sq km, Russia 17 098 242 sq km, Canada 9 984 670 sq km, USA 9 826 675 sq km, China 9 596 960 sq km. Compared to the UK how many times bigger is China? Compared to Russia, how much smaller is China?   **/***

4   **Made in China**   China is the world's top exporter of goods (just ahead of the EU). Work in small groups. What products are made in China? What do you own that is made in China? Check your clothes, shoes, phones and other devices. Which group has the most things made in China?   */**

The rise of China

5   **Mao Zedong**   China is ruled by the Communist Party, and its first leader was Mao Zedong. Find out about him and write a short biography.   **

6   **One-child policy**   China's one-child policy has been controversial. It has prevented many births, but those who had more than one child were punished in different ways. Find out about the one-child policy and decide whether the policy should be abandoned altogether (it has been relaxed) or whether it should be kept.   **/***

7   **Shenzhen**   Shenzhen is in southeast China. Until 30 years ago, it was a small fishing village, but today it's one of the world's fastest growing cities with lots of foreign companies building new factories there. Millions of people have flocked to Shenzhen from other parts of China to find better-paid work. Use Google Maps to find Shenzhen in China. Zoom in to get a scale of the developments there.   */**/***

8   **Cut pollution!**   China is spending lots of money trying to tackle pollution. Draw a poster to show the causes and effects of pollution. Include your ideas of how pollution could be tackled.   */**/***

China's Southwest region

9   **Fiendish anagrams**   Make anagrams from the names of the five areas in Southwest China (or use an anagram generator on the internet). See how long it takes for the class to work them out. Have they spelt them all correctly?   **/***

10   **GDP per person**   This gives you an idea of how well off people in a place are, *on average*. These figures are the same as the ones in the students' book.

	GDP per person PPP(dollars)
Tibet	6138
Sichuan	7642
Chongqing	10 077
Guizhou	3100
Yunnan	4160
UK	37 000

Draw a bar chart for this data. Annotate your graph with labels to explain the differences between the GDP for the different areas, using the information in this unit to help you.   ***

11   **Wall display**   Collect as many interesting and varied images of one area in Southwest China as you can. Find a way to group them, for example, by landscape, buildings, people, animals etc.   *

12   **Tourist leaflet**   Create a leaflet to encourage tourists to come to Yunnan to see the amazing karst scenery. Include lots of examples of photos of the scenery and explain how it was formed.   */**/***

Chongqing

13   **Plan a trip ...**   to Chongqing. Will you fly? If so where can you fly from, and where do you fly to? How long will it take? What is the time difference between the UK and China? How will you get from the airport to Chongqing city? You will need to do some research for this activity.   **/***

14   **My time in Chongqing**   You are visiting Chongqing. Write a blog to describe your first few days. Describe what you have done in the city and the sights you have seen. You might need to do some research.   */**/***

15   **Chongqing crossword**   Create a crossword about Chongqing. Think carefully about your clues before you try it out on a partner.   */**

16   **No slums in Chongqing**   If you went to many large cities in developing countries which have experienced rapid urbanisation, you would find slums. Chongqing has grown rapidly and is still growing at an incredible pace. But there are no slums. Explain.   **

17   **Chongqing Wordle**   Find a video of Chongqing on YouTube. Watch the video and then create a Wordle to describe Chongqing, its size and scale.   */**

Life in Chongqing

18   **A day in the life....**   of Liu Jian. Liu Jian is a bang-bang man. His story is on page 128 of the students' book. Write a diary entry for a day in his life.   */**/**

19   **Ten years later**   You are Wang Hua from page 128 of the students' book. It is ten years later. What is your life like now? Have you got urban hukou? Has your son come to join you

in Chongqing? Aim to write about 100 words for 'ten years later'. */**/***

20 **Rhyme time** Write a poem about hukou – the Chinese system about status and how it depends on where you were born. */**/**

21 **Spider diagram** Create a spider diagram to show the effects of large numbers of people moving from rural areas to Chongqing. Start with three legs for Economic, Social and Environmental, and take it from there. **/***

Tops for biodiversity!

22 **Endangered!** Choose either the golden monkey or the snow leopard. Find out exactly where they live, and how many are left in the wild. What are they most at risk from? Prepare a one-minute sound-bite for a radio broadcast. Note that the golden monkey is properly known as the golden snub-nosed monkey (don't confuse it with the golden monkey which lives in Africa). **/***

23 **Stop hunting** Snow leopards are at risk from hunters who kill them for their fur and bones, which are used in Chinese medicine. Write a letter to the hunters to explain why their actions are putting the snow leopards at risk, and why they should stop. */**/***

24 **Extinction** Once a species becomes endangered, it could be heading for extinction. The Chinese river dolphin – small, white and almost blind – was declared extinct in 2006. Does it matter if a species becomes extinct? What effect do you think it might have on other species, if one species becomes extinct? Prepare a presentation for your classmates on why we should aim to protect species to prevent them becoming extinct. **/***

25 **Say no to deforestation!** Design a leaflet to persuade people not to cut down trees. Explain why deforestation is a problem, and some of the issues it can create. Your leaflet should be clear and simple. Use photos and drawings to make it attractive. */**/***

Tibet

26 **Plan a trip to Tibet** When will you go? (Perhaps you should look at a climate graph – or do activity 28 first). What will you see? Where will you stay? How will you get there? **/***

27 **Everest – who is famous?** Who first climbed Everest? When? What nationalities were they? Write a short account of their achievement – you will need to do some research. */**/***

28 **Tibet climate** Use the climate figures below to draw a climate graph for Lhasa, the capital of Tibet. Look at the climate graph of London on page 83 of the students' book to see what your climate graph should look like.

	Jan	Feb	Mar	Apr	May	Jun	Jul	Aug	Sep	Oct	Nov	Dec
Temperature °C	-2	2	5	8	12	16	16	15	13	9	3	-1
Rainfall mm	1	1	3	6	28	71	117	121	69	9	2	1

Now describe the climate for Lhasa and see if you can explain why the climate is like that. **/***

29 **Acrostic** Write TIBET down the side of your page. Make each letter the first letter of a word or phrase to do with Tibet. *

All change in Tibet

30 **Take the train** – from Lhasa to Beijing. How far is it? How long will it take? What will you see on the way? Will you be able to sleep? What will you eat? Find out. **/***

31 **Two sides** Print out a blank map of China and colour in Tibet. There are tensions in Tibet – China is working to develop Tibet, but many Tibetans want to be free of China. Using two different colours, write as many different arguments for and against China's involvement in Tibet as you can think of inside your map of China. */**/***

32 **Choice for Bemba Sonam** Write an interview with Bemba Sonam – the questions and his responses – about his life. How has he ended up in a settlement village for nomads? If he had a free choice, what would he do now? Has his life improved at all? Do all nomads think the same as him? */**/***

The rivers and dams

33 **For or against 1?** Work with a partner and create two spider diagrams. One should show all the arguments why dams are a good idea, and the second, all the arguments against dams. Include all the ideas in this Unit, and any others you can think of. */**/***

34 **For or against 2?** Work in three groups. One group are conservationists, one are local people and the other group represent the government. Watch a video clip about the impacts and benefits of dams in China – use the Three Gorges Dam as an example – and note the points that are relevant to your group. Discuss whether you are for or against more dams being built in China. **/***

35 **Rivers wordsearch** Create a wordsearch for all the rivers that rise in the Plateau of Tibet. Try it out on a partner. Be careful with your spelling as some of the rivers have tricky names. If you think your partner is up to the challenge, you could write the letters in reverse order. */**/***

36 **Conflict?** China's neighbours are uneasy about China's plans for dams. Could it lead to conflict? Work with a partner and write a discussion between China and one of the countries downstream about China's plans for more dams on the Mekong river. **/***

37 **Huge class Wordle!** As a class think of as many words as you can to do with Southwest China. Then create a huge Wordle. The words that most students come up with should appear the largest, and others should be smaller. If you can make your Wordle in the shape of Southwest China, that's even better! */**/***

Glossary

A

abrasion – scraping away material

aerial photo – a photo taken from the air

air mass – a huge block of air moving over Earth; it can be warm or cold, damp or dry, depending on where it came from

air pressure – the force pressing down on us because of the weight of the atmosphere

altitude – height of a place above sea level

anemometer – use it to measure wind speed

arch – the curved structure left when the sea erodes the inside of a cave away

atmosphere – the layer of gas around Earth

B

barometer – use it to measure air pressure

bay – a smooth curve of coast between two headlands

beach – an area of sand or small stones, deposited by waves

beach replenishment – adding sand to a beach to replace the sand the waves carried away

biodiverse – has many different species of plants and animals

biome – a very large area with a similar climate, plants, and animals

C

capital city – the city where the country's government is based

climate – what the weather in a place is usually like, over the year; they take measurements over long periods and calculate the average

climate change – all aspects of climate are changing because Earth is getting warmer

coast – where the land meets the sea

coastal defences – barriers to protect the coast from erosion or flooding

condense – to change from gas to liquid

confluence – where two rivers join

coniferous – describes trees which bear cones (such as pine trees)

continent – one of Earth's great land masses; there are seven continents

convectional rainfall – the Sun heats the ground, convection currents of warm air rise, the water vapour condenses, and rain falls

correlation – a relationship or connection between two different things

country – humans have divided continents into political units called countries

D

dam – a structure built across a river to control water flow; it usually contains turbines which the water spins, generating electricity

data – information collected for a purpose; for example, names and addresses

deciduous – describes trees which lose their leaves in winter

decline – to fall gradually into a poor state

deforestation – cutting down forests

densely populated – lots of people live there

deposit – to drop material; waves deposit sand and small stones to form beaches

depression – a weather system made up of a warm front chased by a cold one; it brings wet windy weather

desalinate – to turn seawater into fresh water that people can drink, by removing its salt

desert – gets very little rain; it can be a hot or cold desert, and sandy or rocky

desertification – where fertile land becomes like a desert, through overuse or drought

drought – there is less rain than usual, so there is not enough water for our needs

E

earthquake – the shaking of Earth's crust, caused by sudden rock movement

economic – about money and business

economy – all the business activity going on in a country

emissions – waste gases that go into the air, for example from car exhausts

endangered – when so few of a species are left that it's in danger of extinction; for example snow leopards are endangered

environment – everything around you; air, soil, water, animals, and plants form the natural environment

Equator – an imaginary line around the middle of Earth (at 0° latitude)

erosion – the wearing away of rock, stones and soil by rivers, waves, wind, or glaciers

exploit – to make use of a place, or people, or things, for your own benefit

exports – things a country sells to other countries

F

favela – a slum in a South American city

fetch – the length of water the wind blows over, before it meets the coast

flood defences – structures built to prevent flooding; for example an embankment

fossil fuel – coal, oil, natural gas

front – the leading edge of an air mass; a warm front means a warm air mass is arriving

frontal rainfall – rain caused by a warm front meeting a cold one

fuels – thing we use to provide energy; we usually burn them (but not nuclear fuel)

G

GDP (gross domestic product) – the total amount that the population of a country earns in a year

GDP per person – the GDP divided by the population; it's a measure of how wealthy the people are, on average

GDP per person (PPP) – the GDP per person is adjusted to take into account that things cost more in some places than others

glacier – a river of ice

global warming – the rise in average temperatures around the world

gravity – the force of attraction that draws things towards Earth

grazing – land with grass and other vegetation, where animals can feed

greenhouse gases – they trap heat around Earth

groynes – barriers of wood or stone down a beach, to stop sand being washed away

gulf – a large area of ocean that is partly enclosed by land

Glossary

H

headland – land that juts out into the sea

hukou system – in China you have rural or urban hukou (status) depending on where you were born; if your hukou is rural, you don't have full rights in the city

hunter gatherers – they lived by hunting animals and collecting fruit and seeds

hydroelectricity – electricity generated when flowing water spins a turbine, at a dam

I

ice age – when Earth's average temperature is lower than usual, and glaciers spread

imports – things bought in from other countries

independence – when a country that had been a colony begins to govern itself

Industrial Revolution – the period (about 1760 – 1840) when many new machines were invented, and many factories were built

inequality – the unequal sharing of wealth in a society

international – concerns more than one country

K

karst – landscape features that form when rock such as limestone is attacked by acidic rain (containing dissolved carbon dioxide)

L

landform – a feature formed by erosion or deposition (for example a bay)

latitude – how far a place is north or south of the Equator; it is measured in degrees

leeward – sheltered from the wind

life expectancy – how many years a new baby can expect to live for, on average

logging – cutting down trees for timber

longitude – how far a place is east or west of the Prime Meridian; it is measured in degrees

longshore drift – how sand and other material is carried parallel to the shore, by the waves

M

mangroves – trees that grow in salty swamps along the coast

manufacturing – making things in factories

megalopolis – a very large urban area made of a chain of built-up areas

metal ores – rocks from which metals are extracted

migrant – a person who moves to another part of the country, or another country, usually to work

monsoon rains – they fall in summer in some regions, when moist winds are drawn in from over the ocean

N

national – to do with all of one country

natural – occurs without human involvement

nomad – a person who rears animals, and travels with them to find grazing

non-renewable resource – a resource we will run out of one day; for example oil

North Atlantic Drift – a warm current in the Atlantic Ocean; it keeps the weather on the west coast of Britain mild in winter

Northern Hemisphere – the half of Earth above the Equator

O

ocean currents – currents of water in the ocean, that are warmer or colder than the water around them

P

peninsula – land that juts out into the sea, and is almost surrounded by water

permafrost – the ground under the surface that is permanently frozen, in the tundra

plateau – an area of fairly flat high land

population – how many people live in a place

population density – the average number of people living in a place, per square kilometre

population distribution – how the people in a country are spread around

populous – has a large population

postcode – a set of numbers and letters which are added to an address to help mail delivery

precipitation – water falling from the sky (as rain, sleet, hail, snow)

prevailing wind – the wind that blows most often; in the UK it is a south west wind

primary sector (of the economy) – where people earn a living by collecting things from the Earth (farming, fishing, mining)

pull factors – factors that attract people to a place (for example, better wages)

push factors – factors that push people out of a place (for example, there's no work there)

PV cell – converts sunlight into electricity

R

rainforest – has lush vegetation, with many different species of plants and animals

regenerate – to restore an area that was in a poor state, and bring it back to life

relief – how the height of the land varies

renewable resource – a resource that we can grow or make more of; for example wood

republic – does not have a king, queen, or emperor

resources – things we need to live, or use to earn a living; for example food, fuel

rural area – an area that is mainly countryside; it may have villages and small towns

S

salt marsh – a low-lying marshy area by the sea, with salty water from the tides

secondary sector (of the economy) – where people earn a living by making things, mostly in factories

secure – safe from attack

settlement – a place where people live; it could be a hamlet, village, town or city

shanty town – a poor area where the houses are just shacks; another term for slum

shingle – small pebbles

slum – area of very poor housing

sparsely populated – not many live there

species – a type of plant or animal

social – about people and society

software – computer programmes

solar power – when we use sunlight to generate electricity (via PV cells)

sparsely populated – few people live there

speculators – they take a risk, and spend money in the hope of making lots of profit

spit – a strip of sand or shingle in the sea

stack – a pillar of rock left standing in the sea when the top of an arch collapses

steppe – a large flat area of treeless grassland

storm surge – change in sea level caused by a storm

stump – the remains of an eroded stack

sustainable – can be carried on into the future without harming people's quality of life, or the economy, or the environment

T

taiga – region of coniferous forests which lies between the tundra and steppes

temperate – relating to a mild climate: not hot, not too cold

temperature – how hot or cold something is, measured in degrees Centigrade

tertiary sector (of the economy) – people provide services for other people

thermometer – use it to measure temperature

tidal range – the fall in sea level from high to low tide

tides – the rise and fall in sea level, due mainly to the pull of the moon

transnational – crosses country borders

transport – the carrying away of material by rivers, waves, the wind or glaciers

tree line – the line or altitude above which it's too cold for trees to grow

tributary – a river that flows into a larger one

tropics – the area between the Tropics of Cancer and Capricorn

tundra – a cold region where the ground is deeply frozen; only the surface thaws in summer, allowing small plants to grow

U

urban area – a built-up area (large town or city); it's the opposite of rural

urbanisation – the increase in the % of the population living in urban areas, as people move in from rural areas

W

water vapour – water in gas form

wave-cut notch – a notch cut in a cliff face by the action of waves

wave-cut platform – the flat rocky area left behind when waves erode a cliff away

weather – the state of the atmosphere at any given time – for example how warm it is

weathering – the breaking down of rock; it is caused mainly by the weather

wind – air in motion

wind direction – where the wind blows from

wind speed – how fast the wind is blowing

windward – facing into the wind